Lecture Notes in Computer Science   **9053**

Commenced Publication in 1973
Founding and Former Series Editors:
Gerhard Goos, Juris Hartmanis, and Jan van Leeuwen

Editorial Board

T0212901

More information about this series at http://www.springer.com/series/7411

Moritz Steiner · Pere Barlet-Ros
Olivier Bonaventure (Eds.)

Traffic Monitoring and Analysis

7th International Workshop, TMA 2015
Barcelona, Spain, April 21–24, 2015
Proceedings

 Springer

Editors
Moritz Steiner
Akamai Technologies
San Francisco
California
USA

Olivier Bonaventure
Université catholique de Louvain
Louvain-la-Neuve
Belgium

Pere Barlet-Ros
Universitat Politècnica de Catalunya/Talaia
    Networks
Barcelona
Spain

ISSN 0302-9743   ISSN 1611-3349   (electronic)
Lecture Notes in Computer Science
ISBN 978-3-319-17171-5   ISBN 978-3-319-17172-2   (eBook)
DOI 10.1007/978-3-319-17172-2

Library of Congress Control Number: 2015935613

LNCS Sublibrary: SL5 – Computer Communication Networks and Telecommunications

Printed on acid-free paper

Springer International Publishing AG Switzerland is part of Springer Science+Business Media
(www.springer.com)

Preface

The seventh Traffic Monitoring and Analysis (TMA) workshop took place in Barcelona, Spain. TMA initially started as a workshop associated to conferences. Since 2014, TMA is an independent event which is colocated with a PhD school that provides training to PhD students working on Internet measurements. This coupling is important because it allows the PhD students who participate in the PhD school to interact with researchers who present recent results in the field of their PhD. This interaction will not only be beneficial for the PhD students, but also for the researchers who will have to expose their results to fresh minds.

Traditionally, TMA has been particularly focused on the validation (or invalidation) of previous works in the field of network measurements. This year, TMA's Call for Papers broadened its scope to all the aspects related to network monitoring and Internet measurements, covering the entire network stack up to the application layer, with special emphasis on the measurement of cloud services, content distribution networks, social networks, mobile applications, and data centers, but also including more traditional measurement topics, such as traffic classification, anomaly detection, network performance evaluation, and traffic analysis.

As a result, this year's technical program includes papers on various network measurements topics, including measurement tools and methods, mobile and wireless, security, web, and new protocols. This year 54 papers were submitted to the TMA workshop.

The final program, composed of 16 papers, is the result of a detailed review process that has provided feedback to all authors of submitted papers. Each paper received at least three reviews and almost all the reviews were written by members of the Technical Program Committee (TPC) that was composed of 34 researchers with expertise in the workshop topics. The reviews were complemented by online discussions during one week among all the reviewers for each paper and a teleconference was organized to discuss the remaining papers. At the end of this process, authors received detailed feedback and 16 papers covering a broad range of network measurement topics were selected. The accepted papers were chosen based on their technical merits without any logistical constraint on the total number of papers.

The final program contains papers from both academia and industry. While many accepted papers were written by European researchers, there are also papers from Asia and North America.

Thank you all for attending the workshop. We hope you enjoyed the scientific program and had fruitful interactions with other researchers.

February 2015

Moritz Steiner
Pere Barlet-Ros
Olivier Bonaventure

Organization

Workshop Chairs

Pere Barlet-Ros   Universitat Politècnica de Catalunya
BarcelonaTech/Talaia Networks, Spain
Olivier Bonaventure   Université catholique de Louvain, Belgium
Moritz Steiner   Akamai Technologies, USA

Steering Committee

Ernst Biersack   Eurecom, France
Alberto Dainotti   CAIDA, USA
Xenofontas Dimitropoulos   University of Crete/FORTH, Greece
Jordi Domingo-Pascual   Universitat Politècnica de Catalunya
BarcelonaTech, Spain
Christian Kreibich   ICSI/ICIR, USA
Marco Mellia   Politecnico di Torino, Italy
Philippe Owezarski   CNRS, France
Maria Papadopouli   University of Crete/FORTH, Greece
Antonio Pescape   Università degli Studi di Napoli Federico II, Italy
Aiko Pras   University of Twente, The Netherlands
Fabio Ricciato   Austrian Institute of Technology, Austria
Yuval Shavitt   Tel Aviv University, Israel
Steve Uhlig   Queen Mary University of London, UK

PhD School Program

Renata Teixeira   Inria, France

Local Organization

Pere Barlet-Ros   Universitat Politècnica de Catalunya
BarcelonaTech/Talaia Networks, Spain
Josep Solé-Pareta   Universitat Politècnica de Catalunya
BarcelonaTech, Spain

Technical Program Committee

Bernhard Ager	ETH Zurich, Switzerland
Chadi Barakat	Inria Sophia Antipolis, France
Damiano Carra	University of Verona, Italy
Kenjiro Cho	IIJ, Japan
David Choffnes	Northeastern University, USA
Italo Cunha	Universidade Federal de Minas Gerais, Brazil
Alberto Dainotti	CAIDA, USA
Jordi Domingo-Pascual	Universitat Politècnica de Catalunya BarcelonaTech, Spain
Benoit Donnet	Université de Liège, Belgium
Constantine Dovrolis	GeorgiaTech, USA
Nick Duffield	Texas A&M University, USA
Jeff Erman	AT&T, USA
Alessandro Finamore	Politecnico di Torino, Italy
Hamed Haddadi	Queen Mary University of London, UK/Qatar Computing Research Institute, Qatar
Dali Kaafar	NICTA, Australia
Ramana Kompella	Google, USA
Pietro Michiardi	Eurecom, France
Andrew Moore	University of Cambridge, UK
Philippe Owezarski	CNRS, France
Maria Papadopouli	University of Crete/FORTH, Greece
Antonio Pescape	Università degli Studi di Napoli Federico II, Italy
Fabio Ricciato	Austrian Institute of Technology, Austria
Matthew Roughan	University of Adelaide, Australia
Josep Sanjuas	Talaia Networks, Spain
Fabian Schneider	NEC Laboratories Europe, Germany
Georgios Smaragdakis	MIT/Technische Universität Berlin/Akamai Technologies, USA
Anna Sperotto	University of Twente, The Netherlands
Gareth Tyson	Queen Mary University of London, UK
Narseo Vallina-Rodriguez	ICSI/ICIR, USA
Matteo Varvello	Telefónica, Spain
Tanja Zseby	Technische Universität Wien, Austria

TMA Sponsors

PhD School Supporters

Contents

Security

New Protocols

Measurement Tools and Methods

Selective Capping of Packet Payloads for Network Analysis and Management

Víctor Uceda, Miguel Rodríguez, Javier Ramos, José Luis García-Dorado[(⊠)], and Javier Aracil

High Performance Computing and Networking, Universidad Autónoma de Madrid, Madrid, Spain
{vic.uceda,miguel.rodriguez01}@estudiante.uam.es,
{javier.ramos,jl.garcia,javier.aracil}@uam.es

Abstract. Both network managers and analysts appreciate the importance of network traces as a mechanism to understand traffic behavior, detect anomalies and evaluate performance in a forensic manner, among other applications. Unfortunately, the process of network capture and storage has become a challenge given the ever-increasing network speeds. In this scenario, we intend to make packets thinner to reduce both write speed and storage requirements on hard-drives and further reduce computational burden of packet analysis. To this end, we propose to remove the payload on those packets that hardly could be interpreted afterwards. Essentially, binary packets from unknown protocols fall into this category. On the other hand, binary packets from well-known protocols and protocols with some ASCII data are fully captured as potentially a network analyst may desire to inspect them. We have named this approach as selective capping, which has been implemented and integrated in a high-speed network driver as an attempt to make its operation faster and more transparent to upper layers. Its results are promising as it achieves multi-Gb/s rates in different scenarios, which could be further improved exploiting novel low-level hardware-software tunings to meet the fastest networks' rates.

1 Introduction

Traffic monitoring at multi-Gb/s rates poses significant challenges not only for traffic capturing but also for traffic storage and processing. On the one hand, traffic capture at high-speed requires either ad-hoc network drivers that incorporate sophisticated prefetching, core affinity and memory mapping techniques [3] or specifically tailored network interface cards based on network processor devices or FPGA [1]. On the other hand, once the packets have been captured, they must be swiftly transferred to hard disk at the same pace that they are received from the network.

A most important issue in traffic dumping to hard disk is packet size, the larger the packet the more prone the traffic losses and the higher the storage investments. To circumvent this issue, the packet payload is capped to a predefined *snaplen* size. The aim is to reduce the offered write throughput to the hard

© IFIP International Federation for Information Processing 2015
M. Steiner et al. (Eds.): TMA 2015, LNCS 9053, pp. 3–16, 2015.
DOI: 10.1007/978-3-319-17172-2_1

disk, which is the hard disk performance figure of merit and bottleneck. Needless to say, a large share of packets contain a payload that is useless for subsequent analysis, for example encrypted payload packets. Precisely, the motivation of this research is to drop useless payload packets, by selectively capping their length to the mere packet header. The benefit of this approach is threefold: first, the hard disk bottleneck is alleviated, since the write speed requirements decrease. Second, we reduce the storage space, which is very large for a high speed network, even if the capture duration is small. Third, the computational burden required to analyze capped packets is lower, for example the RAM memory requirements of NIDS applications, such as Snort, are less stringent. We call our data thinning technique selective capping. In more detail, we propose marking a packet payload of interest according to two conditions.

First, if it is binary from a well-known protocol –i.e., if it can be interpreted by a traffic dissector. To do so, one has to identify such network services beforehand and only apply selective capping on such services, while leaving the rest untouched –e.g., using flow director filters [5] on port numbers or IP address ranges.

A packet is also interesting if it contains human readable data (more formally, ASCII, UTF-8, UTF-EBCDIC or equivalent) –which can be interpreted by a network analyst or by the application designer. The human readable, ASCII in what follows, case entails a harder work as it embraces not only all-ASCII protocols –e.g, SIP–, but protocols with both binary and ASCII interleaved parts. This is the case of HTTP for example, in which binary content (pictures, videos, etc.) is interleaved with ASCII text. Such binary content is not useful for the most performance analysis such as web profiling or HTTP server response times. Our findings show that for typical HTTP traffic up to 60% of the traffic is made up by binary content. Consequently, if the binary content could be removed on-the-fly then the hard disk input rate would be largely reduced. Similarly to HTTP there is a number of popular protocols that merge binary and ASCII which span all Internet activities. Banking networks leverage protocols such as FIX. Furthermore, routing and login protocols such as Radius and IS-IS, monitoring-oriented protocols like IPFIX and database management systems such as TNS are examples of this behavior. In the case of encrypted protocols such as HTTPS, all packet payloads are useless which motivates even more to discard them. However, it is worth remarking that encryption is not strongly present in enterprise scenarios, where monitoring is performed inside the local network and traffic is unencrypted.

Detection of ASCII packets should be as simple as inspecting the whole payload and checking if every single byte belongs to a given ASCII alphabet. However such alphabets typically encompass close to half possible byte values. As an example, ASCII encodes 128 specified characters into 7-bit binary integers which makes a random byte to fall into the alphabet range one out of two times. In this light, the following two mechanisms are proposed. The first one seeks for a set of consecutive ASCII characters on the payload, namely a run, as an approximation to the idea of a word in the natural language. The second one is based on the percentage of bytes candidates to be classified as ASCII. We have elaborated on these two mechanisms and we present a formal description of the false positive (FP) rate of both. Specifically, we show how to parameterize them to achieve a given error/FP target.

The contributions of this paper go beyond the proposal and evaluation of the selective capping algorithm. The novel algorithm is integrated in a high-speed network driver and the results show multi-Gb/s network-to-hard disk sustainable throughput, whereas the state of the art analysis reveals that no selective capping algorithms have been proposed to date but session-level or flow-record approaches. Those approaches require constructing sessions or flows which is in itself a challenging task on multi-Gb/s scenarios [1].

The rest of this section is devoted to the thorough definition of the problem and the related work on data thinning techniques for traffic captures. Section 2 provides a description of the two proposed methods, while Section 3 presents the architecture and implementation details of a traffic sniffer equipped with selective capping. Section 4 presents the results and discussion, both in terms of compression and speed. Finally, Section 5 outlines the conclusions that can be drawn from this paper and the future work lines.

1.1 Problem Statement

We define a packet payload to be of interest if:

- It is entirely-binary from a well-known service.
- It contains ASCII data –note that we are using the term ASCII as a synonym of human-readable data regardless its codification.

The rationale behind these two conditions is that the payload of a packet (over transport layer) is of interest only if it can be interpreted afterwards. In other words, network analysts may only found of interest those payloads that can be interpreted and eventually turn out useful in their tasks of understanding traffic behavior and its dynamics, detect anomalies or evaluate performance issues among others. Going back to the banking network example, one may be interested in reading error messages from certain transactions, which may be written in plain ASCII in the application-level payload.

The first condition is met by applying network and transport layers filters over traffic. The second one requires identifying ASCII traffic. After inspecting a diverse set of traces that includes academic networks and private networks from banks and large enterprises [10], we have found that the Internet carries ASCII data in diverse ways as so are protocols, services and scenarios on the Internet. Figure 1 shows the taxonomy of the findings. The figure depicts as black the ASCII part of each packet of a given class of protocols while the white part represents binary bytes. Let us elaborate in each of these classes:

- *Class I*: It represents purely binary protocols. RTP and encrypted protocols such as SSL or SSH are examples.

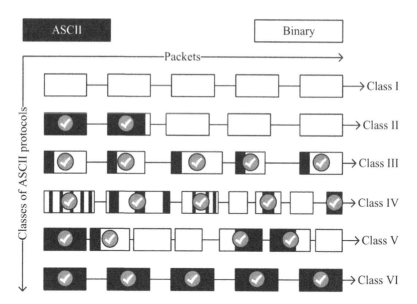

Fig. 1. Taxonomy of classes of protocols according to how ASCII data is carried

- *Class II*: Some protocols exchange ASCII data at the beginning of a connection, typically signaling, and after some sort of content is sent. This content is usually binary such as pictures, documents, or any other object. Often protocols in this class are grouped into the term flow oriented. Non-persistent HTTP is an example of this. Given its importance on Internet aggregates, the amount of bytes that can be saved by cutting the binary part of the connections is promising.
- *Class III*: As third class, we classify protocols where each packet carries an ASCII header along with binary content. They are often referred as packet oriented, Universal Plug-and-Play protocol (UPnP) is a significant example.
- *Class IV*: We define as the fourth class protocols that interleave ASCII and binary content with short runs. In this way, typically most of the packets have a binary and ASCII part and only a small fraction would be either all-ASCII or all-binary. DNS and Skinny Call Control Protocol (SCCP) are examples of this. Especially representative of this pattern are TLV-based (Type-Length-Value) protocols. In these protocols, typically, a binary code states the meaning of the subsequent values, often, ASCII values. Other significant protocols such as Lightweight Directory Access Protocol (LDAP), SNMP, Remote Authentication Dial-In User Service (RADIUS), IS-IS and H.323 among others follow this functionality. In this case, the problem cannot be addresses by keeping only the ASCII bytes of a given packet, but also it is necessary to capture the surrounding binary values which give meaning to the ASCII data. To do so we decided to mark the entire packet of interest as a faster approach to rule out several parts of a packet. In addition, once a piece of TLV behavior is found, it is likely that there will be more occurrences.

– *Class V*: Similar to the previous class but more frequent, we have found protocols that interleave both binary and ASCII data but with long runs of each of them. The most significant example is HTTP-persistent given its contribution on Internet aggregates volumes. According to the measurements in [12] about 60% of all HTTP requests are persistent and they represent more than 30% of the total transferred volume over HTTP. In addition, there are a number of both management and banking protocols that follow this pattern. Such protocols are of paramount importance for network analysts on bank networks as some of them are close protocols and reverse engineering is required to carry any study on them. An important example of them is Oracle's TNS (Transparent Network Substrate) used by databases' transfers which encompass a request –which typically includes ASCII data– and a bulk data transfer for requested objects –a file, a list of records, for example. Other examples are proprietary bank transfers' accounting protocols or communication protocols such as Link Layer Discovery Protocol (LLDP) among others.
– *Class VI*: Finally, this class states for all-ASCII protocols, for example SIP.

As conclusion, the problem we are facing is on the one hand to deploy hardware filters to forward well-known service to hard-drive; and on the other hand, in the rest of the traffic to detect those packets that include ASCII data bearing in mind the diversity of ways ASCII data is carried.

1.2 State of the Art

How to reduce the amount of stored traffic while keeping its most significant pieces of information has received notable attention by the research community given the importance of traffic traces on monitoring tasks [6,7,11,13]. The common factor of these novel works is that they first capture traffic and construct its respective flows. Then they decide what packets or fraction of payloads to rule out or how to apply compressing mechanisms on the headers and payloads of a given flow.

More specifically, the authors in [7] developed a system, named Time Machine, that rules out the last packets of the flows –i.e., packets beyond a arbitrarily-fixed threshold. The rationale behind this proposal is that such packets are often less discriminant for monitoring purposes (e.g., the signaling tends to be at the beginning of communications). This, together with the heavy-tail nature of the Internet flow sizes whereby a small fraction of flows account for most of the traffic, makes that by fixing a maximum flow size of 15 KB the required capacity translates into less than 10% of the original size, while keeping records for most of the flows. Afterwards, the authors in [6] extended the set of possible thresholds to the maximum number of bytes per packet and packets per flow with similar purposes and motivation.

An alternative approach to the problem is to compress packet headers or data. In this sense, the authors in [2] exploited the particularities of network traffic to overcome the compressing capacity of standard tools over traffic headers – such as zip or rar. Specifically, traffic follows a very specific format where some fields appear in the same position and with similarity (e.g., in a capture IP addresses tend to share a prefix and appear in the same positions). Similarly, the authors in [13] leveraged dictionary-based mechanism to reduce workload on both HTTP and DNS traffic. Strings found in such protocols are hash-mapped to numbers and replaced in the capture traces previously indexed in a database. This makes that the trace cannot be accessed directly by typical packet-oriented libraries such as libpcap nor libpcap-like flavors [3]. This is not necessarily an inconvenient in terms of both accessibility and storage capacity, but becomes a challenge in performance terms.

Precisely in this regard, the authors in [11] focused its work on high-speed networks, that is, multi-Gb/s networks. They exploit the modern NICs' capacity to configure hardware filters on-the-fly. Their proposal, Scap, constructs flows similarly to [7] but once the maximum flow size is exceeded, a NIC filter is raised to rule out subsequent packets of the corresponding flow. This makes packets that were going to be rule out at application layer be ruled out before in the network stack thus saving resources. As a result, Scap is able to deal with traffic at ranges between 2.2 and 5.5 Gb/s depending on traffic patterns and configuration. On the downside, note that discarding packets at the lowest level is often an inconvenient as such discarded packets (or at least their headers) may be of interest for monitoring purposes. Additionally, real-time filter reconfiguration becomes a challenge as setting a hardware filter takes 55 μs [5] while the inter-arrival packet can be as small as 68 ns in 10 GbE networks.

We propose to make the decision if the payload of a given packet can be potentially of interest and consequently, entirely captured, as a first step to any other tasks, which are normally resource-intensive. In this way, instead of capping the number of packets or its payload up to an arbitrarily threshold, the byte number reduction is attained by storing only those bytes that have a chance to be analyzed in the future. As mentioned before, we have termed such processed as selective capping and its explained throughout this paper.

With the aim of applying selective capping as soon as possible in the network stack and, importantly, in a transparent way to users, we have entrusted the network driver layer with this task. This implies a carefully low-level hardware-software interaction, but on the upside, a possible way to achieve multi-Gb/s rates in real traffic traces. Additionally note that by modifying driver level, we ensure that all the above-introduced stream-oriented mechanisms still remain valid. That is, after our thinning process, upper-layer proposals can be further applied for additional storage capacity cuts.

2   Detection of ASCII Traffic

Prior to ASCII traffic detection, we must realize ASCII standard and other equivalent text representations span a large fraction of the total 256 possible values for a byte. ASCII codification serves well as a generalization for human-readable data, as UTF-8 is the most used encoding over the Internet, and it uses ASCII representation for Latin characters. In particular, in ASCII alphabet such a fraction accounts for about 40%. Consequently, there are significant chances a random byte falls into the ASCII range regardless it represents an ASCII character or not.

In this scenario, we make two observations that we have translated into two different methods. Essentially, ASCII characters tend to be consecutive one another as they often represent words in natural language. We have named the method based on this observation as ASCII-Runs threshold. On the other hand, we note that is very unlikely that a large set of ASCII characters fall by chance in a randomly-payload packet. In this way, we parameterize the possibility of such a random packet containing more than a given fraction of ASCII bytes by chance. We refer this method as to ASCII-Percentage threshold.

Let us detail these two methods, explain how to parameterize them and provide a final proposal combination of both.

2.1 ASCII-Runs Threshold

In most of the text-based protocols the ASCII characters represent words –often keywords in English such as GET or POST in HTTP case. In a genuine ASCII packet, ASCII will not be randomly distributed, but there will be runs –i.e., ASCII characters located consecutively. Based on this observation, we propose a first method to seek runs of ASCII bytes in packet payload. If at least one significant run is found, we mark such packet as ASCII and otherwise as binary. We formally define a significant run as such a run whose length ensures a parameterized maximum error with respect to a randomly payload distribution in a packet. In other words, this error is the False Positive (FP) ratio, i.e., the probability of a random payload packet to be marked as ASCII when it is binary.

Let us consider a binary packet formed by random bytes. If the byte values are uniformly distributed through 0 to 255, the probability of a byte corresponding to an ASCII character will be around 0.4 (p). Then, error can be modeled using a Markov chain with $L+1$ states, each of it corresponding to have read an ASCII run of L consecutive characters, being then the last state absorbent. The stochastic matrix for this Markov chain is:

$$M_L = \begin{pmatrix} 1-p & p & 0 & 0 & \cdots & 0 \\ 1-p & 0 & p & 0 & \cdots & 0 \\ 1-p & 0 & 0 & p & \cdots & 0 \\ \vdots & \vdots & \vdots & \vdots & \ddots & \vdots \\ 1-p & 0 & 0 & 0 & \cdots & p \\ 0 & 0 & 0 & 0 & \cdots & 1 \end{pmatrix}$$

The i-th row (being zero-row the top one) represents the state where i ASCII characters have been read consecutively. The probability of finding such a run of length L can be computed by observing this Markov chain evolution in n steps, being n the length of the packet. The probability of finding an ASCII run of at least length L is then located on the upper right corner of $(M_L)^n$. By knowing this probability we can state the minimum ASCII run required to

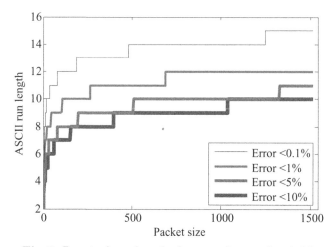

Fig. 2. Required run lengths for several error thresholds

have a pre-parameterized error probability –in the FP sense, likely a low error probability.

Figure 2 shows the required run length for different error threshold and packet sizes. As an example, a false positive ratio of one packet out of 1000, assuming 1000-byte packets entails that a run of 14 consecutive characters that fall into ASCII alphabet range should be found.

2.2 ASCII-Percentage Threshold

The ASCII-Runs threshold method fits with most of the classes showed in the taxonomy section. However, in TLV protocols chances are that the value of a given field is below the required run length. Moreover, it is unlikely that a random payload packet contains many characters falling into ASCII range. Thus, this method works out ASCII characters percentages, and then decides to mark a packet as ASCII contrasting such a percentage with a significant threshold. To calculate this significant threshold, let us consider a packet of length n as a sequence of bytes each with probability p of being 1 (which would correspond to an ASCII character) and probability 1-p of being 0 (some binary value). With this information we can compute the error rate according to the packet length.

Such an error follows a binomial distribution with parameters n and p. Its CDF $F(x)$ represents the probability of having less than x ASCII characters on a packet of length n. By studying the quantiles of this distribution, we work out the minimum ASCII percentage required to guarantee an error threshold on classifying packets. Such percentages depend on the packet length. Figure 3 shows the required ASCII percentages for different packet sizes depending on the chosen error threshold.

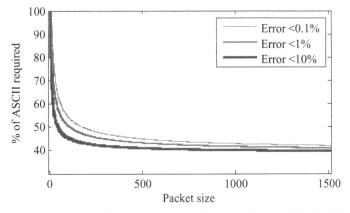

Fig. 3. Required ASCII percentages for several error thresholds

2.3   Multiple Thresholds

Both proposed methods are complementary and they are tailored to different ways ASCII data is distributed over packet payloads. Therefore, we propose to apply both of them and mark a packet as ASCII if any of the methods mark the packet as ASCII. The error threshold in this combination will be at least smaller than the largest one –e.g., if the error thresholds are 0.1 and 1%, respectively, the effective error will be strictly smaller than 1%. This motivates to apply them with the same error threshold –e.g., a low figure of 0.1%. As both are simple and based on similar principles –to seek bytes falling in a given range–, executing both concurrently does not may cause extra overhead on the system, being the slowest which sets the pace.

Note that in our approach, False Negative (FN) cases span those packets that being semantically ASCII have not met our decision thresholds. Such a semantic approach should be based on an in-depth and empirically characterization of run lengths and percentage occurrence of ASCII data in each protocol of each described class –Section 1.1.

3   Selective Capping Sniffer Architecture

The selective capping sniffer follows a two-step architecture. The first step consists on splitting incoming traffic into two categories by means of hardware filters such as Intel Flow Director [5]. Traffic is divided into well-known (in the protocol/port sense) binary traffic that network managers do want to keep, and other traffic over which managers want to cap to transport header or keep in its own if it is ASCII related. Each of these traffic sets is redirected to a different RSS (Receive-Side Scaling) driver queue. The second step is to analyze at driver level the capping candidate traffic and mark packets accordingly. Finally, both capped and uncapped packets are delivered to user level to perform the traffic storage. Figure 4 illustrates the architecture of the proposed system.

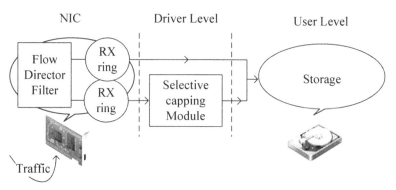

Fig. 4. Selective capping traffic sniffer architecture

Our implementation leverages HPCAP [8] as store engine. Over this base, we have added as a driver level module our implementation of the two capping methods explained previously. Note that neither flow analysis nor DPI can be performed due to time restrictions at this stage, and only simple per-packet operations can be carried out. On the upside, this would provide user level with a transparent thinning process in addition to save the resources that capped bytes do not use along network stack. Furthermore, this also allows for a higher capture throughput.

Actually, this implementation must be extremely efficient in order to cope with multi-Gb/s rates and beyond. Algorithm 1 presents it in pseudocode.

First, both ASCII runs threshold and ASCII percentage threshold are calculated offline using the models described in the previous section to provide a given error (e.g., 0.1%). After, the algorithm traverses all the payload of each packet checking if each byte falls into the printable ASCII value range.

When a run of ASCII characters of length equal to the run threshold is found, the packet is marked for full-content storage. Similarly, if the packet contains a percentage of ASCII characters which is equal to or larger than the percentage threshold, the packet is marked for full-content storage.

Finally, if none of the conditions are met the packet is capped to its transport header length, and only such data is preserved for subsequent analysis. Importantly in terms of performance, to carry out the capping to header, our implementation exploits the advanced packet-descriptor features that modern Intel's NICs offer. Such descriptors provide the protocol stack and protocol header lengths coded in NIC hardware.

After this processing, packets are delivered to user level. Then, an application stores the captured traffic along with a PCAP-like header on a high-performance store solution for subsequent access thereof (e.g., [8]). Alternatively, traffic can be first forwarded to an on-the-fly analysis system [9] or a general-purpose compression system –e.g., gzip, which is specially effective over ASCII content.

Algorithm 1. Selective Capping Algorithm

---

runASCII=0
totalASCII=0
for all bytes in payload **do**
   if MIN_PRINTABLE_ASCII<= byte_value <=MAX_PRINTABLE_ASCII **then**
     runASCII++
     totalASCII+=100
     if runASCII >= ASCII_RUNS_THRESHOLD **then**
       Do not cap packet and process next one
     end if
   else
     runASCII=0
   end if
end for
if totalASCII >= ASCII_PERCENTAGE_THRESHOLD * packet_length **then**
   Do not cap packet and process next one
end if
Cap packet and process next one

Table 1. Evaluation traces summary

Trace	Avg packet size (bytes)	Number of packets	Info.
1	164	1000000	DNS 34%, HTTP 21%, SSH 20% Dropbox 15%, Others 10%
2	786	1000000	HTTP 100%
3	927	4718531	HTTP 43%, HTTPS 13%, SSH 25% Banking protocol 17%, DNS 2%

4   Results and Discussions

We have evaluated both performance and compression ratio using three different traces. To test the performance, the traces have been replayed at different speeds above the original rate in order to explore the limits of our proposal. To test the compression rate, the traces have been replayed at the original rate and the number of capped bytes and packets have been counted. For evaluation purposes, the used flow-director filter redirects all traffic to the selective capping module.

Table 1 shows the most relevant information for each used trace. Trace 1 has been captured in an academic link and contains HTTP, DNS, SSH and Dropbox traffic. Trace 2 contains only HTTP traffic captured from the enterprise network of an important insurance company. Trace 3 has been captured in a large commercial bank network and contains HTTP, HTTPS, SSH, proprietary banking protocols and DNS.

The reception evaluation has been performed on an server with 128 GB of DDR4 memory and two 6-core Intel Xeon processors running at 2.30 GHz. The server motherboard model is Supermicro X9DR3-F. Additionally, to perform the

Table 2. Compression ratio

Trace	Compression ratio	% of capped packets
1	4.28	45
2	3.33	74
3	3.24	81

packet reception, a 10 Gb/s NIC based on an Intel 82599 chip has been used. This NIC is connected using a PCIe 3.0 slot. On the sender side, traffic has been replayed using another Intel 82599 card and a custom software traffic generator based on PacketShader [4] API. Such generator is able to replay PCAP traces at variable rates.

4.1   Compression Ratio

First the compression level of our proposal is evaluated. To this end, the aforementioned traces have been replayed at original rates while capturing and storing into disk. After the replay is complete, the original and captured traces are compared in order to obtain the compression ratio. Table 2 shows the compression ratio values in terms of stored bytes and the amount of capped packets. As it can be observed in Trace 1, almost every packet is capped providing a compression ratio of 4.28. In the case of Trace 2, only 74% of the packets are capped obtaining a compression ratio of 3.33. Finally, in Trace 3 81% of the packets have been capped obtaining a compression ratio of 3.24.

It is worth remarking that although not all the traffic in Trace 3 is HTTP, a large amount of packets have been capped including bank protocols which provides a good idea of the applicability of the capping techniques in both commercial and academic networks where heterogeneous traffic is found.

4.2   Performance Evaluation

Once the compression ratio has been assessed, the aforementioned traces have been replayed at different rates until lossless packet capture and disk storage is achieved, in order to test the performance of the proposed method. The duration of each experiment is 30 minutes. Table 3 shows the average packet capture throughput including our capping methodology for each 30-minute experiment. For the sake of completeness also observed standard deviation is reported.

Table 3. Average capping throughput

Trace	Avg. throughput (Gb/s) ± Std. Dev.	Avg. packet rate (Kpps) ± Std. Dev.
1	3.1 ± 0.13	2221 ± 100
2	2.5 ± 0.08	856 ± 29
3	3.2 ± 0.15	428 ± 21

As shown, our proposal achieves multi-gigabit capture rates. Depending on the payload and packet-rate of each trace different capture rates are achieved. For example, if a trace contains a large amount of binary packets, the workload of the system is greater as each single byte of the binary packet has to be checked before packet is capped.

On the other hand if a trace contains a large amount of text packets, only a small byte-run must be checked before packet is fully captured. An example of this case is Trace 1 where 45% of the packets are text packets. Trace 2 contains a large amount of binary packets and presents a significant average packet rate which results in a reduced performance. Despite the large amount of binary packets present in Trace 3, the average packet rate is smaller than Trace 2 which results in better performance as fewer packets per second must be checked.

Finally, regarding memory consumption, our solution makes use of a static 1GB kernel packet buffer to receive and analyze incoming traffic.

5 Conclusions and Future Work

We have presented a solution for selective packet capping –on-the-fly– to reduce the amount of stored data in multi-Gb/s networks. Our proposal focuses on keeping the payload of those packets that are worth interpreting by network managers and analysts. As a consequence our proposal stores both well-known (in the protocol/port sense) binary protocols and ASCII protocols. The latter has received most of our attention given the difficulties to address it in light of the protocol-diverse and high-speed nature of current business applications. To this end, two methods for ASCII packet identification have been implemented at driver level by modifying a novel high-performance capture engine. The implementation of selective capping allows us to provide a clean and transparent mechanism to cap packets without user-level interaction/tuning. Performance and compression ratio have been assessed using both academic and commercial traffic obtaining compression ratios between 3 and 4. On the other hand, the performance results achieve remarkable multi-Gb/s rates –ranging from 2.5 Gb/s to 3.2 Gb/s– which do not suffice for the fastest network interfaces rates –10, 40 and even 100 Gb/s. Nonetheless, our solution has proven to cope with a real-world OC-192 link such as the one described in [14].

Therefore, as future work we first plan to attack the capping problem in full-loaded 10 GbE links. To this end, we are studying the use of parallelism paradigms, likely at user level and hardware solutions such as NetFPGAs or GPUs. Similarly, we are studying how to reduce the burden of looking for ASCII data. For example, instead of inspecting full packet payload, we could limit the inspection to one or several randomly-chosen windows.

Moreover, we have realized that packet payloads sometimes contain constant values for long runs. Such runs do not provide network analysts with any interesting piece of information and should be capped. As a result, we are measuring the dispersion of the values of bytes in payloads as an attempt to find a formal threshold below which packet payloads render useless. Similary, we are studying if some legibility indicators –e.g., vowels, punctuation or entropy– could be useful to separate semantically-worth ASCII from the total traffic classified as ASCII.

Finally, throughout this paper we have focused on ASCII standard as an illustrative example of codification scheme. We are currently extending our work to other popular schemes such as Base64 and full UTF-8.

References

1. Forconesi, M., Sutter, G., López-Buedo, S., López de Vergara, J.E., Aracil, J.: Bridging the gap between hardware and software open-source network developments. IEEE Network **28**(5), 13–19 (2014)
2. Fusco, F., Vlachos, M., Dimitropoulos, X.: Rasterzip: compressing streaming network monitoring data with support for partial decompression. In: ACM Internet Measurement Conference, pp. 51–64 (2012)
3. García-Dorado, J.L., Mata, F., Ramos, J., Santiago del Río, P.M., Moreno, V., Aracil, J.: High-Performance network traffic processing systems using commodity hardware. In: Biersack, E., Callegari, C., Matijasevic, M. (eds.) Data Traffic Monitoring and Analysis. LNCS, vol. 7754, pp. 3–27. Springer, Heidelberg (2013)
4. Han, S., Jang, K., Park, K.S., Moon, S.: PacketShader: a GPU-accelerated software router. In: ACM SIGCOMM, pp. 195–206 (2010)
5. Intel: 82599 10 Gbe controller datasheet (2012). http://www.intel.com/content/www/us/en/ethernet-controllers/82599-10-gbe-controller-datasheet.html (December 1, 2014)
6. Lin, Y.D., Lin, P.C., Cheng, T.H., Chen, I.W., Lai, Y.C.: Low-storage capture and loss recovery selective replay of real flows. IEEE Communications Magazine **50**(4), 114–121 (2012)
7. Maier, G., Sommer, R., Dreger, H., Feldmann, A., Paxson, V., Schneider, F.: Enriching network security analysis with time travel. In: ACM SIGCOMM, pp. 183–194 (2008)
8. Moreno, V., Santiago del Río, P.M., Ramos, J., García-Dorado, J.L., Gonzalez, I., Gómez-Arribas, F.J., Aracil, J.: Packet storage at multi-gigabit rates using off-the-shelf systems. In: IEEE Conference on High Performance and Communications, pp. 486–489 (2014)
9. Moreno, V., Santiago del Río, P.M., Ramos, J., Muelas, D., García-Dorado, J.L., Gómez-Arribas, F.J., Aracil, J.: Multi-granular, multi-purpose and multi-Gb/s monitoring on off-the-shelf systems. International Journal of Network Management **24**(4), 221–234 (2014)
10. naudit: Detect-pro (2013). http://www.naudit.es/ (December 1, 2014)
11. Papadogiannakis, A., Polychronakis, M., Markatos, E.P.: Scap: Stream-oriented network traffic capture and analysis for high-speed networks. In: ACM Internet Measurement Conference, pp. 113–124 (2012)
12. Schneider, F., Ager, B., Maier, G., Feldmann, A., Uhlig, S.: Pitfalls in HTTP traffic measurements and analysis. In: Taft, N., Ricciato, F. (eds.) PAM 2012. LNCS, vol. 7192, pp. 242–251. Springer, Heidelberg (2012)
13. Taylor, T., Coull, S.E., Monrose, F., McHugh, J.: Toward efficient querying of compressed network payloads. In: USENIX Annual Technical Conference, pp. 113–124 (2012)
14. Walsworth, C., Aben, E., Claffy, K., Andersen, D.: The CAIDA anonymized 2009 Internet traces. http://www.caida.org/data/passive/passive_2009_dataset.xml (December 1, 2014)

Youtube Revisited: On the Importance of Correct Measurement Methodology

Ossi Karkulahti$^{(\boxtimes)}$ and Jussi Kangasharju

Department of Computer Science, University of Helsinki, Helsinki, Finland
{karkulah,jakangas}@cs.helsinki.fi

Abstract. Measurements of large systems typically rely on sampling to keep the measurement effort practical. For example, Youtube's video popularity has been measured by crawling either related videos or videos belonging to certain categories or by using a list of, e.g., the most recent videos as the data-source. In this paper we demonstrate that all these methods lead to a biased sample of data when compared to a random sample. We demonstrate the bias by comparing the differently sampled data sets in terms of different commonly used metrics, such as video popularity, age, length, or category. The results show that different sampling methods lead to significantly different values in the metrics, thus potentially leading to very different conclusions about the system under study. The goal of the paper is not to provide yet-another-set-of-numbers for YouTube; instead we seek to emphasize the importance of using correct measurement methodologies and understanding the inherent weaknesses of different methodologies.

1 Introduction

Measuring large systems or services is challenging and typically measurements are performed via sampling since analyzing the complete system is either prohibitively expensive or even impossible. Naturally, the way the sampling is performed has a strong effect on the measurement results and the conclusions that can be drawn from them. Ideally, the sampling should be done in a way as to produce a random, representative sample of the total system, but in many cases technological limitations on the sampling may skew the process away from getting a representative sample. Using such a biased sample may yield incorrect conclusions about the properties of the system and further affect any derivative work which uses those results as its basis.

In this paper we show the effects of three different sampling methods on YouTube. YouTube is the largest and most popular video service on the Internet and has been an active focus in research for many years. Previously, YouTube's video popularity has been measured, for example, by crawling related videos [2], selecting videos belonging to certain categories [1], or by using a list of, e.g., the most recent videos [6] as the data-source. The problem with these methods is that, while the corresponding results of the measurements are valid as such, the methods lead to a biased sample, and thus, the results are not representative of

© IFIP International Federation for Information Processing 2015
M. Steiner et al. (Eds.): TMA 2015, LNCS 9053, pp. 17–30, 2015.
DOI: 10.1007/978-3-319-17172-2_2

YouTube in all respects. Since other works may base their assumptions on the measured values, it is important that they indeed do represent the whole service and not a subset of it.

To demonstrate our case, we have collected three datasets, two by using methods from earlier research, and one by using a method that is based on random video IDs that has previously been used to estimate the number of videos on YouTube. We will show that, even though all data is obtained from the same source, via the YouTube API, there are noticeable discrepancies in the video popularity and other metrics depending on the method used.

Our main goal is to highlight the importance of using proper sampling techniques and show how different sampling methods can lead to different conclusions. The main contributions of the paper are the following:

- We review prior YouTube measurements and data collection methodologies and show their differences.
- We compare three existing methods for collecting YouTube video metadata.
- We demonstrate the differences in various metrics between the different sampling methods.

We also argue that, while out of the scope of this paper, the value of the result and the implications drawn from results span multiple research areas such as storage, replication, bandwidth and even wider disciplines such as marketing, user experience and user behavior.

The rest of the paper is organized as follows. In Section 2 we discuss related work and review previous measurement methods that have been used on YouTube. Section 3 presents our data collection process. The results are presented in Section 4 where we compare several key metrics obtained by the different methods and demonstrate their differences. Finally, Section 5 concludes the paper.

2   Related Work

Cha et al. [1] analyzed the video popularity of YouTube in 2006-2007. Their dataset consists of video metadata formed by crawling the indexed pages and getting videos belonging to certain categories. They had 1.7 million videos from Entertainment category and another 250,000 from Science category. Their results showed that the video popularity ranking of both categories exhibited power-law behavior "across more than two orders of magnitude" with "truncated tails" but "the exact popularity distribution seems category-dependent." The authors called for further research on the subject. The traces collected by the study have been a source for [7].

Cheng et al. [2] also measured and examined, among other things, the popularity of YouTube videos. They collected metadata for three million videos in 2007 and for further five million in 2008, using bread-first search (BFS) starting with initial video and asking its related videos and then their related videos until the fourth depth. Looking at video popularity they observed that: "though the plot has a long tail on the linear scale, it does not follow the well-known Zipf distribution." and found "that the Gamma and Weibull distributions both fit better than the Zipf, due to the heavy tail that they have".

Since the authors were concerned that the BFS method would be biased towards more popular videos, they formed another dataset by collecting meta-data of videos from the recently added list for four weeks. Comparing the two datasets they concluded that also the videos from the recently added list exhibit popularity where: "There is a clear heavy tail" and "verifying that our BFS crawl does find non-popular videos just as well as it finds popular ones".

Szabo and Huberman took a slightly different approach and wanted to see whether it is possible to predict content popularity. In the case of YouTube they measured the popularity and view counts of new videos for 30 days [6]. Their data is from 2008 and consists of 7,146 videos selected daily from the recently added list. They chose the list over other alternatives in order to get "an unbiased sample". They concluded that the popularity of a YouTube video on the 30th day can be predicted with a 10 % relative error after 10 days.

In the research mentioned above, the data has been collected either by BFS crawling, or by selecting videos of a certain category or by picking most recent videos. We will show in the results section the problems that are associated with the methods and popularity distributions they produce.

Another method is used e.g. by Gill et al. [3] who analyzed the traffic between a university campus and Youtube servers. They concluded that "video references at our campus follow a Zipf-like distribution". They reasoned it to be partly because Youtube did not allow video downloading, meaning that a user had to issue another request to see the same video again. They also found out that on a longer time frame the most popular categories were Entertainment, Music, and Comedy. Zink [9] et al. also measured the Youtube viewing and traffic patterns on a campus level and studied the effects of proxy caches to reduce traffic.

On a more general level, the importance of a correct sampling method has been noted e.g. by Krishnamurthy et al. [4] who used three different data collection methods and analyzed their strengths and weaknesses in order to examine Twitter and improve the prior research, and by Stutzbach et al. [5] who introduced a technique for a more accurate and unbiased sampling for unstructured peer-to-peer networks.

3   Data Collection

We have collected data using three different approaches. In the first approach, we started by periodically asking a list of the 50 most recently published videos using the YouTube API version 2 and later version 3. The list included information of the videos such as ID, view count, and publish date. Having obtained the IDs of the videos, we later collected their view counts after 30 days. We had done similar surveys in 2009 and 2011 and we wanted to compare the results by doing the same procedure again in late 2013 and early 2014. We refer to this method as MR (Most Recent). The inherent problems of the MR method are that it is a slow way of collecting data and that videos for which data is collected are limited to similar age. The method is similar to one used in [6] and [2].

However, as it is not known in which manner videos end up on the MR list and thus it is not possible to know whether they constitute a representative sample, we simultaneously started collecting data using a different method in order to the verify our results. In this approach, we generated random character strings and requested through the API a list of video IDs which include the string. Hence we call this method RS (Random Strings). In more detail, the method can be described as follows. We formed four characters long strings using random characters from 'a-Z', '0-9', '-', and '_'. As the YouTube video IDs are 11-character long strings generated with the same character set, we used the strings as keywords to request video IDs containing the random strings (4 characters were the shortest strings that returned matches consistently via the search). Resulting data also included video metadata such as duration, category, etc., and on average a random string yielded 6.9 video IDs. Besides randomness, the benefits of the method are that we were able to collect a very large number of video IDs with corresponding metadata and it provided a way to get a comprehensive sample of different-aged videos. Given that different strings might match to same ID, we further pruned out the duplicates.

Interestingly, for reasons unknown to us, with this method the YouTube API only returns video IDs that have at least one '-' in them, even though, in general, video IDs do not need to contain a '-'. The "-" was usually the fifth character of the ID. However, we argue that as the search strings are randomly generated (and the IDs are likely similarly generated, although this cannot be proven), statistically the sample obtained in this manner is equivalent to a random sample over all the videos; obviously this is a potential weakness of this method. Incidentally, Zhou et al. [8] provide a detailed description and discussion of the same method, with evidence to support that it indeed provides a random sample of the videos. However, their focus is on estimating the number of videos on YouTube and they do not investigate different metrics for the videos. They also mention a potential bias in other collection methodologies, such as BFS, but do not present any evidence of that. While we strongly conjecture that the RS method provides a random sample, for the purposes of this paper, i.e., to demonstrate the differences between different sampling methods, it is not strictly necessary for the method to actually produce a random sample. A further limitation of this method is that it will not return videos with 0 views or deleted videos.

Our third method to collect data was to randomly select a video ID and then ask for its related videos and after that the related videos for all those videos up until to the fourth level. We set a limit of 50 related videos per one video, so theoretically one seed video could return up to 125,000 videos (50x50x50). The actual number of unique videos is naturally lower, due to overlap in the related videos. This can been seen as similar to breadth-first search and we shall refer to the method as BFS. As mentioned in Section 2 this method has been used earlier by [2]. This method is a fast way of obtain a large set of IDs, since the API allows getting the information of 50 videos with just one API request compared to the average of 6.9 obtained with the random strings. Because a video can be, and usually is, related to multiple videos, the method also needs pruning to remove duplicates.

Table 1. Description of datasets

Set name	Method	Time period	N
MR-09	Most recent videos	summer 2009	9,405
MR-11	Most recent videos	summer 2011	8,766
MR-14	Most recent videos	late 2013 - early 2014	10,000
RS	Random id	early 2014	5M
BFS	BFS related videos	early 2014	5M

Table 1 shows an overview of the different datasets that we collected using the three methods described above. All of the data we have collected will be made available. In the following, we refer to the different datasets by their names and in some cases combine all three MR datasets into a single set, called MR.

4   Results

As described in the previous section, we have three datasets collected using three different methods. Now we are going to show how the datasets differ according to different typical metrics that have been used in previous research on YouTube. We start with the video popularity ranking and then use number of views, age, length, and categories to further compare the datasets. Obviously, as the MR dataset is much smaller and the videos are by definition very recently uploaded (to the time when the dataset is collected), thus it does not allow one-to-one comparison with the other two methods in some metrics.

4.1   Popularity

Figure 1 plots the videos of RS and BFS datasets ranked based on the view count in log-log scale. Both datasets have 5 million videos. As can be obviously seen, there is a clear difference in the view count distributions provided by the two methods. The data collected using BFS method has a clear two-part distribution, with a quick-dropping tail. The RS data follows more closely a Zipf distribution, with a truncated tail. Across the board, the distribution of BFS data exhibits much higher popularity (higher view counts), being in parts four orders of magnitude higher (around the millionth most viewed video). Since RS represents a random sample, it can be argued that the BFS method provides videos which significantly over-estimate the actual view counts in YouTube. We suspect that when determining which videos to show as related videos, YouTube proposes videos that are more popular than average, and, thus, BFS datasets are prone to have inflated number of videos with high view counts.

A simple analysis reveals that the 10 most viewed videos in RS dataset account for 5 % of the total views, 100 most viewed for 17 %, 1000 for 43 %, and 10,000 (0.2 % of the total sample) for 74 %.

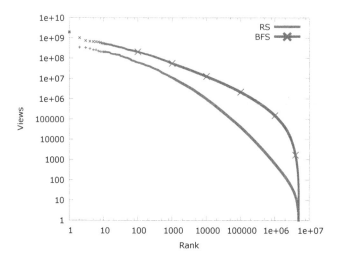

Fig. 1. Video popularity

Popularity Per Category. Figure 2 plots the popularity distributions of different categories. We show view counts for categories Music and People & Blogs as well as the view counts for a random selection; all other categories fall somewhere between Music and People. The data is taken from RS dataset and the sample size is 100,000. While the shapes of the curves are qualitatively similar, the actual numerical values (between the categories shown here) can differ by an order of magnitude or more in terms of number of views. This illustrates that while a category-based video selection may yield qualitatively correct results, it cannot be relied to provide quantitatively correct results.

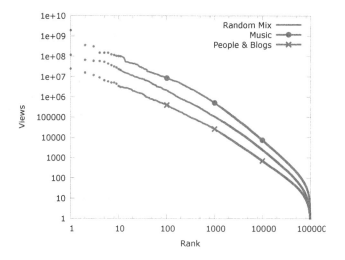

Fig. 2. Video popularity per category

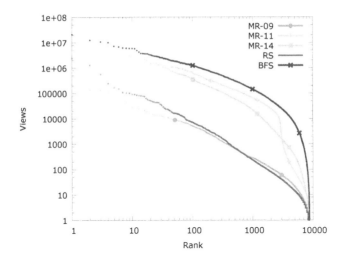

Fig. 3. 30-day view count ranking comparison

These results highlight the pitfalls in sampling method selection. Different methods may yield qualitatively, even quantitatively, similar results on some metrics, but fail on other metrics as we demonstrate below.

Popularity After 30 Days. Figure 3 shows the view counts of videos 30 days after their uploading, on a log-log scale, i.e., the plot captures the popularity of one month old videos. We show all three MR datasets separately and the x-axis is limited to 8766 which is the size of the MR-11 dataset (the smallest dataset in our study) to make the curves comparable. As can be seen, the datasets have noticeably different popularity distributions. In general, both MR and BFS methods seem to overestimate the video popularity when compared to RS (Recall Figure 1 which shows the same result between BFS and RS across a larger dataset). Interestingly, the MR-09 shows a relatively straight line, close to that of RS, with a truncated tail, resembling the observations of Cha et al. [1], whereas the MR-11 would seem at least bipartite, pivoting around 12,000 views.

The view counts of MR-11, MR-14, and BFS are orders of magnitude higher than those of RS. We suspect that this is because either a) new videos on the most recent list are such that are more likely attract more views or b) being on the list will make the videos gain more views. The same conjecture applies also more or less to the related videos.

4.2 Views

Table 2 list the view count statistics for the datasets. It should be noted that the numbers for the MR dataset are not directly comparable with the others, since the dataset includes mostly new videos and thus they have had a shorter time to accumulate views. As already stated, the BFS method favors more popular

Table 2. View count statistics of the datasets

	N	Mean	Std. Dev	Median	Min	Max
RS	5M	16,260	1,115,835	81	1	1,920,284,708
BFS	5M	260,019	2,595,870	19,217	1	1,950,573,461
MR	21K	68,553	1,205,992	461	1	111,762,034

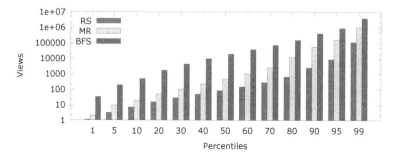

Fig. 4. View count percentiles

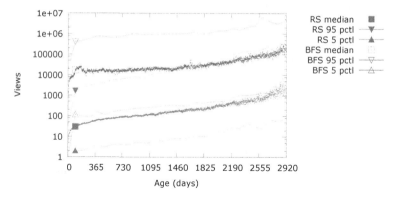

Fig. 5. Median and 5th and 95th percentiles of RS and BFS

videos, which can be seen in the much higher mean and median values. In other
words, in general, the videos of the BFS dataset are more viewed than those
of RS. Figure 4 shows the different percentiles of the view counts. We can see
that e.g. the 5th percentile of BFS is higher than the median of RS and across
the board the BFS view counts are at least one order of magnitude higher than
the RS ones. Figure 5 further illustrated this point by showing the median and
the 5th and 95th percentiles of the RS and BFS datasets for eight years. For
example, in the RS dataset the median value of 730-day-old videos is approximately 100 views. Looking at the percentiles we can see that there is overlap in
the datasets, but the median of BFS is most of the time two orders of magnitude
higher than the median of RS.

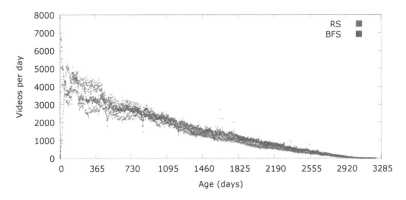

Fig. 6. Video age distribution

4.3   Age

Figure 6 illustrates the age distribution of the videos gathered by the RS and BFS methods. The MR data is left out as the age is already determined by the way the method works, limiting the data to new videos only. The plot is made by calculating the number of videos published on each day. The BFS set has less videos that are newer than three years, when compared to the RS dataset. However, for very recent videos, the BFS dataset shows a considerable increase, reaching up to more than three times the number of videos with similar age in the RS set. It therefore appears that the selection of related videos is biased towards recent videos and implies that the BFS dataset has a disproportionate number of recent videos, when compared to the RS set.

RS dataset shows a sharp decrease in the number of recent videos, but this is an artifact of the sampling method. This is because the method can only match existing videos and therefore videos that were uploaded after the data collection began have had a smaller probability of being selected, thus artificially reducing their number in the set. This effect can be eliminated simply by not counting the videos published during the data collection period.

On a more general note, looking at the RS data, we can see that that number of videos has grown rapidly, (even exponentially in some points), and continues to do so. Videos that are less than six months old make up 14 % of all video, less than one year 29 % and less than two years 53 %. In other words, majority of the YouTube content is newer than two years and 80 % newer than four years. Hence, the rate at which videos are uploaded to YouTube is still increasing and majority of videos have been published in the past two years.

4.4   Categories

Figure 7a shows the fraction of videos in different categories in the different datasets. The bars for MR combine all the three MR datasets MR-09, -11, and -14. Interestingly, the category with most videos is different in each dataset and the differences are significant. RS has most videos from the People & Blogs

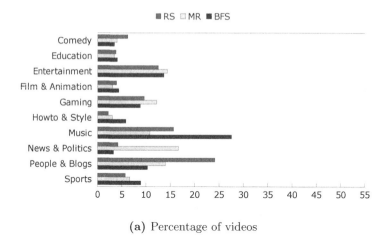

(a) Percentage of videos

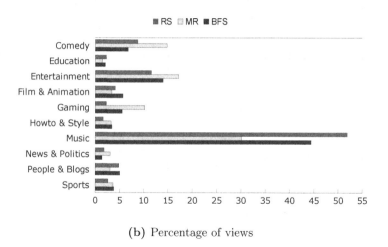

(b) Percentage of views

Fig. 7. Video categories

category, MR's biggest category is News & Politics, and Music is the largest category for BFS. When uploading a video, YouTube requires that the user sets a category for the video. If user does not not explicitly define a category, YouTube sets the video's category to the category of the last video that the user uploaded. If no prior upload exists, YouTube sets the video's category to People & Blogs, which is a very likely explanation why the RS dataset has the most videos in the People & Blogs category. Likewise, since MR takes the videos from the (curated) most recent list, it is not surprising that topical events dominate the list. For BFS, the high number of music videos is also not surprising since suggesting another music video as a related video to another music video seems intuitive.

However, even though the number of videos in different categories is very different for the three datasets, Figure 7b shows that the distribution of number of views across categories in the three datasets is very similar. Music is the most watched category for all three datasets, followed by Entertainment and then Comedy. Again, this highlights that the results from different methods may end up looking similar on some metrics, but not on others.

4.5 Length

YouTube used to cap the video duration to 10 minutes, but now the default limit has been extended to 15 minutes and a user can remove the limit completely by verifying the account. Table 3 shows the length statistics. The lengths are in seconds. We have checked that the maximum value for the BFS dataset is valid. The median video length is the highest for the videos of the BFS dataset, followed by MR and RS, whereas MR has the highest mean and standard deviation.

Figure 8a shows how the lengths of the videos in the different datasets vary; the videos have been rounded to the next minute for plotting. Both RS and MR show that the most common length of a YouTube video is 60 seconds or less and that majority of video are less than three minutes long. The BFS in turn indicates that most videos between three and five minutes. This can be considered further evidence that BFS promotes certain type of videos forming a biased sample; as we already saw that BFS contains more music videos which are typically three to five minutes long. Interestingly, MR and RS differ only in that MR has more videos over 15 minutes whereas RS has more videos of one minute or less.

However, Figure 8b shows videos between three and five minutes have the most views in all datasets. If this data were used to produce an estimate of how much traffic YouTube sees, all three datasets would yield similar values, with MR being likely slightly below the others as it contains proportionally more videos of around 3 minutes.

Figure 9 show total duration of videos uploaded per day as a function of the age of the videos. This could also be used to obtain a rough estimate of total storage requirements of YouTube service. Again, BFS over-estimates the video length. As the figure shows, the amount of data has risen almost exponentially for years. 40 % of the amount consists of less than one year old videos and 80 % of videos newer three years.

Table 3. Length statistics of the datasets

	N	Mean	Std. Dev	Median	Min	Max
RS	5M	296	614	157	1	131,516
BFS	5M	512	1,181	247	1	800,492
MR	21K	545	1,535	190	1	45,122

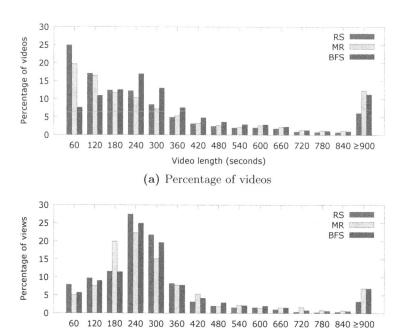

(a) Percentage of videos

(b) Percentage of views

Fig. 8. Video length

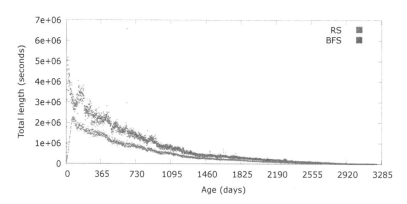

Fig. 9. Total video length per day

4.6 Summary of Results and Methods

When comparing the three methods among themselves, BFS tends to over-estimate most of the metrics we used and cannot therefore be considered a reliable method; however, it is the fastest of the three for collecting a large data-set. MR, on the other hand, is a very slow method, limited to new videos only, and it also tends towards over-estimation of the metrics. While we consider the

RS method to be the most reliable, its weakness is that it is not very fast (recall that it returns on average 6.9 videos per query). Also, since all returned videos contain '-', there is potential for a bias in the returned videos, in case video IDs are not assigned randomly.

5   Conclusion

In this paper we have argued that data collection methodology can have a significant impact on what kinds of results can be obtained from measurements. We have used YouTube as an example and considered three different data collection methods, two from existing research and one adapted from previous work. By comparing the datasets obtained with the three different methods, we have shown that they differ, sometimes greatly, in many of the key metrics used in past research on YouTube. Even a large sample is not immune to the bias introduced by a particular measurement methodology, as the results of the BFS dataset demonstrate.

The random sampling method behind the RS dataset has not been used to measure different metrics on YouTube whereas MR and BFS have been used in previous research to characterize YouTube. Given the large difference between RS and the others on several key metrics, it is natural to raise questions about the general applicability of previously obtained results on YouTube done via MR or BFS methods. As we have shown in this paper, depending on the metric and the collection methodology, results may differ either qualitatively, quantitatively, or both, or they might not differ from the RS dataset. While we have strong reasons to believe that the RS method produces a representative sample of YouTube, we cannot exclude a potential bias in its selection methodology; further research would be needed to ascertain that.

In essence, our results demonstrate that there is a need to understand the strengths and weaknesses of the different measurement methodologies in order to understand their impact on the measurement results. We believe that on the whole, a more critical approach to measurement methodologies is required in order to ensure that the measurements capture the essence of the measured system, to the extent that it is feasible.

References

1. Cha, M., Kwak, H., Rodriguez, P., Ahn, Y.-Y., Moon. S.: I tube, you tube, everybody tubes: analyzing the world's largest user generated content video system. In: Proceedings of the 7th ACM SIGCOMM Conference on Internet measurement, pp. 1–14. ACM (2007)
2. Cheng, X., Liu, J., Dale, C.: Understanding the characteristics of internet short video sharing: A youtube-based measurement study. IEEE Transactions on Multimedia 15(5), 1184–1194 (2013)
3. Gill, P., Arlitt, M., Li, Z., Mahanti, A.: Youtube traffic characterization: a view from the edge. In: Proceedings of the 7th ACM SIGCOMM Conference on Internet Measurement, pp. 15–28. ACM (2007)

4. Krishnamurthy, B., Gill, P., Arlitt, M.: A few chirps about twitter. In: Proceedings of the Tworkshop on Online Social Networks, pp. 19–24. ACM (2008)
5. Stutzbach, D., Rejaie, R., Duffield, N., Sen, S., Willinger, W.: On unbiased sampling for unstructured peer-to-peer networks. IEEE/ACM Transactions on Networking (TON) **17**(2), 377–390 (2009)
6. Szabo, G., Huberman, B.A.: Predicting the popularity of online content. Communications of the ACM **53**(8), 80–88 (2010)
7. Valancius, V., Laoutaris, N., Massoulié, L., Diot, C., Rodriguez, P.: Greening the internet with nano data centers. In: Proceedings of the 5th International Conference on Emerging Networking Experiments and Technologies, pp. 37–48. ACM (2009)
8. Zhou, J., Li, Y., Adhikari, V.K., Zhang, Z.-L.: Counting youtube videos via random prefix sampling. In: Proceedings of the 2011 ACM SIGCOMM Conference on Internet Measurement Conference, pp. 371–380. ACM (2011)
9. Zink, M., Suh, K., Gu, Y., Kurose, J.: Characteristics of youtube network traffic at a campus network-measurements, models, and implications. Computer Networks **53**(4), 501–514 (2009)

Zen and the Art of Network Troubleshooting: A Hands on Experimental Study

François Espinet[1], Diana Joumblatt[2]([✉]), and Dario Rossi[1,2]

[1] Ecole Polytechnique, Paris, France
{François.Espinet,Dario.Rossi}@polytechnique.edu
[2] Telecom ParisTech, Paris, France
Diana.Joumblatt@enst.fr

Abstract. Growing network complexity necessitates tools and methodologies to automate network troubleshooting. In this paper, we follow a crowd-sourcing trend, and argue for the need to deploy measurement probes at end-user devices and gateways, which can be under the control of the users or the ISP.

Depending on the amount of information available to the probes (e.g., ISP topology), we formalize the network troubleshooting task as either a clustering or a classification problem, that we solve with an algorithm that (i) achieves perfect classification under the assumption of a strategic selection of probes (e.g., assisted by an ISP) and (ii) operates blindly with respect to the network performance metrics, of which we consider delay and bandwidth in this paper.

While previous work on network troubleshooting privileges a more theoretical vs practical approaches, our workflow balances both aspects as (i) we conduct a set of controlled experiments with a rigorous and reproducible methodology, (ii) on an emulator that we thoroughly calibrate, (iii) contrasting experimental results affected by real-world noise with expected results from a probabilistic model.

1 Introduction

Nowadays, broadband Internet access is vital. Many people rely on online applications in their homes to watch TV, make VoIP calls, and interact with each other through social media and emails. Unfortunately, dynamic network conditions such as device failures and congested links can affect the network performance and cause disruptions (e.g. frozen video, poor VoIP quality).

Currently, troubleshooting performance disruptions is complex and ad hoc due to the presence of different applications, network protocols, and administrative domains. Typically, troubleshooting starts with a user call to the ISP help desk. However, the intervention of the ISP technician is useless if the root cause lies outside of the ISP network, which possibly includes the home network of the very same user – hence, for the ISP, it would be valuable to extend its reach beyond the home gateway by instrumenting experiments directly from end-user devices. While (tech savvy) users can be assisted in their troubleshooting efforts

© IFIP International Federation for Information Processing 2015
M. Steiner et al. (Eds.): TMA 2015, LNCS 9053, pp. 31–45, 2015.
DOI: 10.1007/978-3-319-17172-2_3

by software tools such as [4,6,17,19] which automate a number of useful measurements, these tools do not incorporate network tomography techniques [9,21] to identify the root causes of network disruptions (e.g., faulty links). Additionally, these tools are generally ISP network-agnostic, hence, they would benefit from cooperation with the ISP.

In this paper, we propose a practical methodology to automate the identification of faulty links in the access network based on end-to-end measurements. Since the devices participating in the troubleshooting task can be either under the control of the end-user or the ISP, the knowledge of the ISP topology is not always available for the measurement probes. Consequently, we formalize the troubleshooting task as either a *clustering* or a *classification* problem – where respectively end-users are able to assess the severity of the fault, or ISPs are able to identify the faulty link.

This paper makes several contributions. While our troubleshooting *model* (Sec. 3), *algorithm* (Sec. 4) and *software implementation* (Sec. 5) are interesting per se, we believe our major contribution is the rigour of the *evaluation* methodology (Sec. 6), which overcomes state of the art limits (Sec. 2). Indeed, on one hand, previous practical troubleshooting efforts [4,6,16,17,19] are valuable in terms of domain knowledge and engineering, but lack theoretical foundations and rigorous verification. On the other hand, prior analytical efforts are cast on solid theoretic ground [9,21], but their validation is either simplistic (e.g. simulations) or lacks ground truth (e.g. PlanetLab).

In this work, we take the best of both worlds, as we (i) propose a practical methodology for network troubleshooting with an open source implementation; (ii) provide a model of the expected fault detection probability that we contrast with experimental results; (iii) use an experimental approach where we emulate controlled network conditions with Mininet [13]; (iv) perform a calibration of the emulation setup, an often neglected albeit mandatory task; (v) in spirit with Mininet and the TMA community, we further make all our source code available for the scientific community at [1,2].

2   Related Work

Our work complements prior network troubleshooting efforts [3,4,6–8,16–19,23] that we overview in this section. Without attempting at a full-blown taxonomy, we may divide the above work as having a more *practical*[3,4,6,16,17,19] or *theoretic*[7,8,18,23] approach. While most work, including ours, uses active measurements [4,6–8,17–19,23], there are exceptions that use passive measurements [16] or logs[3]. In terms of network segment, previous work focuses on home networks [17], enterprise networks [3], and backbone networks [5,9,18]. Some studies do not target a network segment in particular[7,8,23] and remain at a more abstract level. In this paper, we focus on home and access networks.

Our methodology is based solely on end-to-end measurements to localize the set of links that are the most likely root cause of performance degradations. Closest to our work is the large body of work in network tomography which exploits the similarity of end-to-end network performance from a source to multiple receivers due to common paths to infer properties of internal network links such as network outages[18], delays[23], and packet losses [8]. However, these studies make simplifying assumptions that do not hold in real deployments [9,15] such as the use of multicast [23]. In addition, the proposed algorithms are computationally expensive for networks of reasonable scale and their accuracy is affected by the scale and the topology of the network [9].

In this work, we instead present a practical, general framework to *identify* faulty links that we instantiate on two specific metrics: delays as in [23] and bottleneck bandwidth, which is notoriously more difficult to measure. When full topological information is not available, our algorithm performs a *clustering* of measurement probes as in binary network tomography [21], where the inference problem is simplified by separating links (in our case probes) into good vs failed, instead of estimating the values of the link performance metrics.

Additionally, one major problem of the related literature is the realism of ground truth data to evaluate the accuracy of the algorithms. Even in practical approaches, ground truth in the form of user tickets [3] or user feedback[16] is extremely rare, so that the absence of ground truth is commonplace [4,6,17,19]. Theoretic work builds ground truth with simulations [8], or using syslogs and SNMP data in operational networks [18]. On the one hand, although simulations simplify the control over failure location and duration, they do not provide realistic settings. On the other hand, the ground truth is either completely missing in real operational networks (such as PlanetLab [21]) or partially missing in testbeds [15,18], where network events outside of the control of researchers can happen. Our setup employs controlled emulation through Mininet [13] which is (relatively) fast to implement, uses real code (including kernel stack and our software), and allows testing on fairly large scale topologies. This setup allows full control on the number, duration, and location of network problems. Additionally, by running the full network stack, Mininet keeps the real world noise in the underlying measurements, thus providing a more challenging validation environment with respect to simulation. As a side effect of this choice, the NetProbes software that we release as open source [2] has also undergone a significant amount of experimental validation. Most importantly, any peer researcher is capable of repeating our experiments in order to validate our results, compare their approach to ours, and extend this work.

3   Problem Statement and Model

Considering an ISP network, and focusing for the sake of simplicity on its access tree, faults can occur at multiple levels in the access network hierarchy. The ability to launch measurements between arbitrary pairs of devices in the same access network would significantly enhance the diagnosis of network performance disruptions. In this work we consider two use-cases: *User-managed* probes and *ISP-managed* probes. User-managed probes run only on end-user devices and lack topology information. In contrast, ISP-managed probes can reside in home

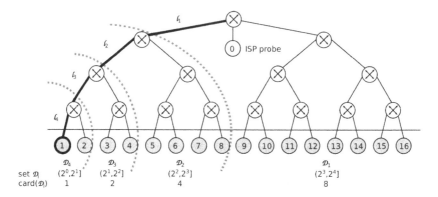

Fig. 1. Synoptic of the network scenario and model notation

gateways, in special locations inside the ISP network, and can also be available as "apps" on user devices (e.g., smartphones and laptops). We address both use-cases with the same algorithm: clustering in the user-scenario separates measurement probes into two sets (i.e., un/affected sets), whereas an additional mapping in the ISP-scenario allows to pinpoint the root cause link.

We formalize the problem and introduce the notation used in this paper with the help of Fig. 1, which depicts a binary access network tree. The troubleshooting probe software runs in the leaf nodes of the tree. However, the ISP can strategically place probes inside the network (e.g. probe 0 in the picture attached to the root). Our algorithm runs continuously in the background to gather a baseline of network performance, and troubleshooting is triggered by the user (e.g., upon experiencing a degradation of network performance) or automatically by a change point detection procedure on some relevant metrics (outside the scope of this work).

For the sake of clarity, let us assume that probe 1 launches a troubleshooting task. In this context, we can safely assume that the root cause is located somewhere in the path from the user device or gateway towards the Internet (links $\ell_4, \ell_3, \ell_2, \ell_1$ in bold in Fig. 1). In order to identify which among $\ell_4, .., \ell_1$ is the root cause of the fault, probe 1 requires sending probing traffic to a number M of the overall available probes N. Let us denote, for convenience, by $D^+ = log_k(N)$ the maximum depth (i.e., height) of a k-ary tree and by $\mathcal{D}_i$ the set of probes $\mathcal{D}_i = \left(k^{D^+-i}, k^{D^+-i+1} \right]$. The set $\mathcal{D}_i$ includes probes whose shortest path from probe 1 passes through ℓ_i, but does not pass through ℓ_{i-1}. In the access tree, whenever a link ℓ_f (located at depth f in the tree) is faulty, all probes whose shortest path from the diagnostic probe (probe 1 in our example) passes through ℓ_f will also experience the problem, unlike probes that are reachable through ℓ_{f+1}: it follows that the troubleshooting algorithm requires probes from both sets $\mathcal{D}_f$ and $\mathcal{D}_{f+1}$ to infer with certainty that the fault is located at ℓ_f. For a k-ary tree, the minimum number of probes that allows to identify the faulty link irrespectively of the depth f of the fault is $M = O(log_k(N))$ – i.e., one probe in each of the $\{\mathcal{D}_i\}_{i=1}^{log_k(N)}$ strata suffices to accurately pinpoint the root cause.

Such a strategic probe selection requires either topology knowledge or the assistance of a cooperating server managed by the ISP (e.g., an IETF ALTO[24] server). However, this strategy is not feasible with user-managed probes, in which probe selection is either uniformly random or based on publicly available information such as IP addresses. It is thus important to assess the detection probability of a naive random selection.

Let us denote by $p^-(f, \alpha)$ the probability that a random selection includes a probe that is useful to locate a fault at depth $f \in [1, D^+]$, with a probe budget $\alpha = M/N$. The deeper is the fault location, the smaller is the number of probes available to identify the faulty link. As the size of $\mathcal{D}_f$ exponentially decreases as f increases ($\mathrm{card}(\mathcal{D}_f) = k^{D^+ - f}$), we expect the random selection strategy to easily locate faults at small depths (close to the root) and fail at large depths (close to the leaves) where a stratified selection is necessary to sample probes in the smaller set $\mathcal{D}_f$. The probability that none of the M vantage points falls into $\mathcal{D}_f$ decreases exponentially fast with the size of $\mathcal{D}_f$, i.e., $(1 - \alpha)^{\mathrm{card}(\mathcal{D}_f)}$. Consequently, the probability to sample at least[1] one probe in $\mathcal{D}_f$ is:

$$p^-(f, \alpha) = 1 - (1 - \alpha)^{k^{(D^+ - f)}} \tag{1}$$

Expression (1) is a lower bound on the expected detection probability with random selection. When a random subset of probes *does not contain* any probe in $\mathcal{D}_f$, it is still possible to correctly guess the root cause link. Here, there will be ambiguity because multiple links are equally likely to be root cause candidates. At any depth d, ambiguity will be limited to the links located between the fault and the root of the tree (i.e., $\ell_d, .., \ell_1$): since, at depth d, ambiguity involves d links, the probability of a correct guess is $1/d$. To compute the average probability of a correct guess $\mathbb{E}[p^{guess}]$, we have to account for the relative frequency of the different ambiguity cases, which for depth d happen proportionally to $k^d / k^{\log_k(N)} = k^d / N$,

$$\mathbb{E}[p^{guess}] = \sum_{d=1}^{\log_k(N)} \frac{1}{d} \frac{k^d}{N} = \frac{1}{N} \sum_{d=1}^{\log_k(N)} \frac{k^d}{d} \tag{2}$$

We can then compute the expected discriminative power of a random selection, expressed in terms of the probability to correctly identify a fault at depth f as:

$$\mathbb{E}[p] = p^-(f, \alpha) + \left(1 - p^-(f, \alpha)\right) \mathbb{E}[p^{guess}] \tag{3}$$

where the first term accounts for the proportion of random selection that is structurally equivalent to a stratified selection (so that the root cause link can be found with probability 1), and the second term accounts for the proportion of

---

[1] Note that this probability would be better expressed with the hypergeometric distribution, that models sampling without replacement; however the formulation reported here differ by less than 1% from the hypergeometric results, and further allows to express the loss of discriminative power due to random selection in a more intuitive way.

random selection able to pinpoint the faulty link by luck (thus with probability $\mathbb{E}[p^{guess}]$). By plugging (1) and (2) into (3) we get:

$$\mathbb{E}[p] = 1 - (1-\alpha)^{k^{(D^+ - f)}} + \left[1 - (1 - (1-\alpha)^{k^{(D^+ - f)}})\right]\left(\frac{1}{N}\sum_{d=1}^{log_k(N)}\frac{k^d}{d}\right) \quad (4)$$

$$= 1 - (1-\alpha)^{k^{(D^+ - f)}}\left(1 - \frac{1}{N}\sum_{d=1}^{log_k(N)}\frac{k^d}{d}\right) \quad (5)$$

Notice that (5) has structurally the form $1 - p_{loss}$. The term p_{loss} can be interpreted as the loss of discriminative power with respect to a perfect strategic selection that always achieves correct detection. Clearly, this model is simplistic as it does not consider all combinatorial aspects which could be used to obtain finer-grained expectations at each depth of the tree. Yet, the main purpose of the model is to serve as a reality check for our experimental results.

4   Troubleshooting Algorithm

We treat both clustering and classification problems with a single algorithm, whose pseudocode is reported in Algorithm 1. Assuming the algorithm runs at a source node s, for any performance metric Q (e.g., delay, bandwidth), s collects baseline statistics $Q_0(p)$ with low-rate active measurements towards other peers p. When the troubleshooting is triggered, s iteratively selects up to R batches of B of probes, so that $R \cdot B$ represents a tuneable probing budget. Selection is made according to a selection policy $\mathcal{S}_p$, based on a probe score $S(p)$. The probe selection is iterative because $S(p)$ can vary, and thus the next batch is selected based on the results of the previous batch.

At each step, upon doing B measurements, we compute, for each probe p, $Q(p) - Q_0(p)$ and add it to the set P: K-means clustering partitions P into P^+ and P^-. Two points are worth stressing: first, the algorithm does not associate any semantic to clusters: e.g., a node in P^+ can be affected by large delay, whereas a node in P^- can be affected by a bottleneck bandwidth. Second, in case of a single failure, it can be expected that probes in one of the two clusters exhibit $Q(p) - Q_0(p) \approx 0$, so P^+ and P^- should be interpreted as a syntactical difference. Once the probe budget is exhausted (or once other stop criteria, that we don't mention for the sake of simplicity, are met), the algorithm either returns P^+ and P^- (user-managed case, line 12), or continues with the mapping. When no clear partition can be established, only one set is returned.

To map probes in P^+ and P^- to links, the algorithm requires the knowledge of the links ℓ in the shortest path $SP(s,p)$. The score $S(\ell)$ of $\ell \in SP(s,p)$ is incremented by +1 for $p \in P^+$ and decremented by -1 for $p \in P^-$. As a consequence of metric-agnosis, the algorithm needs to know if links with the largest (smallest) $S(\ell)$ scores are to be pinpointed, which is done according to a link selection policy $\mathcal{S}_\ell$.

We experiment with $\mathcal{S}_p \in \{random, |IP(s) - IP(p)|, balance\}$ and combinations of the above. Random selection is useful as a baseline and to compare with the model. We additionally consider probe selection policies that are more complex to model such as the absolute distance in the IP space, as well as a policy that attempts at equating the size of P^+ and P^-, by selecting an IP that is close to IPs in the small cluster, and far from IPs in the large cluster (exact definition omitted due to lack of space). Moreover, we consider $\mathcal{S}_\ell \in \{random, proportional, argmax\}$. The naïve random method makes an informed guess by selecting one of the D^+ links in the path $\ell_{D+}, \ldots, \ell_1$ to the root (success probability $1/D^+$, much larger than the $1/2(k^{D^+} - 1) = 1/2(N-1)$ in case of a random guess over all links). We also select links proportionally to their score (proportional policy), or only the link with the largest (smallest) score (argmax policy).

Algorithm 1. Detection algorithm at s

1: Get a baseline $Q_0(p)$ for metric $Q(p)$, $\forall p$ ▷ Initialization, over long timescale
2: **for** round $\in [1..R]$ **do**   ▷ When triggered upon user/ISP demand
3:     select a batch of B probes according to a probe selection policy $\mathcal{S}_p$, based on score $S(p)$
4:     **for** $p \in B$ **do**
5:        perform active measurements with p to get $Q(p) - Q_0(p)$
6:        add probe p to probed set P
7:        partition P into P^+ and P^-, by K-means clustering on $Q(p) - Q_0(p)$
8:     **end for**
9:     update probe scores $S(p)$, $\forall p$
10: **end for**
11: **if** topology is not available **then**   ▷ Clustering results
12:     **return** P^+ and P^-
13: **else**   ▷ Classification results
14:     **for** probe $p \in P$ **do**
15:        **for** link $\ell \in$ shortest path $SP(s, p)$ **do**
16:           $S(\ell) \leftarrow S(\ell) + (p \in P^+) - (p \in P^-)$
17:        **end for**
18:     **end for**
19:     **return** link ℓ according to a link selection strategy $\mathcal{S}_\ell$ based on scores $S(\ell)$
20: **end if**

---

5 Calibration of the Emulation Environment

Before running a full-fledged measurement campaign, it is mandatory to perform a rigorous calibration phase, yet this phase is often neglected [22]. In this work, we follow an experimental approach using emulation in Mininet, to control the duration and the location of the faults. However, it is unclear how well state-of-the-art delay and bandwidth measurement techniques perform in Mininet. In order to disambiguate inconsistencies due to Mininet from measurement errors intrinsic to measurements techniques, we perform calibration experiments for a set of delay (expectedly easy) and bandwidth (notoriously difficult) measurement tools and assess their accuracy in Mininet. In this section, we first briefly describe Mininet and NetProbes, the diagnosis software we develop for this work (Sec. 5.1), then present the calibration results (Sec. 5.2).

5.1   Software Tools

Mininet [13]. Mininet is an open source emulator which creates a virtual network of end-hosts, links, and OpenFlow virtual switches in a single Linux kernel and supports experiments with almost arbitrary network topologies. Mininet hosts execute code in real-time, exchange real network traffic, and behave similarly to deployed hardware. All the software developed for a virtual Mininet network can run in hardware networks and be shared with others to reproduce the experiments. Mininet provides the functional and timing realism of testbeds in addition to the flexibility and full control of simulators. Experimenters configure packet forwarding at the switches with OpenFlow and link network characteristics (e.g., delay and bandwidth) with the Linux Traffic Control (`tc`). Reproducing experiments from tier-1 conference papers [2] indicates that results from Mininet and from testbeds are in agreement.

NetProbes [2]. We design NetProbes, a distributed software written in Python 3.x that runs on end-hosts and executes a set of user-defined active measurement tests. NetProbes agents deployed at end-user devices and gateways form an overlay. They perform a set of periodic measurements to monitor the paths in the overlay and collect a baseline network performance. When the user experiences network performance issues, the NetProbes agent running at the user device launches a troubleshooting task to assess the severity of the performance issue and the location of the faulty link. It is worth pointing out that the set of measurement tasks that can be performed by NetProbes agents (e.g., HTTP or DNS requests, multicast UDP tests, etc.) is far larger than what we consider within the scope of this paper, and that the software is available at[2].

5.2   Delay and Bandwidth Calibration

Setup. We build a Mininet virtual network with the topology depicted in Fig. 1 on a server with four cores and 24 GB of RAM. We run the selected tools on probes 1 and 2. In our delay experiments, we impose five different delay values (0 ms, 20 ms, 100 ms, 200 ms, 1000 ms) on ℓ_3 located at depth $d = 3$ in the tree. At each delay level, probes 1 and 2 perform 50 measurements of round trip delays to probes 7 and 6 respectively (250 measurements in total for each pair of probes). We use Mininet processes through the Python API to issue `ping` and `traceroute` to measure RTTs (we test `traceroute` with UDP, UDP Lite, TCP, and ICMP).

---

[2] Stanford's CS224 blog: http://reproducingnetworkresearch.wordpress.com

Similarly, in the bandwidth experiments, we vary the link capacity of ℓ_3 (100 Mbps, 10 Mbps, 1 Mbps) under three different traffic shapers, namely the hierarchical token bucket (HTB), the token bucket filter (TBF), and the hierarchical fair service curve (HFSC) and we make 20 measurements of the available bandwidth between probes 1 and 7 and probes 2 and 6 (120 in total for each value of the link capacity). There is a plethora of measurement tools designed by the research community to estimate the available bandwidth[11]. In this work we limitedly report the calibration of three popular tools (Abing [20], ASSOLO [10], and IGI [14]) which are characterised by low intrusiveness: Abing and IGI infer the available bandwidth based on the dispersion of packet pairs measured at the receiver. ASSOLO sends a variable bit-rate stream with exponentially spaced packets and calculates the available bandwidth from the delays at the receiver side. We compare the performance of the three bandwidth estimation tools in the absence of cross traffic and under the three traffic shapers mentioned earlier.

Delay. We expect delay measurements to be flawless. Yet we observe that the first packet sent between any two hosts exhibits a large delay variance: this is due to the fact that the corresponding entry for the flow is missing in the virtual switch and thus requires data exchange between the OpenFlow controller and the virtual switch, whereas the forwarding entry is ready for subsequent packets. We thus do the baseline $Q_0(p)$ over multiple packets (50 for delay) to mitigate this phenomenon, so that the impact of the first packet delay is factored out in the warmup phase. Doing a baseline and subtracting it from each delay measurement enables an accurate study of the effect of the imposed delay value on the accuracy of the measurement technique. Further results are shown in Fig. 2. All techniques exhibit a time evolution similar to ICMP `ping` whose experiment is depicted in Fig. 2(a). We report the PDF of the measurement error (i.e., the difference between the measured and the enforced RTT) in Fig. 2(b). Results for `traceroute` with various protocols are similar: we observe that, for all the delay measurement techniques, the bulk of the error distribution is less than 1 ms (with outliers not shown up to 10ms). Moreover, we note that using ICMP brings the absolute error to less than 0.1 ms for both `traceroute` and `ping`. From this calibration phase, we select ICMP `ping` to measure delay: as the measurement noise is insignificant, errors in the classification outcome should be solely attributed to our troubleshooting algorithm.

Capacity. Fig. 3 reports the evolution of the estimated available bandwidth as a function of three link capacity values for the cross product of {Abing, ASSOLO, IGI} × {HTB, TBF, HFSC}. We stress that while comparison of bandwidth estimation tools under the same experimental conditions has already been studied, we are not aware of any study jointly considering bandwidth estimation and bandwidth shaping, especially since many bandwidth measurement tools rely on effects of cross-trafic to estimate available bandwidth. As before, we use a warmup phase to factor out the extra delay incurred by the first packet. We can see that Abing systematically fails in estimating the available bandwidth under HTB and TBF shaping, while the estimation is correct with HFSC. Similarly,

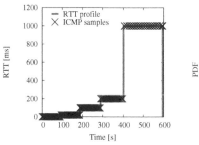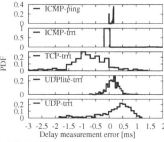

(a) Time evolution of RTTs with   (b) PDF of measurement errors
ICMP Ping

Fig. 2. Calibration of delay measurements

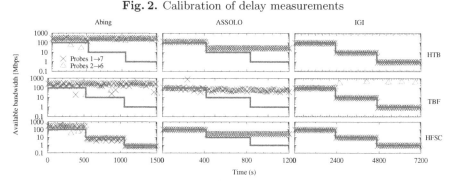

Fig. 3. Calibration of bandwidth measurements: {Abing, ASSOLO, IGI} × {HTB, TBF, HFSC}

ASSOLO fails in estimating 1 Mbps available bandwidth under all shapers, and additionally fails the estimation of 10Mbps under TBF. In contrast, IGI succeeds in accurately tracking changes of available bandwidth at ℓ_3, although outliers are still possible (see IGI+TBF). A downside of IGI is that the measurements last longer than measurements with Abing or ASSOLO. These results and tradeoffs are interesting and require future attention. However, this is beyond the scope of this work. The most important takeaway is that measurement errors of such magnitude would invalidate all experiments, showing once more the importance of this calibration phase. We additionally gather that the IGI+HFSC combination offers the most accurate estimates of available bandwidth. As accurate input is a necessary condition for trobuleshooting success, we use this combination in the remainder of this paper.

6   Experimental Results

We now evaluate the quality of our clustering and classification for various probe budgets (namely 10, 20 and 50 probes) for faults (e.g., doubling delay or halving bandwidth) at controlled depths of the tree. All the scripts to reproduce the

experiments are available at [1]. We first compare experimental results in a cali-
brated Mininet environment (including real-world noise), with those expected by
a probabilistic model (neglecting noise) (Sec. 6.1). We next perform a sensitivity
analysis by varying topological properties, probe selection policies $\mathcal{S}_p$, and link
selection policies $\mathcal{S}_\ell$ (Sec. 6.2).

6.1   Performance at a Glance

We perform experiments over a binary tree scenario ($k = 2$) with depth $D^+ = 9$
and $N = 512$ leaf nodes. In this case, a strategic probe selection would need
$M/N = 9/512$ probes ($\alpha = 1.75\%$) to ensure perfect classification, but we consider larger budget $M = \{10, 20, 50\}$ in our experiments. Unless otherwise stated,
we use a random probe selection $\mathcal{S}_p$ and an argmax link selection $\mathcal{S}_\ell$ policies. We
first evaluate the clustering methodology by comparing the two sets of affected
and unaffected probes obtained from the algorithm with our ground truth, using
the well-known rand index[12], which takes value in $[0, 1] \subset$, with 1 indicating
that the data clusters are exactly the same. Since we have full control over the
location of the fault, we build our ground truth by assigning the label "affected"
to all the available probes (under a given budget constraint) for which the path
to the diagnostic probe passes through the faulty link. The remaining probes
constitute the unaffected set. Fig. 4-(a) shows that, provided measurements are
accurate, the clustering methodology successfully identifies the set of probes
whose paths from the diagnostic software experience significant network performance disruptions (and as a consequence accurately identifies nodes in the
complementary set of unaffected probes). For budgets of 10, 20 and 50 probes,
the rand index shows perfect match between the ground truth and the clustering
output in the case of delay measurement. Results degrade significantly instead
for bandwidth measurement: we point out that the loss of accuracy is not tied
to our algorithm, but rather to measurements that are input to it, which was
partly expected and confirms that calibration is a necessary, but unfortunately
not sufficient, step.

Abstracting from limits in the measurement techniques, these result indicates
that in practice our clustering methodology works well in assessing the impact
of a faulty link without requiring knowledge of the network topology. Yet, root
cause link identification is a clearly more challenging and important objective,
which we analyze in the following by restricting our attention to delay experiments: as the classification step is a deterministic mapping from the clusters,
as long as the measurement error remains small, the results of the classification
task are not affected by the specific metric under investigation. We expect classification results to apply at large, as opposite to merely illustrating the algorithm
performance under delay measurement (although they are not representative of
bottleneck localization as per Fig. 4-(a)).

We next show that the experimental and modelling results are in agreement,
with a random probe selection policy and a budget of $M = 50$ probes, which corresponds to $\alpha = 9.75\%$. For each fault depth f, we perform 10 experiments by ran-
domizing the set of destination probes. Results, as reported in Fig. 4-(b), depict

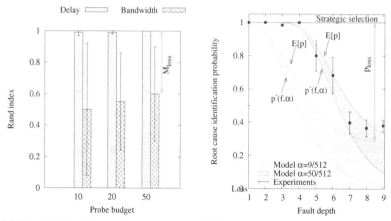

(a) Rand index of experimental output (b) Probability of correctly identifying
of clustering algorithm vs ground truth the faulty link (models (1) and (3) vs
clusters   experiments)

Fig. 4. Experimental results at a glance: (a) Clustering and (b) Classification

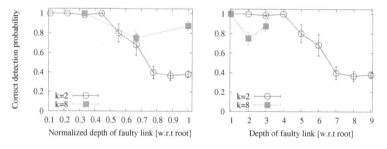

Fig. 5. Sensitivity analysis: Impact of network topology properties

the correct classification probability of the model vs the experiments. Recall that
equation (1) gives a lower bound $p^-(f, \alpha)$ to the experimental results, while (3)
models the average expected detection probability $\mathbb{E}[p]$. We consider $\alpha = 9.75\%$,
to directly compare with experimental results, as well as $\alpha = 1.75\%$, to assess the
loss of discriminative power from a strategic selection, that could achieve perfect
classification in this setting, to a random selection (denoted with p_{loss} in the figure).

6.2 Sensitivity Analysis

Impact of Topology. We study the impact of the network topology on the
classification performance. We use two trees with 512 probes (i.e. leaves) each.
The first tree has a depth $d = 3$ and a fanout $k = 8$ while the second tree
has a depth $d = 9$ and a fanout $k = 2$. Fig. 5 reports the correct detection
probability of the faulty link as a function of the depth of the injected fault

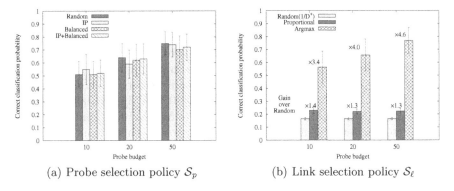

(a) Probe selection policy $\mathcal{S}_p$ (b) Link selection policy $\mathcal{S}_\ell$

Fig. 6. Sensitivity analysis: Impact of selection policies

in the tree, using variance bars. As expected, results indicate that the correct detection probability decreases as the fault depth increases[3]. Thus, when the root cause link is located close to the *leaves* of the tree, it is harder to randomly sample another probe which is also affected by the fault: we thus need a smarter probe selection strategy to improve the link classification performance.

Impact of the Probe Selection Policy $\mathcal{S}_p$. We consider policies based on IP-distance (IP), cluster-size (balance), and a linear combination of both. We average the results over all the depths of the binary tree and contrast them with a random selection policy. Unfortunately, our attempts are so far unsuccessful as shown in Fig. 6(a), where the discriminative power is roughly the same over all probe selection policies. This is due to the fact that the current set of metrics we consider to select probes do not encode useful information to bias the selection. The absence of a notion of net masks and hierarchy with IP-distance for example makes it hard to extract information about how topologically close/far probes are from each other. An obvious improvement would be to consider the IP-TTL field. However, since Mininet uses virtual switches to construct the network, the IP-TTL field remains unchanged. As a consequence, we could not conduct experiments with this field and we leave it as future work.

Impact of the Link Selection Policy $\mathcal{S}_\ell$. Finally, we use three different policies to select the faulty links: $\mathcal{S}_\ell \in \{\text{random}, \text{proportional}, \text{argmax}\}$. Results, averaged over all depths of the binary tree, are reported in Fig. 6. The plot is futher annotated with the gain factor over the random selection: while proportional selection brings a constant improvement of about 40%, the argmax policy brings considerable gains (in excess of a factor 4) which grow with the probe budget.

---

[3] We use variance, instead of stdev, to reduce visual noise: thus the increase for $k=8$ at depth $d = 3$ is only apparent, as the corresponding standard deviation bars are large.

7   Conclusions and future work

In this work, we present a troubleshooting algorithm to diagnose network performance disruptions in the home and access networks. We apply a clustering methodology to evaluate the severity of the performance issue and leverage the knowledge of the access network topology to identify the root cause link with a correct classification probability of 70% using 10% of the available probes. We follow an experimental approach and use an emulated environment based on Mininet to validate our algorithm. Our choice of Mininet is guided by our requirements to have flexibility in designing the experiments, full control over the injected faults, and realistic network settings. We contrast the experimental results with an analytical model that computes the expected correct classification probability under a random probe selection policy. We also evaluate the impact of topology, probe and link selection policies on the algorithm.

Our proposed solution is a first step towards the goal of having reproducible network troubleshooting algorithms – for which we make all our code publicly available. Our future work will focus on extending the algorithm to different network topologies and to diversify the set of network performance metrics, to verify its generality. Also, while simplicity was one of the goals of this paper, and allowed to compare analytical vs experimental results, our future work will address more practical issues, such as how our design can be integrated and complement troubleshooting systems already deployed by ISPs.

Acknowledgments. This work has been carried out at LINCS http://www.lincs.fr and funded by the FP7 mPlane project (grant agreement no. 318627).

References

1. Emulator scripts. https://github.com/netixx/mininet-NetProbes
2. NetProbes. https://github.com/netixx/NetProbes
3. Bahl, P., Chandra, R., Greenberg, A., Kandula, S., Maltz, D.A., Zhang, M.: Towards highly reliable enterprise network services via inference of multi-level dependencies. In: Proc. ACM SIGCOMM (2007)
4. Bischof, Z., Otto, J., Sánchez, M., Rula, J., Choffnes, D., Bustamante, F.: Crowd-sourcing ISP characterization to the network edge. In: Proc. SIGCOMM WMUST (2011)
5. Dhamdhere, A., Teixeira, R., Dovrolis, C., Diot, C.: Netdiagnoser: troubleshooting network unreachabilities using end-to-end probes and routing data. In: Proc. CoNEXT (2007)
6. Dhawan, M., Samuel, J., Teixeira, R., Kreibich, C., Allman, M., Weaver, N., Paxson, V.: Fathom: A browser-based network measurement platform. In: Proc. ACM IMC (2012)
7. Duffield, N.G., Horowitz, J., Lo Presti, F., Towsley, D.: Multicast topology inference from measured end-to-end loss. IEEE Transactions on Information Theory (2002)
8. Duffield, N.G., Presti, F.L., Paxson, V., Towsley, D.F.: Network loss tomography using striped unicast probes. IEEE/ACM Trans. Netw. (2006)

9. Ghita, D., Karakus, C., Argyraki, K.J., Thiran, P.: Shifting network tomography toward a practical goal. In: Proc. CoNEXT (2011)
10. Goldoni, E., Rossi, G., Torelli, A.: Assolo, a new method for available bandwidth estimation. In: ICIMP (2009)
11. Goldoni, E., Schivi, M.: End-to-End available bandwidth estimation tools, an experimental comparison. In: Ricciato, F., Mellia, M., Biersack, E. (eds.) TMA 2010. LNCS, vol. 6003, pp. 171–182. Springer, Heidelberg (2010)
12. Halkidi, M., Batistakis, Y., Vazirgiannis, M.: On clustering validation techniques. Journal of Intelligent Information Systems 17(2–3), 107–145 (2001)
13. Handigol, N., Heller, B., Jeyakumar, V., Lantz, B., McKeown, N.: Reproducible network experiments using container-based emulation. In: Proc. CoNEXT (2012)
14. Hu, N., Steenkiste, P.: Evaluation and characterization of available bandwidth probing techniques. IEEE J. Selected Areas in Communications (2003)
15. Huang, Y., Feamster, N., Teixeira, R.: Practical issues with using network tomography for fault diagnosis. ACM SIGCOMM Computer Communication Review (2008)
16. Joumblatt, D., Teixeira, R., Chandrashekar, J., Taft, N.: HostView: annotating end-host performance measurements with user feedback. In: ACM HotMetrics Workshop (2010)
17. Kim, K., Nam, H., Singh, V.K., Song, D., Schulzrinne, H.: DYSWIS: crowdsourcing a home network diagnosis. In: ICCCN (2014)
18. Kompella, R., Yates, J., Greenberg, A., Snoeren, A.: Detection and localization of network black holes. In: Proc. IEEE INFOCOM (2007)
19. Kreibich, C., Weaver, N., Nechaev, B., Paxson, V.: Netalyzr: Illuminating the edge network. In Proc. ACM IMC (2010)
20. Navratil, J., Cottrell, R.L.: Abwe: a practical approach to available bandwidth estimation. In: Proc. of PAM (2003)
21. Nguyen, H.X., Thiran, P.: The boolean solution to the congested IP link location problem: Theory and practice. In: Proc. IEEE INFOCOM (2007)
22. Paxson, V.: Keynote: reflections on measurement research: crooked lines, straight lines, and moneyshots. In: Proc. ACM SIGCOMM (2011)
23. Presti, F.L., Duffield, N.G., Horowitz, J., Towsley, D.F.: Multicast-based inference of network-internal delay distributions. IEEE/ACM Trans. Netw. (2002)
24. Seedorf, J., Burger, E.: Application-Layer Traffic Optimization (ALTO) Problem Statement. IETF RFC **5693** (2009)

Mobile and Wireless

Vivisecting WhatsApp in Cellular Networks: Servers, Flows, and Quality of Experience

Pierdomenico Fiadino$^{(\boxtimes)}$, Mirko Schiavone, and Pedro Casas

Telecommunications Research Center Vienna - FTW, Vienna, Austria
{Fiadino,Schiavone,Casas}@ftw.at

Abstract. Instant Multimedia Messaging (IMM) applications are increasing their popularity in cellular networks, rapidly taking over the traditional SMS and MMS messaging service. This paper presents the first large-scale characterization of WhatsApp, the new giant in IMM. Understanding how it works is paramount for cellular operators and service providers, both to assess its impact on the network as well as gaining know how for tracking its growing usage. Through the combined analysis of passive measurements at the core of a European national-wide cellular network, geo-distributed active measurements using RIPE Atlas, live traffic captures at end devices, and subjective Quality of Experience (QoE) lab tests, our study shows that: (i) the WhatsApp hosting architecture is highly centralized and exclusively located in the US; (ii) multimedia sharing covers about 75% of the total WhatsApp traffic volume, with 36% of it being video content; (iii) flow characteristics depend on the OS of the end device; (iv) despite achieving download throughputs as high as 1.5 Mbps, about 35% of the total file downloads are potentially badly perceived by the users, showing the impacts of the long latencies to WhatsApp servers. Our analysis additionally overviews the worldwide WhatsApp outage occurred in February 2014.

Keywords: WhatsApp · Large-Scale measurements · Cellular networks · Traffic characterization · Quality of experience

1 Introduction

WhatsApp is doubtlessly the leading instant multimedia messaging service in cellular networks. WhatsApp is a cross-platform mobile application which allows users worldwide to instantly exchange text messages and multimedia contents such as photos, audio and videos. It currently handles more than 64 billion messages per day, including 700 million photos and 100 million videos [16]. With half a billion of active users, it has become the fastest-growing company in history in terms of users [15]. Such an astonishing popularity does not only have a major impact on the traditional SMS/MMS business, but might also have a remarked impact on the traffic, especially due to the sharing of multimedia messages.

The goal of this paper is to provide the first large-scale characterization of the WhatsApp service. By analyzing a week of cellular traffic flows collected in February 2014 at the cellular network of a major European ISP, we shed light on the

© IFIP International Federation for Information Processing 2015
M. Steiner et al. (Eds.): TMA 2015, LNCS 9053, pp. 49–63, 2015.
DOI: 10.1007/978-3-319-17172-2_4

WhatsApp hosting network architecture, the characteristics of the generated traffic, and the performance of media transfers, specially as perceived by the end users. As WhatsApp runs on top of encrypted connections, our measurements are complemented with a dissection of the WhatsApp protocol through hybrid measurements, enabling a subsequent passive monitoring at the large-scale. In addition, due to its large worldwide popularity, the WhatsApp dataset is augmented with geo-distributed DNS active measurements using more than 600 RIPE Atlas boxes distributed around the globe [14]. As we shall see next, this paper it is not just about finding which flows belong to the WhatsApp service and analyze them. Indeed, there are many measurement challenges associated to the characterization of such a service: the data gathering, the processing and the interpretation are already very complex per se, given the number of different measurement sources and datasets.

Recent papers have partially addressed the characterization of the WhatsApp traffic [2,3], but using very limited datasets (i.e., no more than 50 devices) and considering an energy-consumption perspective. Our study follows previous papers characterizing popular Internet services such as YouTube [6], Facebook [5], Google+ [8], Skype [4], and Dropbox [7] among others. This paper represents an extended version of a recently presented abstract on the topic [1].

Our main findings are the following: (i) Despite its worldwide popularity, **WhatsApp is a fully centralized service hosted by the cloud provider SoftLayer at servers located in the US**. (ii) While the application is mainly used as a text-messaging service in terms of transmitted flows (more than 93%), **video-sharing accounts for about 36% of the exchanged volume** in uplink and downlink, and **photo-sharing/audio-messaging for about 38%**. (iii) Despite achieving **flow download throughputs of 1.5 Mbps on average**, about **35% of the total file downloads are potentially badly perceived by users**. (iv) **Flow duration characteristics depend on the device OS**. In particular, different platforms employ different app-level timeouts.

Besides these contributions, our study also provides an overview on the worldwide WhatsApp outage reported on February the 22nd of 2014 [17], characterizing the event as observed from the analyzed dataset. The measurements are complemented with external Online Social Networks (OSNs) feeds (Twitter in this case) to verify that the outage was negatively perceived by the users, immediately at the time were the event occurred, additionally demonstrating the feasibility of using OSNs data to provide near real-time evidence of user quality impairments in large scale service outages. We believe that the information provided in this paper is highly useful for cellular operators to better understand how WhatsApp works and performs, and specially to provide means for analyzing and tracking its evolution inside their networks, including a Quality of Experience (QoE) perspective. To the best of our knowledge, we are the first to provide a large-scale characterization of the complete WhatsApp service running on its live environment.

The remainder of this paper is organized as follows: §2 briefly describes the client application work-flow in terms of exchanged messages and server roles as identified from hybrid end-device measurements. §3 explains the procedure used to detect the WhatsApp flows in the large-scale cellular passive measurements, and characterizes the underlying hosting network. The analysis of the WhatsApp traffic is presented in §4, including both the flow characteristics per communication and end-device types and the performance in terms of transfer throughputs. §5 presents the results of subjective QoE tests performed with customers downloading multimedia files through WhatsApp, and applies them to the analyzed large-scale traffic dataset. §6 provides an overview of the WhatsApp outage. Finally, §7 concludes this work.

2   An Overview on WhatsApp

WhatsApp uses encrypted communications, therefore the first step to analyze its functioning in the wild is to better understand its inner working. To this end, we rely on the manual inspection of hybrid measurements. We actively generate WhatsApp text and media flows at end devices (both Android and iOS), and passively observe them at two instrumented access gateways. We especially paid attention to the DNS traffic generated by the devices.

WhatsApp uses a customized version of the open eXtensible Messaging and Presence Protocol (XMPP) [20]. XMPP is a protocol for message oriented communications based on XML. Not surprising, our measurements revealed that WhatsApp servers are associated to the domain names `whatsapp.net` (for supporting the service) and `whatsapp.com` (for the company website). As indicated in table 1, different third level domain names are used to handle different types of traffic (control, text messages, and multimedia messages). When the client application starts, it contacts a *messaging* or *chat server* `{e|c|d}X.whatsapp.net` listening on port 5222, where `X` is an integer changing for load balancing. This port is assigned by IANA to clear-text XMPP sessions. Nevertheless, the connection is SSL-encrypted. This connection is used for text messages as well as control channel, and is kept up while the application is active or in background. If the connection is dropped, a new one with the same or another messaging server is immediately re-established. In case the application client is not running, the message notification is delivered through the OS push APIs.

The application also offers the capability of multimedia contents transfer, including photos, audio and video. Transfers are managed by HTTPS *multimedia (mm) servers* listening on port 443. Those servers are associated to different domain names depending on their specific task: `mmsXYZ.whatsapp.net` and `mmiXYZ.whatsapp.net` are both used for audio and photo transfers, while `mmvXYZ.whatsapp.net` are exclusively reserved for videos. For each object, a dedicated TLS-encrypted connection towards a *mm server* is established. Uploads

Table 1. Third level domain names used by `whatsapp.net` and communication types

domain	protocol (port)	type
cX,eX,dX	XMPP (5222, 443)	chat & control
mmiXYZ,mmsXYZ	HTTPS (443)	media (photo/audio)
mmvXYZ	HTTPS (443)	media (video)

are started immediately, while downloads of large objects need to be manually triggered by the receiving user to avoid undesired traffic. These servers do not perform any transcoding. As we shall see in §4, the two server classes have very different network footprints. While connections to chat servers are characterized by low data-rate and long duration (specially due to the control messages), media transfers are carried by short and heavy flows.

3   Hosting Infrastructure

The first part of the study focuses on discovering where the servers are located. For doing so, we rely on the analysis of a complete week of WhatsApp traffic traces, consisting of more than 150 million flows collected at the core of a European national-wide cellular network, from 18.02 till 25.02. Flows are captured at the well-known Gn interface [22], using the METAWIN cellular network monitoring system [12]. To preserve user privacy, any user related data are anonymized, while packets' payload is removed on the fly. Using the MaxMind GeoIP databases [13], the ASes serving the corresponding flows are included in the dataset. Traffic flows are continuously imported and analyzed through DBStream [11], a data stream warehouse tailored for large-scale traffic monitoring applications. In the following analysis, volume and flow counts are normalized to preserve business privacy, and time-series are constructed with 10-min time slots resolution.

3.1   Methodology

WhatsApp communications are encrypted, thus we firstly devised a classification approach to identify WhatsApp flows. The approach is based on the HTTPTag classification system [10] running on DBStream. HTTPTag classification consists in applying pattern matching techniques to the `hostname` field of the HTTP requests. Given the usage of encryption, and the need to also classify non-HTTP traffic, the approach was extended to consider the analysis of DNS requests, similar to [9]. Every time a user issues a DNS request for the Fully Qualified Domain Name (FQDN) `*.whatsapp.net`, HTTPTag creates an entry mapping this user to the server IPs provided in the DNS reply. Each entry is time stamped and contains the TTL replied by the DNS server. Using these mappings, all the subsequent flows between this user and the identified servers are assumed to be WhatsApp flows. The approach also allows for a finer-grained classification, using more specific patterns, i.e. `(c|d|e)*.whatsapp.net` for chat flows and `mm*.whatsapp.net` for media flows. To avoid miss-classifications due to out-of-date mappings, every entry expires after a TTL-based time-out. To increase the robustness of the approach, the list of IPs is augmented by adding the list of server IPs signing the TLS/SSL certificates with the string `*.whatsapp.net`. Indeed, our hybrid measurements revealed that WhatsApp uses this string to sign all its communications. Finally, we use reverse DNS queries to verify that the list of filtered IPs actually corresponds to a WhatsApp domain.

Table 2. Number of server IPs and prefixes used by WhatsApp

Service/AS	# IPs	#/24	#/16	#/8
WhatsApp	386	51	30	24
SoftLayer (AS 36351)	1,364,480	5330	106	42

3.2   Measurements Analysis

The complete one-week server IP mappings resulted in a total of 386 IPs identified as hosting the service, belonging to a single AS called SoftLayer (AS number 36351) [19]. To avoid biased conclusions about the set of identified IPs from a single vantage point, we performed an active measurements campaign using the RIPE Atlas measurement network [14], where we analyzed which IPs were obtained when resolving the same FQDNs from 600 different boxes around the globe during multiple days. These active measurements confirmed that the same set of IPs is always replied, regardless of the geographical location of the requester. SoftLayer is a US-based cloud infrastructure provider consisting of 13 data centers and 17 Points of Presence (PoPs) distributed worldwide. Using MaxMind geoloacalization capabilities, we observed that despite its geographical distribution, WhatsApp traffic is handled mainly by the data centers in Dallas and Houston. Given that the city-location accuracy of public GeoIP databases such as MaxMind is questionable [21], we confirmed through traceroutes and active RTT measurements that the servers are indeed located in the US.

Tab. 2 reports the different number of prefixes covered by the identified IPs in SoftLayer. Note that we consider different netmasks (e.g., /24, /16, /8) for simple counting and aggregation purposes, i.e., we do not claim that the prefixes are fully covered/own by the ASes. The range of server IPs is highly distributed, covering 51 different /24 prefixes and 24 /8 ones. The table additionally shows the total number of SoftLayer IPv4 IPs. Fig. 1(a) shows the intersection of both IP address ranges. As depicted in Fig. 1(b), when weighting the IP ranges by volume, the majority of the traffic corresponds to IPs falling in 3 /16 ranges. However, in terms of flows and activity (measured as 10-min active slots), the range 50.22.225.0/24 captures a main share.

To complement the picture of the servers location, we investigate the distance to the vantage point in terms of RTTs, analyzing the minimum RTT values. RTTs are obtained from active ping measurements, performed during the span of the dataset from a single location in Europe. Every unique IP hosting WhatsApp is pinged with trains of 100 ICMP echo request packets every 10 minutes. Fig. 2 plots the distribution of the minimum RTT to (a) all the server IPs hosting WhatsApp, and (b) the same min RTT values, weighted by the previously considered 4 features (i.e., flows, active slots, and traffic volumes) to get a better understanding of the traffic sources. The distribution presents some clear steps indicating the existence of different data centers or hosting locations. The min RTT is always bigger than 100ms, confirming that WhatsApp servers are located outside Europe, where our vantage point is located. Fig. 2(b) shows that the service is evenly handled between

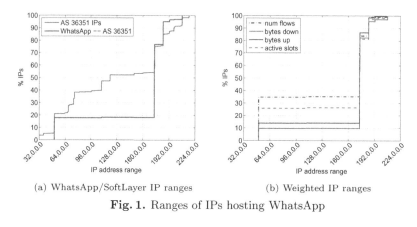

(a) WhatsApp/SoftLayer IP ranges   (b) Weighted IP ranges

Fig. 1. Ranges of IPs hosting WhatsApp

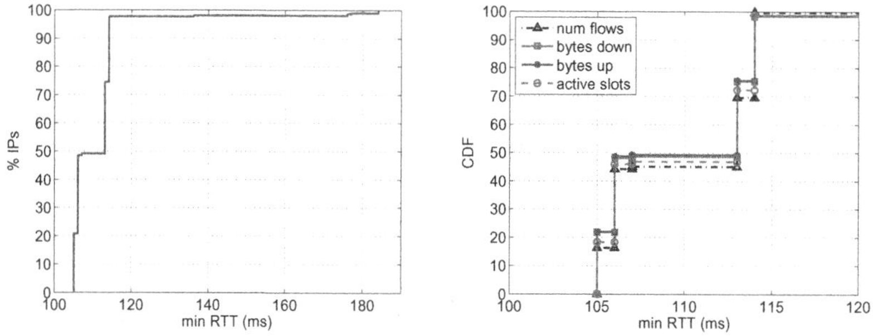

(a) min RTT per WhatsApp IP   (b) Weighted min RTTs

Fig. 2. min RTT to WhatsApp server IPs

two different yet potentially very close locations at about 106 ms and 114 ms, which is compatible with our previous findings.

To further understand how the hosting infrastructure of WhatsApp is structured, Fig. 3 depicts the distribution of server IPs over the same previous 4 features. The figures additionally depict chat and multimedia servers to discriminate their roles. Regarding (a) number of flows and (b) active time slots, we clearly observe how chat servers handle the biggest share of the flows, with a highly active set of server IPs. On the contrary, multimedia servers are much less active and handle a limited share of flows. In terms of volume, the picture is completely the opposite when considering traffic volumes in (c) downlink and (d) uplink directions.

Fig. 4 shows the dynamics of WhatsApp for 3 consecutive days, including the number of active server IPs, the fraction of flows and traffic volume shares, discriminating by chat and mm traffic. The mm category is further split into photos/audio (mmi and mms) and video (mmv). The time-series present a clear night/day pattern with two daily peaks at noon and 8pm. Fig. 4(a) indicates that more than 350 IPs serve WhatsApp flows during peak hours. Note that no less

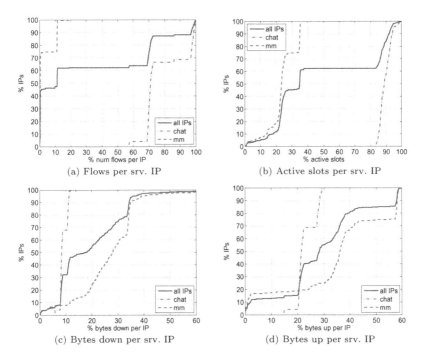

(a) Flows per srv. IP

(b) Active slots per srv. IP

(c) Bytes down per srv. IP

(d) Bytes up per srv. IP

Fig. 3. WhatsApp server IPs in terms of volume, flows, and activity shares

than 200 IPs are active even in the lowest load hours. When analyzing the active IPs per traffic type, we see how chat servers are constantly active, as they keep the state of active devices to achieve an efficient and fast push of the messages to the device. Fig. 4(b) shows the flow count shares, revealing how chat flows are clearly dominating. Once again we stop in the mmi and mms servers, which seem to always handle the same share of flows, suggesting that both space names are used as a mean to balance the load in terms of photos and audio messages. Finally, Figs. 4(c) and 4(d) reveal that even if the mm volume is higher than the chat volume, the latter is comparable to the photos and audio messaging volume, specially in the uplink. Tab. 3 summarizes these shares of flows and traffic volume. The reader should note that our dataset does not include flows transmitted over WiFi, thus some of these results might be biased due to users potentially using WiFi for large file transfers. We are currently analyzing this potential bias as part of our ongoing work, and our first results confirm that our observations are still valid.

As a conclusion, our measurements confirmed that WhatsApp is a centralized and fully US-based service. This is likely to change in the near future after Facebook's WhatsApp acquisition. As for now, all messages among users outside the US are routed through the core network. Being Brazil, India, Mexico and Russia the fastest growing countries in terms of users [16], such a centralized hosting infrastructure is likely to become a problematic bottleneck. Indeed, as

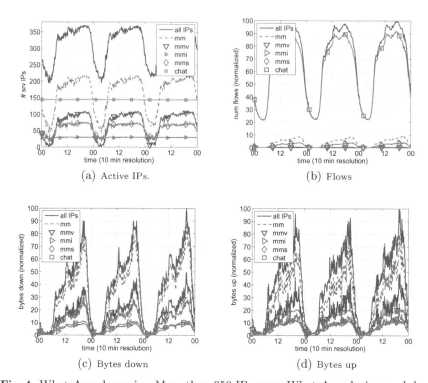

(a) Active IPs.

(b) Flows

(c) Bytes down

(d) Bytes up

Fig. 4. WhatsApp dynamics. More than 350 IPs serve WhatsApp during peak hours.

Table 3. Volume and flows per traffic category

features	chat	mm	mmv	mmi	mms
# bytes$_{down}$	16.6%	83.0%	38.8%	12.8%	29.8%
# bytes$_{up}$	29.5%	70.2%	35.2%	15.0%	17.9%
# flows	93.4%	6.2%	0.3%	2.9%	2.9%
$\frac{\# \ bytes_{down}}{\# \ bytes_{down+up}}$	60.6%	76.3%	75.1%	70.0%	81.9%

we show in §5, the high latencies to US servers are a potential cause of bad QoE for users downloading multimedia files, due to an increased download time and a reduced TCP throughput.

4   Traffic Analysis

We study now the characteristics of the WhatsApp traffic in terms of size and duration. Additionally, we evaluate the performance of the service, computing the transfer throughputs as the Key Performance Indicator (KPI). Flow durations are measured with a coarse-grained resolution of one second (this is a

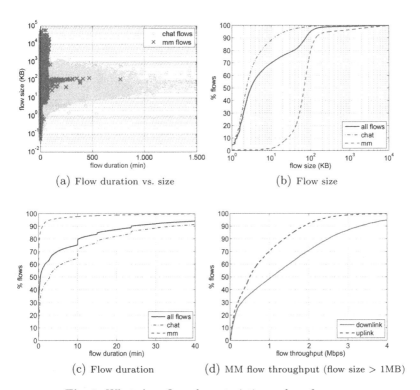

(a) Flow duration vs. size

(b) Flow size

(c) Flow duration

(d) MM flow throughput (flow size > 1MB)

Fig. 5. WhatsApp flow characteristics and performance

limitation of the monitoring system, given the large amount of processed traffic), considering the time-stamps of the first and the last packet of a standard 5-tuple measured flow (note that flows are unidirectional) and adaptive flow time-outs, see [12] for additional details. Flow throughput is estimated as the ratio between the total transferred bytes and the flow duration. Note that given the one second resolution, throughput values are somehow an underestimate of the real throughput. Still, the results obtained in the paper about flow duration allows us to claim that the absolute errors are marginal.

Fig. 5(a) shows a scatter plot reporting the flow duration vs. the flow size, discriminating by chat and mm flows. Whereas mm messages are sent over dedicated connections, resulting in short-lived flows, text messages are sent over the same connection used for control data, resulting in much longer flows. For example, some chat flows are active for as much as 62 hours. The protrusion at around 100KB is due to the fact that the client perform compression of images and most of media flows are close to that size. Fig. 5(b) indicates that more than 50% of the mm flows are bigger than 70 KB, with an average flow size of 225 KB. More than 90% of the chat flows are smaller than 10 KB, with an average size of 6.7 KB. In terms of duration, Fig. 5(c) shows that more than 90% of the mm flows last less than 1 min (mean duration of 1.8 min), whereas chat flows last on average as much as 17 minutes. The flow duration CDF additionally

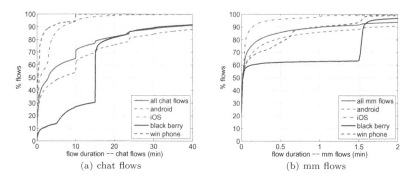

(a) chat flows   (b) mm flows

Fig. 6. Flow duration per different OS

reveals some clear steps at exactly 10, 15 and 24 minutes, suggesting the usage of an application time-out to terminate long idle connections. This behavior is actually dictated by the operating system of the device. To better understand it, we performed a device OS classification based on manual labeling of each device based on its IMEI, covering more than 90% of the observed flows. Note that the device IMEI is not contained in the WhatsApp messages, but comes from other monitoring sources in METAWIN. Fig. 6(a) splits the analysis of the chat flow duration per device OS. The figure clearly shows that the aforementioned time-out is mainly OS-dependent, as different platforms show different values. Three different time-outs are visible for Android devices at 10, 15 and 24 mins; iOS uses a very short time-out of 3 mins, BlackBerry devices have 15 mins. long time-outs, whereas Windows Mobile phones favor 10 mins. time-outs. On the contrary, in the case of mm flows in Fig. 6(b), all the different OS show a similar behavior, with the exception of BlackBerry and Windows Phone, using a 90 secs. time-out. These observations might have a major impact on the performance of the Radio Access Network, due to different OS synchronization times and uneven resources reservation requests. Indeed, it has been recently shown that applications that provide continuous online presence such as WhatsApp can generate a significant burden on the signaling plane in cellular networks [3].

Considering flow throughput, Fig. 5(d) depicts the uplink and downlink throughputs for flows bigger than 1 MB. This filtering is performed as a means to improve the throughput estimations. A-priori, one might expect that the long RTTs involved in the communications to the US servers might heavily impact the achieved performance. This is confirmed for about 30% of the transmitted flows, which achieve a throughput smaller than 250 kbps. However, higher throughputs are obtained for the largest shares of flows, achieving an average per flow downlink/uplink throughput of 1.5 Mbps/800 kbps. Still, as we show next, a big share of the file downloads can actually result in a very poor quality of experience for the users.

5   Quality of Experience in WhatsApp

In the previous section we considered the transfer throughput as the main
KPI reflecting service performance. However, in order to better understand the
impacts of transfer throughputs on the experience of the users, we performed
a QoE-based study of WhatsApp, relying on subjective QoE tests performed
in the lab, following well defined standards for realizing the tests and analyzing the results [23,24]. In a nutshell, 50 participants (45%/55% male/female, 23
average age, 60%/40% students/employees) provided their feedback in terms of
Mean Opinion Scores (MOSs), reflecting their experienced quality while using
WhatsApp for transferring video and music files. The study consisted of users
receiving a multimedia file of 5MB to download on their smartphones as a WhatsApp shared file. Different network conditions were emulated by connecting the
phones to a network emulator, introducing different download throughput profiles via traffic shaping. At the end of each download, the user rates the overall
quality in a 1-to-5 MOS scale, where 5 means excellent experience and 1 means a
very bad one. Note that the file size of 5MB has a clear motivation behind: mp3
music files and short videos have a similar size. While it is clear that the 5MB
flow size reflects only a fraction of the total flows (as depicted in Fig. 5(b)), the
performed study permits to have some rough ideas of what the users perceive
of the service in terms of quality in this case. A deeper WhatsApp QoE-based
study is part of our current work.

Fig. 7(a) shows the QoE results for different download throughput values,
translated into waiting times. Download time is in fact the most relevant feature
as perceived by the user when analyzing file transfers [25], as this is directly
linked to anxiety and satisfaction. The figure shows that users tolerate transfers
of up to 20s long with a good overall experience, whereas transfers lasting more
than 80s are considered as very bad quality. A threshold of about 40s permits to
approximately discriminate between good and bad experience. Fig. 7(b) plots the
Flow Size vs. the Flow Download Time (FDT) for the large-scale dataset, considering only flows bigger than 1MB. If we focus on the range of flows with sizes
around 5MB, we see that while the majority of the flows have a FDT below 40s,
there are many downloads which highly exceed this threshold. Indeed, Fig. 7(c)
shows the distribution of the FDTs, both for all the flows with size between 4MB
and 6MB, as well as for all the flows bigger than 1MB. From these CDFs, one
can say that almost 40% of the WhatsApp downloads with size between 4MB

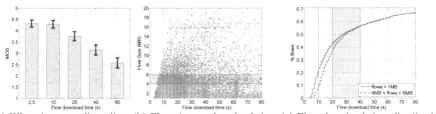

(a) WhatsApp overall quality   (b) Flow size vs. download time   (c) Flow download time distribution

Fig. 7. QoE in WhatsApp, considering flows bigger than 1MB

and 6MB have a FDT lower than 20s, resulting in good user experience. About 60% still result in an acceptable quality, and about 35% are potentially badly or very badly perceived. Finally, if we now assume that users are generally non experts and that file sizes are not taken into account into their quality expectations when downloading a video or a song through WhatsApp, we could say that similar results are observed for the complete dataset of downloaded flows bigger than 1MB. Of course this last observation is rather controversial, but still presents some notions on the experience of the end users. As a main conclusion, we see that the architectural design of WhatsApp, with servers centralized in the US, might actually have an impact on the experience of the users.

6   The WhatsApp Blackout

The last part of the study focuses on the analysis of the major WhatsApp worldwide outage reported since its beginning as observed in our traces. The outage occurred in February the 22nd of 2014, and had a strong attention in the medias worldwide. The event is not only clearly visible in our passive traces, but can also be correlated with the near real-time user reactions on social networks. Through the online downdetector application [18] we accessed the counts of tweeter feeds containing the keyword "whatsapp", coupled with keywords reflecting service impairments such as "outage", "is down", etc.. We refer to these tweets as *error tweets*.

Fig. 8(a) depicts the time series of the share of bytes exchanged with the servers, the share of flows, as well as the number of error tweets during two consecutive days encompassing the outage. The traffic drastically dropped on the 22nd at around 19:00 CEST (event B), and slowly started recovering after midnight, with some transient anomalous behaviors in the following hours (events C and D). Traffic volumes in both directions did not drop completely to zero but some non-negligible fraction of the traffic was still being exchanged, suggesting

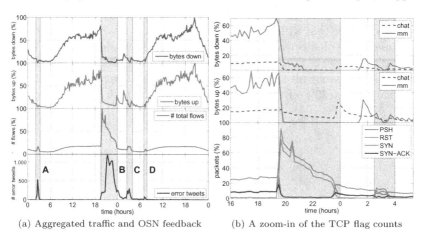

(a) Aggregated traffic and OSN feedback   (b) A zoom-in of the TCP flag counts

Fig. 8. The WhatsApp worldwide outage

an overloading problem of the hosting infrastructure. In terms of number of flows, there is a clear ramp-up on the flow counts. Very interestingly, there is a clear correlation between the events B, C and D and the number of WhatsApp-related error tweets. The users reacted on the social network immediately after the beginning of the outage, with the viral effect reaching its highest point after one hour. There is an additional outage event marked as A, which is clearly observable in the error tweet counts and has exactly the same signature of events B, C and D, i.e., a drop in the traffic volume and an increase in the flows count. As a take away of this social data analysis, one can use such information as ground truth for near real-time detection of QoE-relevant anomalies in popular services such as WhatsApp.

To better drill-down the anomaly, Fig. 8(b) depicts a 12-hour zoom-in of the traffic volume trends, split by chat and mm traffic, along with the counters of TCP flags. The bytes down counters show that the residual downlink traffic exchanged during the first part of the anomaly is due to previously queued mm transfers. In fact, while chat servers stopped working, media servers are still up and running at the beginning of the outage. We recall that connections to chat servers are also used for application control, hence they provide links to media contents. If such links have been delivered before the chat outage, the users might still be able to retrieve media objects. The chat traffic in the uplink direction does not drop to zero but slowly fades out, which actually corresponds to control flows trying to re-establish the lost connections. In particular, the TCP flags counters reveal an steeped increase of SYN packets, indicating that devices were repeatedly trying to reconnect after the servers abruptly flashed the connections (RST flags). This suggests that the servers were still reachable, thus the failure occurred at the application layer. The SYN and RST counters decrease gradually, revealing a back-off mechanism of the client application. These connection attempts explain the high increase in the flow counts during events A-D, as well as the persistence of uplink traffic to chat servers. This behaviour affected the whole WhatsApp addressing space.

7   Concluding Remarks

WhatsApp is the fastest-growing company in history in terms of users, and this paper presented the first large-scale characterization of the service from passive measurements collected at a national-wide cellular network. Our study fully dissected the well structured internal naming scheme used by WhatsApp to handle the different types of connections, which shall enable an easy way to monitor its traffic in the network. We discovered that WhatsApp is a centralized service, fully hosted in the US. We showed that such a centralized hosting infrastructure might negatively impact the experience of the end users. Even more, we believe that having a poorly geo-distributed network of servers might be highly harmful in terms of failures for such Internet-scale services, as revealed by the characterized worldwide outage. Finally, we showed that WhatsApp uses two different approaches for handling the messages exchanged among its users, keeping persistent connections to handle text messages and short-lived flows to send multimedia contents.

The datasets collected and analyzed in this paper correspond to a very interesting point in time in the history of WhatsApp, in which Facebook acquired the service. Given the highly distributed nature of the Facebook network [5], we expect a significant change in the WhatsApp network architecture in the next couple of years, and we are currently collecting a very large-scale WhatsApp dataset to further investigate such changes in an upcoming study.

Acknowledgments. This work has been performed in the framework of the EU-IP project mPlane, funded by the European Commission under the grant 318627.

References

1. Fiadino, P., et al.: Vivisecting WhatsApp through Large-Scale Measurements in Mobile Networks. Extended Abstract in ACM SIGCOMM (2014)
2. Vergara, E., Andersson, S., Nadjm-Tehrani, S.: When mice consume like elephants: instant messaging applications. In: ACM e-Energy (2014)
3. Aucinas, A., Vallina-Rodriguez, N., Grunenberger, Y., Erramilli, V., Papagiannaki, K., Crowcroft, J., Wetherall, D.: Staying online while mobile: the hidden costs. In: ACM CoNEXT (2013)
4. Chen, K., Huang, C., Huang, P., Lei, C.: Quantifying skype user satisfaction. In: ACM SIGCOMM (2006)
5. Fiadino, P., D'Alconzo, A., Casas, P.: Characterizing web services provisioning via cdns: the case of facebook. In: TRAC (2014)
6. Finamore, A., Mellia, M., Munafo, M., Torres, R., Rao, S.G.: YouTube Everywhere: Impact of Device and Infrastructure Synergies on User Experience. In: ACM IMC (2011)
7. Drago, I., Mellia, M., Munafo, M., Sperotto, A., Sadre, R., Pras, A.: Inside Dropbox: Understanding Personal Cloud Storage Services. In: ACM IMC (2012)
8. Magno, G., Comarela, G., Saez-Trumper, D., Cha, M., Almeida, V.: New kid on the block: exploring the google+ social graph. In: ACM IMC (2012)
9. Bermudez, I., Mellia, M., Munafo, M., Keralapura, R., Nucci, A.: DNS to the rescue: discerning content and services in a tangled web. In: ACM IMC (2012)
10. Fiadino, P., Bär, A., Casas, P.: HTTPTag: a flexible on-line http classification system for operational 3G networks. In: IEEE INFOCOM (2013)
11. Bär, A., Casas, P., Golab, L., Finamore, A.: DBStream: an online aggregation, filtering and processing system for network traffic monitoring. In: TRAC (2014)
12. Ricciato, F.: Traffic Monitoring and analysis for the optimization of a 3G network. IEEE Wireless Communications 13(6) (2006)
13. MaxMIND GeoIP Databases. http://www.maxmind.com (accessed on August 20, 2014)
14. The RIPE Atlas measurement network. https://atlas.ripe.net/ (accessed on September 02, 2014)
15. Blodget, H.: Everyone Who Thinks Facebook Is Stupid To Buy WhatsApp For $19 Billion Should Think Again. http://www.businessinsider.com/why-facebook-buying-whatsapp-2014-2 (accessed on August 15, 2014)
16. WhatsApp Blog. http://blog.whatsapp.com/ (accessed on September 07, 2014)
17. WhatsApp Status in Twitter. https://twitter.com/wa_status (Accessed on August 13, 2014)

18. Downdetector.com. http://downdetector.com/ (accessed on October 07, 2014)
19. SoftLayer: Cloud Servers. http://www.softlayer.com (accessed on October 01, 2014)
20. Saint-Andre, P.: Extensible Messaging and Presence Protocol (XMPP): Instant Messaging and Presence. RFC-6121, March 2011
21. Poese, I., Uhlig, S., Kaafar, M., Donnet, B., Gueye, B.: IP Geolocation Databases: Unreliable? ACM SIGCOMM Computer Communication Review, 53–56 (2011)
22. Bannister, J., Mather, P., Coope, S.: Convergence Technologies for 3G Networks: IP, UMTS, EGPRS and ATM. Wiley (2004)
23. International Telecommunication Union, Methods for Subjective Determination of Transmission Quality, ITU-T Rec. P. 800 (1996)
24. International Telecommunication Union: Estimating End-to-End Performance in IP Networks for Data Applications. ITU-T Rec. G. 1030 (2005)
25. Casas, P., et al.: A First Look at Quality of Experience in Personal Cloud Storage Services. In: ICC Workshops (2013)

Device-Specific Traffic Characterization for Root Cause Analysis in Cellular Networks

Peter Romirer-Maierhofer[✉], Mirko Schiavone, and Alessandro D'Alconzo

Forschungszentrum Telekommunikation Wien (FTW), Vienna, Austria
{romirer,schiavone,dalconzo}@ftw.at

Abstract. Nowadays mobile devices are highly heterogeneous both in terms of terminal types (e.g., smartphones versus data modems) and usage scenarios (e.g., mobile browsing versus machine-to-machine applications). Additionally, the complexity of mobile terminals is continuously growing due to increases in computational power and advances in mobile operating systems. In this scenario novel traffic patterns may arise in mobile networks, and it is highly desirable for operators to understand their impact on the network performance. We address this problem by characterizing the traffic of different device types and Operating systems, analyzing real traces from a large scale mobile operator. We find the presence of highly time synchronized spikes in both data and signaling plane traffic generated by different types of devices. Additionally, by investigating a real case, we show that a device-specific view on traffic can efficiently support the root cause analysis of some type of network anomalies. Our analysis confirms that large traffic peaks, potentially leading to large-scale anomalies, can be induced by the misbehavior of a specific device type. Accordingly, we advocate the need for novel analysis methodologies for automatic detection and possibly mitigation of such device-triggered network anomalies.

1 Introduction

In the last decade operators of mobile networks have witnessed the spread of heterogeneous mobile devices. Their heterogeneity stems from several respects: Mobile devices include different terminal types, operating systems and support a large variety of different applications. The level of device complexity is increased by the permanent evolution of their computational power, the introduction of novel mobile services and upgrades of the respective mobile APPs and Operating Systems (OSs). In such a heterogeneous and complex network scenario it is very appealing for mobile network operators i) to verify that device-specific traffic patterns are conform with the assumptions taken during dimensioning of network capacity, and ii) to identify device-specific traffic patterns that may induce undesirable events (such as temporary overload due to large device populations issuing synchronized downloads). This aspect is even more critical due to today's dynamics of mobile OSs making the assessment of device-specific traffic patterns a moving target.

© IFIP International Federation for Information Processing 2015
M. Steiner et al. (Eds.): TMA 2015, LNCS 9053, pp. 64–78, 2015.
DOI: 10.1007/978-3-319-17172-2_5

In this study we present a device-specific view on traffic behavior in an operational cellular network by first categorizing device types and mobile OSs present in the network, and second by characterizing traffic patterns at different protocol layers for the resulting device- and OS- categories. Additionally, we show how device-specific traffic characterization can be exploited for the identification of the root causes of detected network anomalies, a task which is typically resource-intensive in operational networks [1]. Monitoring device-specific traffic behavior enables the discrimination of anomalies caused by large populations of specific devices from other, network-triggered anomalies, such as e.g., malfunctioning of network equipment typically affecting all device types at the same time.

The remainder of this paper is organized as follows. We present our monitoring setup and approach to device categorization in §3. In §4.1 we characterize device-specific traffic behavior at the data plane. Additionally, we report on observed similarities and differences compared to the previous work in [2]. We investigate the device characteristics in Third Generation Partnership Project (3GPP)-specific signaling at sub-minute granularity in §4.2. To the best of our knowledge this is the first work investigating device-specific 3GPP signaling at sub-minute granularity. In §4.3 we report about a device-specific network anomaly detected from the analysis of Domain Name System (DNS) traffic for different device categories and mobile OSs. Finally, we discuss lessons learned and derive guidelines for future work in §5.

Our findings collectively suggest that the extraction and analysis of device-specific traffic patterns becomes more and more important for dimensioning and troubleshooting mobile networks. Accordingly, novel methodologies to detect and mitigate undesirable device-specific traffic behavior are required in the near future.

2   Related Works

In order to enable a consistent taxonomy for describing heterogeneous mobile devices Gansemer *et al.* presented a scalable database approach for classifying devices, according to their features [3], into three categories: smartphones, mobile phones and Personal Digital Assistents (PDAs). While the focus of that work lies on enabling the selection of the optimal devices for development of specific mobile applications, we use our device categorization for studying their network-layer behavior. The authors in [4] presented the classification of mobile devices by means of fingerprinting of their specific traffic behavior at the network and transport layer. To this purpose the authors deploy supervised machine learning techniques for processing passively monitored traffic features such as Time-To-Live or TCP congestion-window size. However, the experimental measurements presented in [4] cover only a limited number of devices, while we characterize the traffic behavior of the entire population of mobile devices within an operational mobile network. Kumar *et al.* report about large spatio-temporal differences between smart-phones and laptops in [5]. Their study relies on MAC address-based device classification and has been conducted by means of large-scale trace analysis within a campus Wireless Local Area Network (WLAN). Our work includes also additional device categories and is based on characterizing the

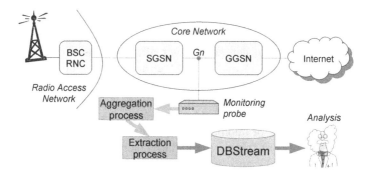

Fig. 1. Monitoring infrastructure and measurement setup

traffic behavior of a device population that is several orders of magnitudes larger than the one studied in [5].

The characterization of Machine-to-Machine (M2M) device-specific traffic behavior in operational cellular networks has been presented earlier in [2,6,7]. The work presented in [6] includes the characterization of traffic volume behavior and radio performance of M2M devices. The authors in [2] study volume time series, session durations, mobility, applications and network performance of M2M devices. While our approach to device categorization is similar to these earlier studies, we do not limit ourselves to the characterization of M2M devices, but rather we encompass additional device categories such as tablets and USB modems. Additionally, we complement the studies presented in [2,6,7] by *i*) characterizing the traffic behavior of two different types of mobile operating systems, *ii*) studying the 3GPP-signaling protocol behavior and *iii*) investigating traffic behavior at shorter time-scales enabling us to characterize device synchronization at sub-minute granularity. Finally, we compare the traffic volume characteristics in the network under study with the characteristics presented in [2] and discuss observed similarities and differences.

3   Methodology

Traces were collected at the core network of a large scale European mobile operator. The results reported in the paper are based on several consecutive weeks of observation in the fourth quarter of 2013. The measurement setup is depicted in Fig. 1. Packet-level traces are captured at the Gn links between the GGSN and SGSN — for details about 3G network structure please refer to [8]. We analyze anonymized data captured by the METAWIN monitoring system developed in a previous research project [9]. This monitoring system relies on Endace DAG cards [10], and packets are recorded with Global Positioning System (GPS)-synchronized timestamps offering an accuracy of ±100 ns.

Our measurement setup enables the investigation not only of data traffic, but also of 3GPP-specific signaling traffic, e.g., mobile data sessions set-up and tear-down , that is PDP contexts in the terminology of 3GPP (see [11] for more details). Signaling information is exploited for associating an anonymized Mobile

Device Identifier (MDID) and the observed device type to each monitored packet. This latter is achieved by extracting the Type Allocation Code (TAC) digits from the International Mobile Equipment Identity (IMEI), while the serial number digits of the IMEI are anonymized by means of an irreversible hash function. Additionally, anonymized traffic data is transformed into high-level records of e.g. aggregate IP flows or signaling events (ref. "Aggregation Process" in Fig. 1). Finally, the recorded measurements are forwarded within an extraction process (ref. Fig. 1) to DBStream [12], a PostgreSQL-based parallel data processing system. In this paper, we use DBStream as our main analysis system. Note that all results presented in this work report normalized values to protect confidentiality of business-relevant information. Therefore, we cannot report the exact number of devices in our dataset, nor the number of devices per category.

3.1 Device Categorization

Studying device-specific traffic behavior relies on a proper categorization of the device types observed in the monitored traffic. To this purpose we follow the approach presented in [2,6]. To determine the hardware model we started inspecting the device TAC codes and matching them with the publicly available GSM Association database [13]. For categorizing M2M devices we adopt the base template scheme defined in [14]. Then, similarly to [2] we used public information (e.g., production brochures, specification sheets) to manual supplement and verify this template. Furthermore, we distinguish the categories *tablet*, *feature phone* and *smartphone*. In particular, we label as feature phone all devices that are only capable of transferring data via 2G, i.e., General Packet Radio System (GPRS) or Enhanced General Packet Radio System (E-GPRS), while we consider smartphones all devices that are at least Third Generation (3G)-capable, i.e., support data transfer via Universal Mobile Telecommunications System (UMTS) or High Speed Packet Access (HSPA). We also distinguish between *USB modems* and *modems*. The first category includes devices connected via USB to PCs or Laptops, the latter refers to PCs or Laptops built-in modems. Finally, devices specifically designed for offering 3G-connectivity via local WLAN connections are labeled as *router*.

By relying on this approach we managed to label up to 96% of the devices observed within our study. As there is no standardized definition of M2M devices some might have multiple uses (e.g., PC built-in card and M2M device modem), thus the accuracy of our categorization is affected. In these cases, we adopted a conservative approach and we labeled as M2M, devices which were exclusively advertised as such by vendors.

3.2 Operating System Classification

In addition to previous works, our study includes the characterization of traffic behavior for two different types of mobile OS in §4.3. The different OS types have been derived from publicly available TAC information. For example, the TAC codes assigned to Apple devices can be associated to the iOS operating system, whereas TAC codes assigned to Nexus devices can be labeled as Android OS).

While we are aware that such a manual labeling provides only moderate classification coverage, as shown in §4.3, it still enables us to study important OS specific traffic characteristics. For obtaining larger classification coverage, information from higher protocol layers would be required — refer to the earlier study presented in [4] for an illustrative example.

4   Results

We start our study of device-specific traffic characteristics by analyzing aggregate traffic volume behavior for different types of devices.

4.1   Device-specific Characteristics at the Data Plane

As reported in [2] the introduction of new device types, as e.g., M2M devices, induce novel traffic usage patterns that may question current assumptions for optimization of network capacity. For instance, Shafiq *et al.* report that careful allocation of network resources is required due to uplink-heavy M2M devices contradicting optimization approaches relying on downlink asymmetry of network traffic [15].

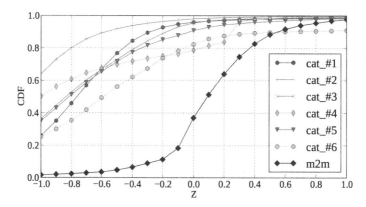

Fig. 2. CDF of ratio log(Uplink/Downlink), 7 day aggregate

For investigation of this aspect in the network under study, we plot the ratio of uplink traffic volume to downlink traffic volume for different device categories over a period of 7 days in Fig. 2. We plot the ratio for the device category M2M and all other device categories separately. The latter categories are named according to their ranked share of the overall traffic volume during the observation period[1]. For enabling a comparison of our results with the findings presented in [2, Fig. 2c] we also plot the ratios after taking their logarithm, referred to as Z. Negative values of Z indicate larger volume in downlink than in uplink, while positive values of Z refer to larger uplink volume than downlink

---

[1] In order to obfuscate business-sensitive information the specific category labels have been substituted by their rank.

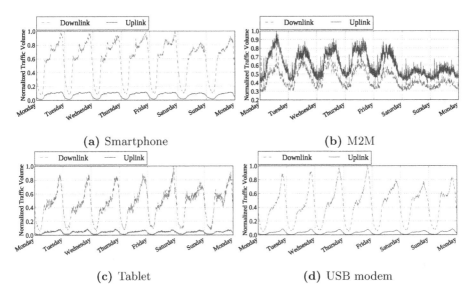

(a) Smartphone   (b) M2M

(c) Tablet   (d) USB modem

Fig. 3. Downlink and uplink traffic volume time series, time bins of 5 minutes

volume. In Fig. 2 we observe a clear separation of the distribution of M2M devices and all other devices. This is consistent with the finding presented in [2, Fig. 2c]. However, while Shafiq *et al.* report that ≈40% of smartphones have $Z < -0.4$ and ≈20% of smartphones have more uplink than downlink traffic (i.e. $Z > 0$), in our study we cannot identify any device category exhibiting the reported qualitative shape (compare Fig. 2 and [2, Fig. 2c]). Another dissimilarity to the work in [2] is observed in the volume share of M2M devices. While we observe $Z \leq 0$ for almost 40% of M2M devices, Shafiq *et al.* report less than 10% of M2M devices exhibiting larger downlink volume than uplink volume.

For further study of the device-specific data volume behavior, in Fig. 3 we plot data volume time series for different device categories, in time bins of 5 minutes, over a period of one week in the fourth quarter of 2013. We observe diurnal patterns for all time series of Fig. 3. In case of smartphones (ref. Fig. 3a) the daily peak volume is reached in the evening hours of each day. This represents a strong difference compared with the observation provided in [2, Fig. 3a] where the authors report a decrease of overall traffic volume for the evening hours. This might be explained by the different pricing models used in the two networks. In the case of [2] users may be encouraged by higher tariff models to switch from cellular connectivity to WLAN connections available in private homes.

The local volume peaks observed in Fig. 3a at noon during lunch time are a further deviation from the results presented in [2]. This specific characteristic is not visible for any other device type (ref. Fig. 3c and Fig. 3d). Our comparison with the work in [2] suggests that even conceptually simple metrics such as e.g., volume time series may exhibit significant dissimilarities for different networks.

An aspect which should be specifically regarded when establishing generic traffic models based on observations derived from real networks.

From the time series of M2M devices (ref. Fig. 3b) we may establish following findings which are consistent with the results presented in [2, Fig. 3b]: *i*) there is a clear difference of the time series between working days and week days, *ii*) M2M devices are the only device types that show higher aggregate uplink volume than downlink volume, and *iii*) we observe distinct spikes in the traffic volume indicating the presence of M2M devices sending data traffic in a synchronized manner. The aspect of synchronized traffic patterns will be further addressed in the next section.

Summarizing our investigation of traffic volume behavior, we may confirm earlier works reporting the presence of uplink-heavy, synchronized M2M terminals. However, we report distinct differences in the aggregate time series, specifically for the smartphone device category.

4.2   Device-Specific Characteristics at the Signaling Plane

As reported in [16], 3G wireless networks are currently designed for traditional human-type communication rather than for synchronized, machine-type communication patterns as they may be triggered by M2M applications or mobile APPs relying on periodic transfers of data. Accordingly, it is highly desirable for mobile network operators to assess the effect of synchronized communication patterns onto available network capacity. This is specifically important since large increases of M2M-devices are expected until 2020. Such a perspective makes an evolution from high data rate networks to M2M-optimized low cost networks very appealing for network operators [16].

In this section we characterize the signaling behavior of different device classes. In In this section we characterize the signaling behavior of different device classes. In particular we focus on the PDP-context establishment procedure. Whenever a mobile client requires the establishment of a mobile data session, it is required to send a PDP-context create request message (ref. to [8] for more details).

Fig. 4 shows the Cumulative Distribution Function (CDF) of the number of Packet Data Protocol (PDP)-context create requests for the device class M2M and the two most popular device categories, computed over an aggregation period of 7 consecutive days[2]. We observe similar characteristics for M2M devices and the top category. While the second category converges quickly to 1, suggesting that the devices of this category are operated by means of lower amounts of PDP context create procedures. Moreover, we observe that the CDF of M2M devices converges slower to 1 than in case of other device types. This suggests that a small fraction of M2M devices relies on frequent session establishments, an aspect which we address further below.

---

[2] In order to obfuscate business-sensitive information the specific category labels have been again substituted by their rank according to the overall volume during the observation period.

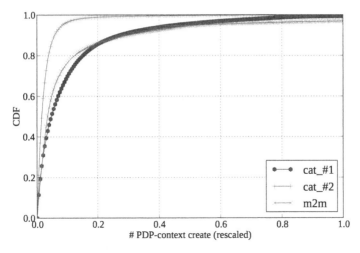

Fig. 4. CDF of number of PDP-context create, different categories, 7 days (rescaled)

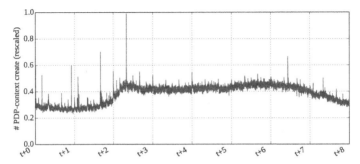

Fig. 5. Time series of PDP-context creates, 1 day, time bins of 10 sec

Fig. 5 depicts the overall time series of PDP-context create request messages over a period of one day. We observe a time-of-day variation in the PDP-context create request messages indicating more context establishments during day-time and less connection establishments during night hours. However, in addition to this daily cycle, we report distinct short-term spikes arising every full-hour and also smaller spikes occurring at a periodicity of 15 minutes.

For further investigation of these spikes in the connection establishment process, we plot the time series of PDP-context creates for different device classes over a period of two days in Fig. 6. Comparing Fig. 5 and Fig. 6 we discover that the reported peaks are triggered by different device classes. In particular M2M devices are responsible for the higher peaks (e.g. refer to the largest spike in the morning hours depicted in Fig. 6b). Additionally, we observe that M2M devices exhibit their largest spikes during night hours indicating that a certain population of M2M devices relies on periodic session establishments during off-peak hours. It is interesting to note that also smartphones exhibit some sort of synchronized behavior recognizable by the first three prominent spikes persistently re-occurring

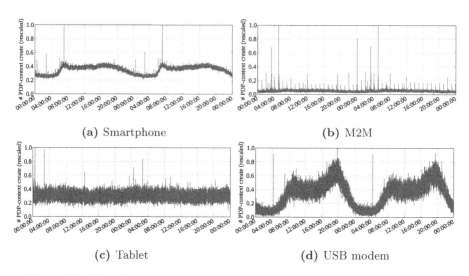

(a) Smartphone

(b) M2M

(c) Tablet

(d) USB modem

Fig. 6. Signaling: PDP-context create event time series, time bins of 10 seconds

in the morning hours (ref. Fig. 6a). By isolating these spikes for the different OS types derived from the publicly available TAC identifier, we find that those are caused by different types of mobile OSs. This suggests that specific types of OS may in fact exhibit different behavior in the context establishment process. For instance, the first two prominent spikes can be mapped to iOS-related TAC identifiers while the third peak can be associated to Android OS-specific TAC identifiers. The aspect of OS-specific signaling behavior will be further discussed in§4.3. Additionally, Fig. 6d shows distinct spikes every day at 04:00 for the device category of USB modems. This behavior may be triggered by an M2M-like application relying on periodic data transfers once a day. For further investigation of the synchronization level exhibited by the different device classes, we introduce the following indicator functions and sets.

Be e and E the generic device and the set it belongs, respectively. We denote by $d = 1, 2, ..., 7$ the days of the week, by $m = 1, 2, ..., 1440$ the minutes of the day, and by $w = 1, 2, ...52$ the weeks of the year. For each device, let define the function:

$$\Theta_e(m, d, w) \stackrel{\text{def}}{=} \begin{cases} 1 \text{ if } e \text{ creates a PDP-context within} \\ \quad \text{minute } m \text{ of day } d \text{ on week } w \\ 0 \text{ otherwise} \end{cases} \tag{1}$$

For counting the number of days in the week the device e is creating a PDP-context, at minute m, we introduce the function:

$$\Sigma_e(m, w) = \sum_{d=1}^{7} \Theta_e(m, d, w) \tag{2}$$

For filtering on the devices active in more than τ days per week, we define the following indicator function:

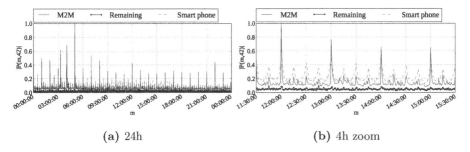

(a) 24h   **(b)** 4h zoom

Fig. 7. Cardinality of $P_{m,42}$, different zoom levels

$$\Lambda_e(m, w) \stackrel{\text{def}}{=} \begin{cases} 1 \text{ if } \Sigma_e(m, w) > \tau \\ 0 \text{ otherwise} \end{cases} \qquad (3)$$

The set of devices active at least τ days at the minute m of the week w, is defined as follows:

$$C_{m,w} \stackrel{\text{def}}{=} \{e \in E : \Lambda_e(m, w) = 1\} \qquad (4)$$

In order to filter those devices that exhibit stable activity patterns across two consecutive weeks, we consider the sets $P_{m,w}$ obtained intersecting the $C_{m,w}$ with the conform set (i.e., the same minute) of the previous week:

$$P_{m,w} = C_{m,w} \cap C_{m,w-1} \qquad (5)$$

Fig. 7a depicts graphical representation of the cardinality of the sets $P_{m,42}$ for the different minutes at week 42. From this plot we notice that M2M and smartphones exhibit similar behavior since both the classes tend to be synchronized with the full hour, and partially synchronized also at a periodicity of 30 and 15 minutes. We found that more than 20% of M2M devices exhibit this behavior while the share of smartphones is around 1%. In Fig 7b we report a zoom on 4 hours of Fig. 7a. We observe that the variation around the spikes is larger for smartphones compared to the case of M2M devices. This suggests that smartphones are synchronized at a coarser level, while M2M devices are tightly synchronized in time. This tight time-synchronization is highly undesirable for mobile operators, since it requires allocation of large network resources when the network is dimensioned to keep up with capacity demands during traffic peaks. Consequently, the expected future increase of M2M devices [16] suggests that a continuous monitoring of M2M-triggered communication patterns is needed, such that adequate countermeasures can be timely enforced (e.g., de-synchronization of M2M devices).

4.3   Investigation of a Device-Specific Anomaly

In this section we report about a large-scale network anomaly detected while studying the characteristics of the Domain Name System (DNS) traffic generated by each device category and for different OS.

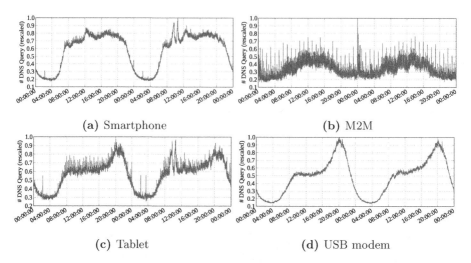

(a) Smartphone **(b)** M2M

(c) Tablet **(d)** USB modem

Fig. 8. Time series of DNS requests per device category, 2 days, time bins of 1 minute

Since the vast majority of Internet applications rely on the proper functionality of the DNS, ensuring the availability and performance of DNS servers is an essential task for operators of mobile networks. Due to the emerging of synchronized traffic behavior, as e.g., shown in §4.2, it is important to know whether a large device population queries the operator's DNS servers in a highly synchronized manner, potentially impairing DNS servers performance. To this purpose, in Fig. 8 we plot the time series of DNS queries for different device categories, over a period of two days, aggregated in time bins of 1 minute. In Fig. 8b we observe that M2M devices trigger several time-synchronized peaks in the DNS query count across both days, showing the largest peaks around midnight. Further manual investigation of the spikes depicted Fig. 8b showed that these spikes are deterministic and re-occur every day at the same time of day. Since network capacity is typically dimensioned in a peak-oriented manner, the presence of short-term peaks results in higher capacity demands and wastage of resources in non-peak intervals. Both aspects are highly undesirable at the network dimensioning stage. Our observation suggests the need for deploying randomization strategies for de-synchronization of network traffic in order to optimize network dimensioning. The expected large increase of (synchronized) M2M devices by 2020 [16] urges for the adoption of such mitigation strategies in the near future. However, in Fig. 8 we observe that not only M2M devices, but also smartphones and tablets exhibit synchronized peaks in the DNS query counts. For instance, we report smaller spikes throughout the whole day and larger, persistent spikes in the night hours every day (ref. Fig. 8a and Fig. 8c).

Interestingly, Fig. 8 shows a sudden and large increase of DNS queries in the morning hours of the second day. This clear anomaly only affects smartphones and tablets, but no other device types (ref. e.g., USB modem in Fig. 8). For further investigation of the anomaly, we plot the time series of DNS query

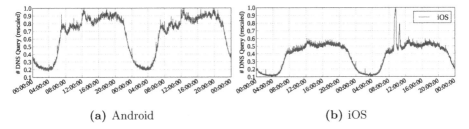

(a) Android   (b) iOS

Fig. 9. Time series of DNS requests per operating system, 2 days, time bins of 1 minute

counts separately for TAC identifiers related to Android OS and iOS (recall §3)
in Fig. 9. From this figure we observe that only iOS-based devices are affected
by the anomaly. This confirms that the misbehavior of a large population of a
certain device type may in fact trigger macroscopic, network-wide anomalies.
As mobile devices nowadays rely on frequent updates of mobile apps and operating systems, it cannot be excluded that novel device-specific (mis-)behavior
are induced by such software updates over time. Accordingly, the assessment
whether software-updates result in new device-specific traffic characteristics or
even might induce novel network anomalies, requires continuous monitoring of
device-specific behavior across different types of devices and OSs. Hence, we
consider the the analysis of device-specific traffic behavior a moving target.

We further investigate the iOS-based anomaly depicted in Fig. 9 as follows.
Our monitoring system allows for the extraction of IP-level flow counters aggregated in time bins of 1 minute. That is, in each time bin traffic volumes (i.e., IP
packets transferred in uplink and in downlink) are aggregated per flow, where a
flow is identified by the anonymized MDID, destination IP address, source port
and destination port. These flow aggregates enable the analysis of three different flow types: flows where traffic has been transferred exclusively in uplink, i.e.,
data has been sent from the mobile devices towards the Internet. Such flows are
referred to as "uplink-only" flows. Conversely, "downlink-only" refers to flows
where traffic has been transferred only from servers in the Internet towards
mobile devices, and "two-way" flows refer to the case where traffic volume has
been transferred in both directions. As mentioned in [17] one-way traffic is caused
by different sources, such as scanning, peer-to-peer applications, back-scatter and
unreachable services. As noticed in [17] the latter type is particularly helpful for
large scale monitoring of network and service outages.

In Fig. 10 we plot the (rescaled) number of different flow types versus time
during the interval of the iOS-based anomaly. Fig. 10a depicts the flows involving
servers located in the anomalous IP range, while Fig. 10b shows flows involving
the residual server IP addresses. In order to enable direct comparison both figures
have been rescaled by the same undisclosed factor. In Fig 10b we observe that
all flow types are rather stable over time. The number of two-way flows shows
two slight bumps during the anomaly, which are likely caused by the anomalous increase of DNS queries that has been presented in Fig. 9b. In contrast, we
observe two distinct bumps for all flows of the anomalous IP range in Fig. 10a.

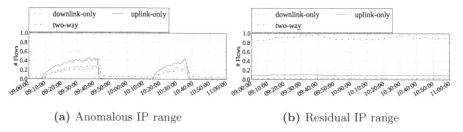

(a) Anomalous IP range   (b) Residual IP range

Fig. 10. Time series of flow types during observed anomaly, 1 min. time bins (rescaled)

The majority of these flows is unanswered by the destined servers within the same time bin, resulting in two bumps of uplink-only flows (indicated by the solid line). This finding and the fact that we observe a simultaneous increase of uplink DNS queries, suggest that the anomaly is induced by a large set of iOS-based devices issuing connection requests in uplink (e.g., by sending TCP SYN packets). While we find that still some of the flows are answered by the servers (see "two-way" flows in Fig. 10a), we also report two bumps for the class of downlink-only flows. Such downlink-only flows may be present if connection requests in uplink are answered late (e.g. by TCP reset packets) such that the downlink packet is counted in one of the subsequent time bins after the corresponding uplink flow. The pattern shown in Fig. 10a suggests that the servers located in the anomalous IP range suffered from temporary faults leading to a large number of unanswered and rejected client connection requests. In fact the mobile devices reacted upon these unsuccessful connection requests by triggering even more uplink-only flows (indicated by the persistently increasing height of the bumps in Fig. 10a). Such a behavior is highly unwanted, since the scheduling mechanisms in the Radio Access Network (RAN) typically rely on assigning higher bandwidth to devices exceeding certain traffic rate thresholds [18]. As a result of this scheduling strategy, anomalies like the reported one may lead to large bandwidth demands for sending unsuccessful connection requests and, hence, to a significant wastage of network resources in the RAN. Since RAN resources are allocated in a shared manner, such incidents may even impair the network performance of those devices not directly involved into an anomaly.

Our findings suggest that new methodologies are required for detecting and mitigating device-specific anomalies. Current protection mechanisms, such as e.g., IP firewalls or intrusion prevention systems, are mainly designed for mitigating anomalies and attacks originating from *external* sources located in the Internet. Accordingly, such protection infrastructure is placed towards the edge of the core network between the Gateway GPRS Support Node (GGSN) and the Internet (ref. Fig 1). However, methodologies for efficiently mitigating device-triggered anomalies should be enforced in the RAN section close to the mobile devices, in order to avoid the propagation of anomalies and their negative effects towards the core network. Furthermore, our study illustrates how root causes of anomalies can be efficiently carried out by relying on device- and OS-specific traffic characteristics. Further work along this direction has been documented in [19]. There, we provide guidelines for designing an automatic diagnosis system for network anomalies, which relies on entropy metrics calculated from device-specific traffic features.

5   Conclusions and Future Work

In this paper we present a device-specific view on the traffic within an operational cellular network, taking into account both, data plane and signaling plane traffic. By discussing previous works on traffic characterization in mobile networks we show that comparing data sets collected from different networks is not trivial, since even simple metrics such as, e.g., traffic volume time series, may exhibit significantly different patterns across different networks. This is specifically critical in case generic traffic models are derived from network-specific traffic behavior.

Moreover, we report the presence of time-synchronized peaks at different protocol layers (e.g., DNS and PDP-context create) and at different time of the day. In particular we find that such spikes are not only triggered by synchronized M2M devices, but are also observed in other device categories (e.g., smartphones, tables and USB modems). This finding suggests that de-synchronization of mobile devices for mitigating the negative effects of synchronized traffic peaks should not only be carried out for M2M devices, but also for all the other device classes.

Finally, we also report about a device-specific network anomaly detected from the analysis of DNS traffic. Analyzing this anomaly we show that device-specific traffic characterization supports investigation of device-induced network anomalies, and the identification of their root causes.

Acknowledgments. This work has been performed in the framework of the EU-IP project mPlane, funded by the European Commission under the grant 318627.

References

1. D'Alconzo, A., Coluccia, A., Romirer-Maierhofer, P.: Distribution-Based Anomaly Detection in 3G Mobile Networks: From Theory to Practice. International Journal of Network Management, September 2010
2. Shafiq, M.Z., et al.: Large-Scale Measurement and Characterization of Cellular Machine-to-Machine Traffic. IEEE/ACM Transactions on Networking (2013)
3. Gansemer, S., Groner, U., Maus, M.: Database classification of mobile devices. In: Intelligent Data Acquisition and Advanced Computing Systems Technology and Applications (IDAACS) (2007)
4. Granell, E., et al.: Smart devices fingerprint detection. In: IEEE Globecom Workshops (2012)
5. Kumar, U., Kim, J., Helmy, A.: Changing patterns of mobile network (WLAN) usage: smart-phones vs. laptops. In: Wireless Communications and Mobile Computing Conference, IWCMC 2013 (2013)
6. Marjamaa, J.: A measurement-based analysis of machine-to-machine communications over a cellular network. Master's thesis, Aalto University, Helsinki, June 2012

7. Baer, A., Svoboda, P., Casas, P.: MTRAC - discovering M2M devices in cellular networks from coarse-grained measurements. In: International Conference on Communications, ICC (2015)
8. Bannister, J., Mather, P., Coope, S.: Convergence technologies for 3G networks: IP, UMTS. John Wiley and Sons, EGPRS and ATM (2004)
9. Ricciato, F., et al.: Traffic monitoring and analysis in 3G networks: lessons learned from the METAWIN project. Elektrotechnik und Informationstechnik (2006)
10. Endace measurememt systems. http://www.endace.com
11. ETSI. 3GPP TS 129.060, version 7.9.0 (2008)
12. Baer, A., et al.: Large-scale network traffic monitoring with DBStream, a system for rolling big data analysis. In: International Conference on Big Data (2014)
13. GSMA IMEI Database. http://imeidb.gsm.org/imei/
14. AT&T, Florham Park, NJ, USA. AT&T specialty vertical devices. http://www.rfwel.com/support/hw-support/ATT_SpecialtyVerticalDevices.eps
15. Law, L.K., Krishnamurthy, S.V., Faloutsos, M.: Capacity of hybrid cellular-ad hoc data networks. In: The 27th Conference on Computer Communications on IEEE INFOCOM 2008 (2008)
16. Laner, M., et al.: Traffic models for machine type communications. In: International Symposium on Wireless Communication Systems, ISWCS 2013 (2013)
17. Glatz, E., Dimitropoulos, X.: Classifying internet one-way traffic. In: Proceedings of the 2012 ACM Conference on Internet Measurement Conference (2012)
18. Laner, M., et al.: A comparison between one-way delays in operating HSPA and LTE networks. In: Symposium on Modeling and Optimization in Wireless Networks, WiOpt (2012)
19. Schiavone, M., et al.: Diagnosing device-specific anomalies in cellular networks. In: ACM CoNEXT 2014 Workshop, Sydney, Australia (2014)

Tracking Middleboxes in the Mobile World with TraceboxAndroid

Valentin Thirion, Korian Edeline, and Benoit Donnet$^{(\boxtimes)}$

Université de Liège, Liège, Belgium
{benoit.donnet,korian.edeline}@ulg.ac.be

Abstract. Middleboxes are largely deployed over cellular networks. It is known that they might disrupt network performance, expose users to security issues, and harm protocols deployability. Further, hardly any network measurements tools for smartphones are able to infer middlebox behaviors, specially if one cannot control both ends of a path. In this paper, we present TraceboxAndroid a *proof-of-concept* measurement application for Android mobile devices implementing the `tracebox` algorithm. It aims at diagnosing middlebox-impaired paths by detecting and locating rewriting middleboxes. We analyze a dataset sample to highlight the range of opportunities offered by TraceboxAndroid. We show that TraceboxAndroid can be useful for mobile users as well as for the research community.

1 Introduction

It has been a while, now, the Research Community has tried to use computing resources made available by end-users. One of the most famous tentative is probably SETI@home [1]. SETI@home provides a screensaver that users can freely install, and that downloads and analyzes radio-telescope data for signs of intelligent life. The project obtains a portion of the computing power of the users' computers, and in turn the users are rewarded by the knowledge that they are participating in a collective research effort, by attractive visualizations of the data, and by having their contributions publicly acknowledged. This model has been followed by others, in particular for performing large-scale Internet topology data collection [2,3].

Meanwhile, we have seen the rise of mobile devices at the expense of a drop in desk-based and notebook computers [4]. Mobile data usage is increasing rapidly in part due to a growing release of mobile devices and the availability of a wide variety of mobile phone applications. For instance, a large number of users nowadays use their mobile devices to watch video on demand (e.g., YouTube) while on the move. Naturally, the idea of using crowdsourcing with mobile devices to measure the Internet has emerged. However, the particularities of those devices make network measurements a difficult task [5].

This work is funded by the European Commission funded mPlane ICT-318627 project.

M. Steiner et al. (Eds.): TMA 2015, LNCS 9053, pp. 79–91, 2015.
DOI: 10.1007/978-3-319-17172-2_6

In addition, the Internet infrastructure has strongly evolved. In particular, we have seen the growing importance of *middleboxes* (i.e., "an intermediary box performing functions apart from normal, standard functions of an IP router on the data path between a source host and destination host" [6]). For instance, Sherry et al. [7] obtained configurations from 57 enterprise networks and revealed that they can contain as many middleboxes as routers. Wang et al. [8] surveyed 107 cellular networks and found that 82 of them used NATs. Those middleboxes has shown to have a negative impact on the evolvability of the TCP/IP protocol suite [9].

Combining the rise of mobile devices and the importance of middleboxes leads to a natural question: are the middleboxes a cause of degraded performance in mobile networks and can we provide tools for monitoring and discovering problems with end-user Quality of Experience (QoE) due to their presence. The first part of the question has already been answered. Wang et al. [8] have demonstrated that middleboxes are, indeed, a brake to mobile network performance in mobile networks.

In this paper, we tackle the second part of the question by proposing a proof-of-concept tool called *TraceboxAndroid*. TraceboxAndroid is based on `tracebox` [10], a `traceroute` extension that is able to reveal the presence of middleboxes along a path. We have ported `tracebox` under the Android system, allowing so the user to detect the presence of a middlebox that could be the cause of a degraded performance on a path. We describe the architecture of TraceboxAndroid and deploy it on several mobile devices across the world in order to demonstrate its potentialities. In addition, TraceboxAndroid is lightweight for mobile devices in terms of battery and memory consumption. TraceboxAndroid is freely available (http:// androidtracebox.org).

The remainder of this paper is organized as follows: Sec. 2 explains how `tracebox` works; Sec. 3 presents TraceboxAndroid, our `tracebox` port into Android devices; Sec. 4 explains our TraceboxAndroid deployment, data collection, and results we obtained; Sec. 5 positions this paper regarding the state of the art; finally, Sec. 6 concludes this paper by summarizing its main achievements.

2   Tracebox

To reveal the presence of middleboxes along a path, we use `tracebox` [10], an extension to the widely used `traceroute`.

`tracebox` mechanism is illustrated in Fig. 1. It relies on RFC1812 [11] and RFC792 [12] stating that the returned ICMP `time-exceeded` message should quote the IP header of the original packet and respectively the complete payload or the first 64 bits. `tracebox` uses the same incremental approach as `traceroute`, i.e., it sends packets with different IP, UDP, or TCP fields and options with increasing TTL values. By comparing the quoted packet to the original, one can highlight the modifications and the initial TTL value allows us to localize the two or more hops between which the change took place. In Fig. 1, packet a is the originally sent one. The first hop, that happens to be a middlebox, modifies

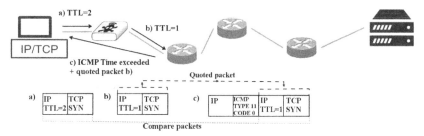

Fig. 1. Example of middlebox detection with tracebox

its TCP Initial Sequence Number (ISN) and sends the rewritten packet b to the next hop. When the next hop receives the expired packet, it sends back to the client an ICMP `time-exceeded` packet c containing packet b as a payload. When the `tracebox` client receives it, it is able to compare packet a and the payload of packet c to detect any changes and the initial TTL value, i.e., 2, allows `tracebox` to bound the middlebox location.

It is worth to notice that in 80% of the cases [10], a path contains at least one router which implement RFC1812 [11], that recommends to quote the entire IP packet in the returned ICMP. This means that, in most cases, `tracebox` is able to detect any modification performed by upstream middleboxes.

3   TraceboxAndroid

`tracebox` has been originally developed to work on desk-based computers, on a UNIX-like system. We have ported `tracebox` on Android mobile devices. Our application is called *TraceboxAndroid*.

Fig. 2 illustrates the general TraceboxAndroid architecture. As shown, it is made of three main components: the *system core* where the `tracebox` intelligence has been included (coded in C, under the front office), the *front office* (or the *application*) corresponding to the Android application (coded in Java) and the *back office* (or *server* – coded in PHP and HTML) that is used to store data and make offline analysis.

The front office communicates with the server using an XML API that gives the application the destinations to be probed and allows it to send back the data collected by the system core. The core itself implements `tracebox` (as described in Sec. 2) and sends probes to the destinations using sockets by system calls.

The front office and the system core are freely available[1] since mid-2014. In the subsequent sections, we deepen each component.

3.1   System Core

TraceboxAndroid is based on BusyBox [13], a software written in C that aims at providing Unix tools for operating systems with limited resources. In particular, it contains a basic networking tool suite (e.g., `ping`, `netstat`, `netcat`,

---

[1] http://www.androidtracebox.org

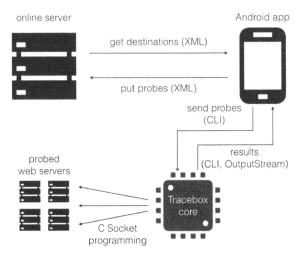

Fig. 2. General overview of the TraceboxAndroid architecture

`traceroute`, etc). We started from the latter source code to port `tracebox` into Android systems.

The main challenge we had to address is that `tracebox` requires the use of raw sockets to manually set IP fields, TCP fields, and TCP options, and retrieve the received headers. As the use of raw sockets is restricted to users that can grant the `CAP_NET_RAW` POSIX capability (i.e., super users), we chose to exclude non-*rooted* devices and call the TraceboxAndroid BusyBox implementation from the JAVA app as a super user. While this limitation is crippling for extended use, as already stated by Faggiani et al. [5], it seems reasonable for a *proof-of-concept* implementation.

TraceboxAndroid *system core* consists in a C applet which is called by a lightweight BusyBox version. The underlying `tracebox` implementation is based on the algorithm described in Sec. 2 and supports TCP/IPv4 and diverse TCP options (e.g., SelectiveACK, Timestamp, MSS, WindowScale, MultipathTCP).

3.2   Front Office

The *front office* (or application) purpose is to send `tracebox` probes to predetermined or user-chosen destinations, compute the result, and send it back to the *back office*. In some sense, it acts as a proxy between the system core and the back office.

On the first execution or when a new version is released, three actions are automatically performed: check if the phone is rooted, download and install our custom lightweight BusyBox version containing the `tracebox` implementation, and retrieve an XML file containing the destination set (detailed in Sec. 4.1).

Three probing mechanisms are available in the Front Office menu:

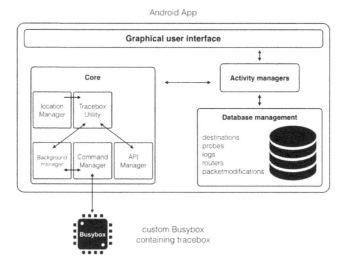

Fig. 3. Front Office organization

- *Background Probing*: background probes are sent by a scheduled task that is executed several times a day while the phone is connected to a network, even if the user shuts down the application.
  The user is able to edit the configuration of the scheduled probing by setting the number of destinations to be probed during one probing session and the maximum duration of a session.
- *Instant Probing*: an Instant probe is a one-time single measurement sent to a random destination within the destination set. The user can choose to run an Instant probe at any time and retrieve the results.
- *Custom Probing*: the Custom probing mode is similar to the Instant Probing but allows the user to set the destination.

Background Probing is mostly for research purposes. The two others are much more dedicated to given network monitoring/analysis in case of a drop in the QoE observed by the user.

The user is also able to check the results, consult the logs, and get information about the application and all the tools that were used to create it.

The architecture of the front office is displayed in Fig. 3. It is divided in three packages; (*i*) the `Main` package that is mainly composed of Activity classes that are responsible for drawing the views, monitoring the state of the app, receiving user commands, and launching `AsyncTask` to perform various operations (e.g., send an Instant Probe, parse an XML file, etc); (*ii*) the `Core` package contains utility and long-lived action managing classes that executes Unix commands and fetch the results, sends the result to the *back office* component and runs the `tracebox` applet; (*iii*) finally, the `Data` package is composed of classes maintaining information about processes and is responsible of managing an internal SQLite database.

The database stores information about destinations, probes, routers, packet modifications, and the logs. In addition to the probed routers inferred characteristics, the GPS position of the device at the probing time, Internet connection mode (i.e., WiFi, cellular, or Bluetooth), the cellular mode and carrier name (in case of a cellular network connection), and the battery consumption are saved into the local database before being sent to the *back office*.

3.3 Back Office

The *back office* is the server-side application that stores data collected by the mobile devices. It also manages the destinations probed by the application.

The *back office* has no other purpose than research (i.e., conserving collected data and off line analysis). The user cannot access the *back office* directly but has the opportunity to analyze data if he selected Instant or Custom probing, or to download the dataset on the website.

4   Evaluation

In this section, we explain our evaluation of TraceboxAndroid. In particular, we discuss our measurement methodology, describe our dataset, and analyze our results.

4.1 Methodology

We built an initial probe target set from the Alexa top-500 websites list, that we pre-resolved using Google Public DNS into 406 unique addresses, avoiding so a resolution on every mobile device that could consume undue resources and that could lead to completely different probed paths, making statistics meaningless. This address set is used by TraceboxAndroid *Background Probing* and *Instant Probing* features. It is, however, obvious that in case of selecting the *Custom Probing* feature, the DNS resolution will be done by the app.

Between May, 2014 and September, 2014 TraceboxAndroid has been downloaded by 23 users from Belgium, Italy, USA, China, and Nigeria. Measurements performed by those users during this period reached a total of 1,756 probes sent. Participating mobile devices were connected to the Internet via WiFI or cellular data networks via different carriers (Mobistar, O2, Mobile Vikings, E-Plus, BASE, T-Mobile, Movistar, KPN) using different mobile technologies (HSPA, HSPAP, HSDPA, LTE, UMTS, and EDGE).

On the whole set of probes sent, 1,372 (78.13%) were done through WiFi connections. The remaining 384 probes (21.87%) were sent through cellular connections.

This dataset is limited but sufficient to demonstrate the extent of TraceboxAndroid capabilities. Moreover, as the Android app was still under development during most measurements, the following results and figures should be considered as illustrations of the variety of the app capabilities rather than rigorous observations.

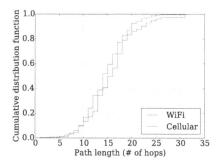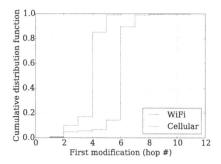

Fig. 4. Path lengths distribution

Fig. 5. Location of first observed middlebox modification

4.2 Results

We first look at paths collected and, in particular, at their length distribution. Path lengths are computed on a subset of the paths collected. From the whole set, we select those that have unique <source;destination> address pairs to compute their lengths. This subset contains 606 paths, 388 of them were obtained via WiFi connections (64.9%) and 218 via cellular connections (35.97%).

The results are displayed in Fig. 4. We see that WiFi paths are 1.14 hops longer on average than cellular networks paths, their respective path length means being 15.8 and 14.67 hops.

The location of the first observed middlebox, in number of hops away from the probing source, is shown in Fig. 5. We see that 272 among 361 (75.32%) WiFi paths and 147 among 215 (68.37%) cellular paths that involves a middlebox had their first probe modified close to the mobile device, respectively at hops 6 and 4.

WiFi probes have crossed 180 different different ASs (Autonomous Systems) and cellular probes have crossed 139 different ASs. The AS overlap between the two types of probes includes 111 ASs. The three autonomous systems that WiFi probes have traversed the most are HIBERNIA TripartZ,NL, BELGACOM-SKYNET, BE and TTNET,TR, for cellular probes these are BASE-AS,BE, KPN Interational, NL and UUNET,US. The types of crossed ASs are somewhat equivalent, whatever the type of network connection of the device (i.e., WiFi or cellular), consisting mainly in Transit networks.

We next check IP and TCP modifications. They are inferred using the tracebox algorithm described in Sec. 2. As probes have common subpaths, we counted each answering device only once based on the source IP addresses. The resulting set is composed of 3,109 routers, 175 (5.63%) of them exhibit middlebox behaviors. We have observed that 2,304 routers answered through WiFi connections and 1,392 were probed through cellular connections, among them tracebox respectively detected 103 (4.47%) and 87 (6.25%) middleboxes. Note that 587 routers have been probed via WiFI and cellular data networks.

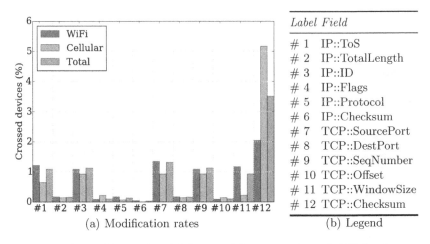

(a) Modification rates

Label	Field
# 1	IP::ToS
# 2	IP::TotalLength
# 3	IP::ID
# 4	IP::Flags
# 5	IP::Protocol
# 6	IP::Checksum
# 7	TCP::SourcePort
# 8	TCP::DestPort
# 9	TCP::SeqNumber
# 10	TCP::Offset
# 11	TCP::WindowSize
# 12	TCP::Checksum

(b) Legend

Fig. 6. Observed middlebox modification in IP and TCP headers

The amount of detected middleboxes in this set has to be put in perspective with their strategic positioning; from the unique paths set explained above, 576 among 606 (95.05%) paths are crossing at least one middlebox that modifies at least one IP header, TCP header field, or TCP option. 361 among 389 (93.04%) WiFi paths and 215 among 218 (98.62%) cellular network paths involves a rewriting middlebox.

Fig. 6 summarizes those modifications. The TCP checksum is recomputed by many middleboxes, those that modifies IP pseudo-header fields, TCP fields, and TCP options. It is natural to see that 3.5% of the total observed routers are modifying it. Besides the TCP checksum, four fields are rewritten more often: IP ToS, IP-ID, TCP source port and TCP sequence number. This modification set exactly matches NATs rewriting behavior.

IP ToS rewriting can either come from routers using its DiffServCodePoints (DSCP) sub-field to mark packets for differentiated services, or modifying the last two Explicit Congestion Notification (ECN) bits. The latter modification can either be the action of legacy routers trying to modify the legacy 8-bits ToS field instead of the 6-bits DSCP field, unintentionally modifying ECN-related bits, or a systematic clearance of ECN bits [14].

In several operating systems, IP-ID fields of self-forged packets are filled with the value of a globally-incremented packet counter, which is known to be a side-channel leaking information about other connections [15]. Security consequences when end-points use such a counter to write IP-ID have been discussed multiple times and involves enabling attackers to perform idle scan attacks, NATted hosts counting, facilitating TCP injections and more [16–19], but consequences when it is performed by middleboxes for either self-forged or certain non self-forged packets have been less discussed. One of the most harmful known exploitation of middleboxes using a globally-incremented IP-ID is when it is combined with TCP window-checking, as it enables attackers to gain feedback on in-window/out-of-window packets to infer the TCP sequence number, and perform off-path TCP injections [18,20,21].

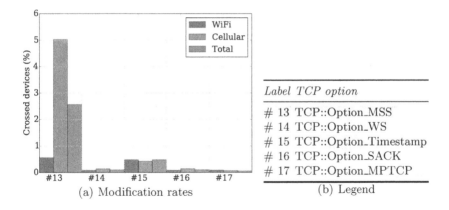

(a) Modification rates   (b) Legend

Fig. 7. Observed middlebox modification in TCP options

Source port modification is a common practice of Carrier-Grade NATs (CGNs), which makes it difficult for traffic intended for machines located behind it to pass through (e.g., active FTP). However, solutions to this problem have been proposed [22]. TCP ports modification by middleboxes also makes it difficult to achieve transport layer security (e.g., IPSEC) [23].

TCP sequence number modification is mostly due to initial sequence number (ISN) re-shuffling middlebox policies, which aim at mitigating ISN prediction attacks [10]. Such policies are known to create inconsistencies with TCP options using absolute sequence numbers such as Selective ACKnowledgement (SACK), and to reduce substantially the maximum achievable bandwidth [24,25].

TCP Options modifications are shown in Fig. 7. We witnessed multiple middleboxes rewriting the MSS in cellular networks to 1,392 bytes, which is probably designed to obtain packets of 1,500 bytes taking into account the sizes of the desired headers. Among the other options, MultiPathTCP have been cleared by some middleboxes to forbid its use, and is also prone to be blocked by middleboxes that are not familiar with it [25]. WindowScale have been modified by a few middleboxes to custom values, probably for network performance optimization purposes. WindowScale is also known to cause connectivity problems with certain firewalls that do not implement it as defined in RFC1323 [26,27].

Overall, we showed that TraceboxAndroid can be used efficiently for deducing certain network disruption causes from inferred middlebox policies. This can be useful to users for fast on-demand troubleshooting purposes, for researchers that could analyze the collected dataset to get insights such as the permeability of a TCP option, and for network managers to understand what is *really* happening to packets crossing their networks.

Table 1. Observed Memory and CPU consumption

Case	Samsung Galaxy SII	Arnova 10d G3
Memory	10.8Mb	6.45Mb
CPU (app)	< 1 %	< 1 %
CPU (instant probe)	12.5 %	12.5%

4.3 Impact on Mobile Devices

To test the impact of the use of TraceboxAndroid on mobile phones, we used the Android Monitoring tool [28]. In more than 99% of the cases, a *Background Probing* session with 10 destinations consumes less than one percent of battery. The same probing session never sent more than 165Kb of data, including the XML result file sent to the *back office*. We also did CPU and memory consumption measurements whose results are shown in Table 1. The experiments were made on a Samsung Galaxy SII (1,4Ghz, 1GB RAM, Android 4.3) and a Arnova 10d G3 (1,2Ghz, 1GB RAM, Android 4.1.1). Clearly, TraceboxAndroid is lightweight for mobile devices.

5 Related Work

Since the end of the nineties, the Internet topology discovery has been extensively studied [29]. In particular, `traceroute` has been used for revealing IP interfaces along the path between a source and a destination. Since then, `traceroute` has been extended in order to mitigate its intrinsic limitations. From simple extensions (i.e., the types of probes sent [30]) to much more developed modifications. For instance, `traceroute` has been improved to face load balancing [31] or the reverse path [32]. Its probing speed and efficiency has also been investigated [33,34].

Medina et al. [24] report one of the first detailed analysis of the interactions between transport protocols and middleboxes. They rely on active probing with `tbit` and contact various web servers to detect whether Explicit Congestion Notification (ECN), IP options, and TCP options can be safely used. The `TCPExposure` software developed by Honda et al. [9] is closest to `tracebox`. It also uses specially crafted packets to test for middlebox interference. Wang et al. [8] analyzed the impact of middleboxes in hundreds of cellular networks. This study revealed various types of packet modifications. More recently, Craven et al. [35] proposed TCP HICCUPS to reveal packet header manipulation to both endpoints of a TCP connection. HICCUPS works by hashing a packet header and by spreading the resulting hash into three fields (in case one is changed). Finally, Xu et al. [36] analyzed the behavior of proxies deployed by four major US cellular carriers. They looked at the HTTP traffic between their clients and their own server. They exhibited mostly application-level proxy features such as caching, HTTP redirection, image transcoding and connection persistence, and quantified their effectiveness.

These tools provide great results, but they are limited to specific paths as both ends of the path must be under control or must implement particular techniques in the TCP/IP stack and, except for Wang et al. and Xu et al., are not dedicated to mobile devices. On the contrary, TraceboxAndroid does not require any cooperation with the service and only the source must install TraceboxAndroid. It allows one to detect middleboxes on any path, i.e., between a source and any destination.

6   Conclusion

In this paper, we introduced TraceboxAndroid, a `tracebox` port under the Android system, allowing so the user to detect the presence of a middlebox that could be the cause of degraded performance on a path. We showed the extent of TraceboxAndroid capabilities for detection and location of middleboxes rewriting IP and TCP headers fields and TCP options as well as for AS path analysis and `traceroute`-like path displaying.

The main limitation of TraceboxAndroid is the impossibility to forge network and transport headers and read ICMP control messages in non-rooted environments. We need raw sockets to achieve this and their use is restricted to users that can grant the `CAP_NET_RAW` POSIX capability (i.e., super users). As a workaround, we chose to develop a *proof-of-concept* app for rooted devices only and call the TraceboxAndroid BusyBox implementation from the JAVA app as a super user, but this requirement is inappropriate for large-scale deployment because it involves a loss of warranty and risks of system instabilities, among others [37]. Note that this limit has already been discussed in the literature [5].

The dataset sample that we analyze in this paper is fairly limited and does not provide particular insight of middleboxes in mobile networks. However, we believe this dataset is enough to describe the potentialities of TraceboxAndroid.

In the near future, we would like to improve TraceboxAndroid. For instance, we would like to extend the *Custom Probing* mechanism to allow the user to select more IP fields, TCP fields, and TCP options to check and to choose the probe transport layer between TCP and UDP. We also plan to support additional TCP options, such as the TCP Authentication Option (TCP-AO) [38] or the TCP Alternate Checksum Request [39]. Additionally, we would like to improve the user experience by displaying more information and statistics (RTTs, values of modified fields, crossed ASs, etc.) within the application itself.

Another interesting improvement would be to implement middlebox TCP option blocking inference. Mobile devices could send multiple probes with different TCP options combinations to infer middlebox blocking behavior and find if in-path middleboxes are forbidding the use of certain option. This would allow user to perform more complete on-demand connectivity tests and the research community would benefit from the compiled results dataset.

References

1. Anderson, D.P., Cobb, J., Korpela, E., Lebofsky, M., Werthimer, D.: SETI@home: An experiment in public-resource computing. Communications of the ACM **45**(11), 56–61 (2002). http://setiathome.berkeley.edu/

2. Shavitt, Y., Shir, E.: DIMES: Let the internet measure itself. ACM SIGCOMM Computer Communication Review **35**(5), 71–74 (2005). http://www.netdimes.org

3. Chen, K., Choffnes, D., Potharaju, R., Chen, Y., Bustamante, F., Pei, D., Zhao, Y.: Where the sidewalk ends: Extending the Internet AS graph using trace-routes from P2P users. In: Proc. ACM SIGCOM CoNEXT, December 2009

4. Rivera, J., Van Der Meulen, R.: Forecast: Devices by operating system and user type, worldwide, 2010–2017. Technical Report 1Q13 Update, Garnter Inc., April 2013. http://www.gartner.com/resId=2396815

5. Faggiani, A., Gregori, E., Lenzini, L., Mainardi, S., Vecchio, A.: On the feasibility of measurement the Internet through smartphone-based crowdsourcing. In: Proc. IEEE International Symposium on Modeling and Optimization in Mobile, Ad-Hoc and Wireless Networks (WiOpt), May 2012

6. Carpenter, B., Brim, S.: Middleboxes: Taxonomy and issues. RFC 3234, Internet Engineering Task Force, February 2002

7. Sherry, J., Hasan, S., Scott, C., Krishnamurthy, A., Ratnasamy, S., Sekar, V.: Making middleboxes someone else's problem: network processing as a cloud service. In: Proc. ACM SIGCOMM, August 2012

8. Wang, Z., Qian, Z., Xu, Q., Mao, Z., Zhang, M.: An untold story of middleboxes in cellular networks. In: Proc. ACM SIGCOMM, August 2011

9. Honda, M., Nishida, Y., Raiciu, C., Greenhalgh, A., Handley, M., Tokuda, H.: Is it still possible to extend TCP. In: Proc. ACM/USENIX Internet Measurement Conference (IMC), November 2011

10. Detal, G., Hesmans, B., Bonaventure, O., Vanaubel, Y., Donnet, B.: Revealing middlebox interference with tracebox. In: Proc. ACM/USENIX Internet Measurement Conference (IMC), October 2013

11. Baker, F.: Requirements for IP version. RFC 1812, Internet Engineering Task Force, June 1995

12. Postel, J.: Internet control message protocol. RFC 792, Internet Engineering Task Force, September 1981

13. Vlasenko, D.: BusyBox: the swiss army knife of embedded Linux. http://www.busybox.net

14. Kühlewind, M., Neuner, S., Trammell, B.: On the state of ECN and TCP options on the internet. In: Roughan, M., Chang, R. (eds.) PAM 2013. LNCS, vol. 7799, pp. 135–144. Springer, Heidelberg (2013)

15. Gilad, Y., Herzberg, A.: Spying in the dark: TCP and tor traffic analysis. In: Fischer-Hübner, S., Wright, M. (eds.) PETS 2012. LNCS, vol. 7384, pp. 100–119. Springer, Heidelberg (2012)

16. Bellovin, S.M.: A technique for counting NATed hosts. In: Proc. ACM SIGCOMM Internet Measurement Workshop (IMW), November 2002

17. Zalewski, M.: Silence on the Wire: a Field Guide to Passive Reconnaissance and Indirect Attacks. No Starch Press (2005)

18. Gilad, Y., Herzberg, A.: Off-path attacking the web. In: Proc. 6th USENIX Workshop on Offensive Technologies (WOOT), August 2012

19. West, M., McCann, S.: TCP/IP field behavior. RFC 4413, Internet Engineering Task Force, March 2006

20. Qian, Z., Mao, Z.M.: Off-path TCP sequence number inference aattack - how firewall middleboxes reduce security. In: Proc. IEEE Symposium on Security and Privacy (SP), May 2012
21. Qian, Z., Mao, Z.M., Xie, Y.: Collaborative TCP sequence number inference attack: how to crack sequence number under a second. In: Proc. ACM Conference on Computer and Communications Security (CCS), October 2012
22. Wing, D., Cheshire, S., Boucadair, M., Penno, R.: Port control protocol (PCP). RFC 6887, Internet Engineering Task Force, April 2013
23. Aboba, B., Dixon, W.: IPsec-network address translation (NAT) compatibility requirements. RFC 3715, Internet Engineering Task Force, March 2004
24. Medina, A., Allman, M., Floyd, S.: Measuring interactions between transport protocols and middleboxes. In: Proc. ACM SIGCOMM Internet Measurement Conference (IMC), October 2004
25. Hesmans, B., Duchene, F., Paasch, C., Detal, G., Bonaventure, O.: Are TCP extensions middlebox-proof? In: Proc. Workshop on Hot Topics in Middleboxes and Network Function Virtualization, December 2013
26. Jacobson, V., Braden, R., Borman, D., Satyanarayan, M., Kistler, J.J., Mummert, L.B., Ebling, M.: TCP extension for high performance. RFC 1323, Internet Engineering Task Force, May 1992
27. Microsoft: Network connectivity fails when you try to use Windows Vista behind a firewall device. Technical report, Microsoft (2012). http://support.microsoft.com/kb/934430
28. Android Developers: Device monitor. http://developer.android.com/tools/help/monitor.html
29. Donnet, B., Friedman, T.: Internet topology discovery: a survey. IEEE Communications Surveys and Tutorials 9(4), December 2007
30. Luckie, M., Hyun, Y., Huffaker, B.: Traceroute probe methode and forward IP path inference. In: ACM SIGCOMM Internet Measurement Conference (IMC), October 2008
31. Augustin, B., Cuvellier, X., Orgogozo, B., Viger, F., Friedman, T., Latapy, M., Magnien, C., Teixeira, R.: Avoiding traceroute anomalies with paris traceroute. In: Proc. ACM/USENIX Internet Measurement Conference (IMC), October 2006
32. Katz-Bassett, E., Madhyastha, H., Adhikari, V., Scott, C., Sherry, J., van Wesep, P., Krishnamurthy, A., Anderson, T.: Reverse traceroute. In: Proc. USENIX Symposium on Networked Systems Design and Implementations (NSDI), June 2010
33. Donnet, B., Raoult, P., Friedman, T., Crovella, M.: Efficient algorithms for large-scale topology discovery. In: Proc. ACM SIGMETRICS, June 2005
34. Beverly, R., Berger, A., Xie, G.: Primitives for active Internet topology mapping: Toward high-frequency characterization. In: Proc. ACM/USENIX Internet Measurement Conference (IMC), November 2010
35. Craven, R., Beverly, R., Allman, M.: Middlebox-cooperative TCP for a non end-to-end Internet. In: Proc. ACM SIGCOMM, August 2014
36. Xu, X., Jiang, Y., Flach, T., Katz-Bassett, E., Choffnes, D., Govindan, R.: Investigating transparent web proxies in cellular networks. In: Mirkovic, J., Liu, Y. (eds.) PAM 2015. LNCS, vol. 8995, pp. 262–276. Springer, Heidelberg (2015)
37. Kingo: Warranty disclaimer (2014). http://www.kingoapp.com/root-disclaimer.htm
38. Touch, J., Mankin, A., Bonica, R.: The TCP authentication option. RFC 5925, Internet Engineering Task Force, June 2010
39. Zweig, J., Partridge, C.: TCP alternate checksum options. RFC 1145, Internet Engineering Task Force, February 1990

Web

Assessing Affinity Between Users and CDN Sites

Xun Fan[1,2](✉), Ethan Katz-Bassett[2], and John Heidemann[1,2]

[1] Information Sciences Institute, USC, Marina Del Rey, California
{xunfan,ethan.kb}@usc.edu
[2] Computer Science Department, USC, Marina Del Rey, California
johnh@isi.edu

Abstract. Large web services employ CDNs to improve user performance. CDNs improve performance by serving users from nearby Front-End (FE) Clusters. They also spread users across FE Clusters when one is overloaded or unavailable and others have unused capacity. Our paper is the first to study the dynamics of the user-to-FE Cluster mapping for Google and Akamai from a large range of client prefixes. We measure how 32,000 prefixes associate with FE Clusters in their CDNs every 15 minutes for more than a month. We study geographic and latency effects of mapping changes, showing that 50–70 % of prefixes switch between FE Clusters that are very distant from each other (more than 1,000 km), and that these shifts sometimes (28–40 % of the time) result in large latency shifts (100 ms or more). Most prefixes see large latencies only briefly, but a few (2–5 %) see high latency much of the time. We also find that many prefixes are directed to several countries over the course of a month, complicating questions of jurisdiction.

1 Introduction

Large web services serve their content from multiple sites to reduce client latency, to spread load, and to provide redundancy against failure. These services use Content Distribution Networks (CDNs) that operate *Front-End (FE) Clusters*, each consisting of multiple servers in a specific location [7,31]. The CDN dynamically directs users to specific FE Clusters at the granularity of network prefix which Google does and perhaps so do other CDNs. The CDN may direct a user to a FE Cluster using routing (anycast with BGP) or using DNS controlled by a mapping algorithm [3,6,14,28].

Ideally user prefixes might map to the nearest FE Cluster to minimize network latency. In practice, user-FE Cluster mapping is often more involved—a FE Cluster may be temporarily down, a nearby FE Cluster may be overloaded, estimates of user location may be incorrect or out-of-date, or peering costs may influence FE Cluster choice, as reported by Facebook [16].

There are several reasons users, regulators, researchers, and CDN operators should care about the dynamics of a CDN's mapping from users to FE Clusters. Users care about performance, and we show that changes in FE Cluster can result in noticeable performance differences (§ 4). Regulators and some users

© IFIP International Federation for Information Processing 2015
M. Steiner et al. (Eds.): TMA 2015, LNCS 9053, pp. 95–110, 2015.
DOI: 10.1007/978-3-319-17172-2_7

may care about *where* their data goes, particularly when different political jurisdictions have different requirements for privacy. Countries have different policies about censorship [29], and requirements for law enforcement access to user data vary by jurisdiction. Recent concerns about surveillance prompted countries to suggest data should be kept domestically [8]. While prior studies enumerated and geolocated CDN networks [1,2,15], an understanding of dynamics helps interpret such mappings. In addition, a better understanding of user-FE Cluster mapping might help CDN operators understand better how other CDNs work.

The first contribution of this paper is to provide the first evaluation of how user prefixes associate with FE Clusters of CDNs from a large number of network prefixes. We regularly collect data for the Google and Akamai CDNs from a very broad range of vantage points for an extended period—we consider over 32k user prefixes, covering 180 countries and 5158 ASes, with data every 15 minutes for four weeks (§ 3). In addition, we use 192 PlanetLab nodes to measure network and application latency of the two CDNs over one week. We find that many user prefixes experience mapping changes frequently. About 20% of Google user prefixes and 70% of Akamai user prefixes see more than 60 mapping changes (twice everyday on average) in a month (§ 4.1).

Second, we show how changes in user/FE Cluster associations may affect user performance (§ 4). We find that, over one month, most prefixes (50–70%) are redirected from one FE Cluster to another that is very distant, and that sometimes (28–40%) these shifts result in large changes in latency. These shifts are usually brief, but a few users (2–5%) receive poor performance much of the time. We also identify several reasons for these changes, including load balancing and servers being temporarily taken out of production and later restored.

Finally, we look at the geographic footprint of which FE Clusters users employ (§ 4.5). We find that many prefixes are directed to several countries over the course of a month, complicating questions of jurisdiction.

2   Background: CDNs and DNS Redirection

CDNs deploy *front-ends* around the Internet. Front-ends (FEs) are servers that users connect to request web pages or services. For our purposes, we are interested in *FE Clusters*, each of which represents the FEs in a single physical and network location that provide the same services.

Some CDNs use DNS to direct users to front-ends. When a user performs a DNS lookup for CDN-hosted content, the CDN's DNS returns IP addresses of a front-end(s) to serve that user. In practice, CDNs generally perform the same redirection for all users in a given network prefix. We call this association between network prefix and front-end the CDN's *prefix-FE Cluster mapping*. Generally, CDNs strive to map prefixes to nearby FE Clusters to reduce network latency, but the mapping may also be influenced by load, maintenance, or other factors. This paper focuses on observing the results of CDN's prefix-FE Cluster mapping; we do not attempt to reverse engineer the CDN's specific algorithm.

When a prefix p is mapped to FE Cluster A at one time, then later mapped to FE Cluster B, we call this a *prefix-FE Cluster mapping change*. We call (A, B)

Table 1. Datasets collected as part of this work

name	where used	target	coverage (prefixes)	frequ- ency	start date (length)
Google-15min-EDNS	§ 4.1 § 4.2 § 4.5	Google	32,871	15 min.	2014/03/28 (30)
Akamai-Apple-15min-ODNS	§ 4.1 § 4.2 § 4.5	Akamai	29,535	15 min.	2014/03/28 (30)
Akamai-Huff-15min-ODNS	§ 4.1 § 4.2 § 4.5	Akamai	28,308	15 min.	2014/11/17 (30)
PlanetLab-DNS-TTL	§ 4.3	both	192	20 s/5 m	2014/04/23 (7)
Google-15min-early	§ 4.4	Google	32,324	15 min.	2013/12/13 (30)
Google-location-EDNS	§ 3.3	Google	10,057,110	1 day	2014/03/28 (30)
Akamai-Apple-location-ODNS	§ 3.3	Akamai	271,357	once	2014/04/14 (-)
Akamai-Huff-location-ODNS	§ 3.3	Akamai	185,370	once	2014/11/12 (-)
ODNS-2013	§ 3	-	271,357	once	2013/10/21 (-)

the *switching pair*. Our goal is to understand these mapping changes—how often do they occur, how many users change, where did they go before and after.

3 Data Collection

We measure Google and Akamai using existing methodology. Our contribution is new long-term observations and analysis of dynamics. Our datasets (Table 1) provide daily observations for a month from 10M prefixes, and frequent (15-minute) observations for a 30k subset of prefixes.

3.1 Enumerating CDN Front-End Servers with DNS

We focus on the Google and Akamai CDNs because they are massively distributed, host popular services, and use DNS (not anycast) to map users to FE Clusters. Following prior work, we enumerate CDN infrastructure by issuing DNS queries for a service hosted by the CDN. For Google, we query for www.google. com. For Akamai, we query www.apple.com in Akamai-Apple-15min-ODNS dataset and www.huffingtonpost.com in Akamai-Huff-15min-ODNS dataset. They are both static websites hosted by Akamai. We query two websites for Akamai because our initial queries for www.apple.com, turned out to only cover a small set of Akamai's FE Clusters while www.huffingtonpost.com has larger coverage. We expect our results for the specific Google and Akamai services that we study to generalize to other services they each operate that also use DNS-based redirection. Since the fundamentals of replica selection are similar, they may also apply to application-level redirection such as in YouTube and Akamai's web caching, but we do not evaluate application-level services in this paper.

To better understand prefix-FE Cluster mapping we use three techniques. We get broad coverage with both *EDNS-client-subnet* and queries through open resolvers. We get more controlled, detailed measurements from PlanetLab.

Broad Probing. We probe Google with the DNS EDNS-client-subnet extension, following prior work [2,24]. This approach allows one to simulate queries

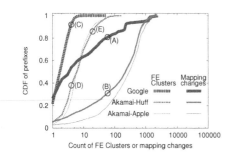

Fig. 1. Number of different FE Clusters and number of mapping changes that user prefixes seen in one month for Google and Akamai. Datasets: Google-15min-EDNS, Akamai-Apple-15min-ODNS and Akamai-Huff-15min-ODNS

Table 2. Statistics on the number of IPs and FEs found for Google and Akamai. Datasets: Google-15min-EDNS and Akamai-Huff-15min-ODNS

	Google		Akamai-Huff	
Total IPs	24,150	100%	9,492	100%
Clustered	22,679	94%	8,843	93%
Un-clustered	1,471	6%	649	7%
Geolocated	22,101	92%	7,953	84%
Un-geolocated	2,049	8%	1,593	16%
Clustered and Geolocated	20,861	86%	7,953	84%
Total FE Clusters	983		1,195	

from any location, but while Google supports it, Akamai added support only in mid-2014, which as part-way through our study [23]. Thus we do not use it with Akamai and instead probe Akamai with open DNS resolvers to make DNS queries from around the globe, again following prior work [9,15]. Open resolvers are often in people's homes, so we use them judiciously to measure Akamai. We choose a subset of global open resolvers that we collected in 2013 (*ODNS-2013*) as the source user prefixes. It contains 32,871 open resolver IPs, each from a unique /24 prefix, and covers 180 countries/regions and 5158 ASes. We use about 32k open resolvers so that our measurement settings can finish a query in 15 minutes. To identify this subset, we start with all open resolvers and take five complete enumerations of mappings for both CDNs over two months. We then discard those that do not respond in every trial, and finally we keep only those necessary to complete the IP-level enumeration that we saw in our five trials.

For Google, we issue DNS EDNS-client-subnet extension queries for the /24 prefixes[1] of the chosen open resolvers. Google hosts front-ends both on its backbone network and data centers (*on-net*) and in other ISPs around the world (*off-net*). We select prefixes to get broad coverage of FE Clusters, thus underrepresenting prefixes that are served directly from on-net FE Clusters. However, we believe our data is not drastically different from what we observe from all routable /24 prefixes, as the difference is moderate (70% of prefixes are mapped to on-net FE Clusters in our data and 88% of all routable /24 prefixes are mapped to on-net FE Clusters from Google-location-EDNS dataset). For Akamai, we probe directly to the chosen open resolvers. We probe both Google and Akamai every 15 minutes for all the 32,871 prefixes. We choose 15 minutes to limit load we impose on open resolvers.

---

[1] We always use /24 prefixes and so just write *prefix* from here.

Since open resolvers sometimes do not respond, we discard prefixes that miss more than 10% of their probes, leaving 29,535 and 28,308 prefixes in Akamai-Apple and Akamai-Huff.

Table 2 shows the total number of front-end IP addresses we find using broad probing. In total, we find 24,150 Google front-end IPs. For Akamai, we find 685 front-end IPs hosting `www.apple.com` (the *Akamai-Apple* dataset, omitted from the table for space) and 9,492 Akamai front-end IPs hosting `www.huffingtonpost.com` in 30 days (*Akamai-Huff*, shown in the table). We will see later that there are also many more FE Clusters hosting `www.huffingtonpost.com` than `www.apple.com`, and we believe this difference comes from the different SLAs used by the two sites. Compared to published reports of the sizes of the Google [2] and Akamai [19] CDNs, we know that our coverage is incomplete, but we believe we cover a good part of Google's CDN (about 70% of prior results [2]). Akamai runs tens of thousands of servers; our methodology tracks only the part of that infrastructure used by our targets. We focus on specific clients hosted by Akamai so we can study user-prefix dynamics for thousands of user prefixes without creating excessive measurement traffic. We observe about three times more IPs in Google's clusters compared to Akamai's. Our methodology of sampling specific URLs means that we do not fully enumerate clusters, and load-balancing and other factors mean IP addresses do not necessarily indicate cluster size, so we focus on clusters rather than IP addresses.

Performance Probing. In order to also study the effects of mapping changes on user-experienced performance, we use PlanetLab to collect ping times to the front-ends and application-level page fetches, as described in § 4.3.

We also issue frequent DNS queries from PlanetLab. Following prior work [25], we probe on DNS TTL intervals (the quickest an end user might experience changes) to capture prefix-FE Cluster mapping changes. (TTL for Google DNS is 5 minutes and Akamai is 20 seconds.)

We collect our *PlanetLab-DNS-TLL* dataset using probing at these rates for 7 days. We use 192 PlanetLab nodes, each in a distinct /24 prefix.

3.2   FE Cluster Identification

Since we are interested in mapping changes between FE Clusters, not IP addresses, we use our previous technique to group IP addresses into FE Clusters based on similarity of round-trip times from PlanetLab [2]. Table 2 shows our clustering results. We find 983 FE Clusters for Google from 22,679 replying IP addresses. We were unable to cluster 1,471 Google IPs because they do not respond to the pings we need for clustering. For Akamai, we find 1,195 Akamai FE Clusters from 9,492 IP addresses in Akamai-Huff dataset, (336 Akamai FE Clusters from 650 IP addresses in Akamai-Apple, not in the table), with 649 IPs we could not cluster. We have no way of identifying, clustering, or geolocating IP addresses that do not reply to measurements, so we must discard them.

3.3   Front-End Geolocation

We geolocate FE Clusters in our datasets using our previous CCG technique (Client-Centric-Geolocation) [2]. CCG geolocates FE Clusters by averaging the locations of the prefixes they serve after aggressively removing prefixes clearly distant from the FE. From that earlier work, we have daily measurements of Google since 2013. We use one month of that data (dataset: *Google-location-EDNS*), selecting the period and subset of prefixes to match our prefix-FE Cluster mapping datasets.

We use an alternate source of data for geolocation since Akamai did not support EDNS-client-subnet queries when our measurements began (§ 3.1). We collect data from open resolvers and apply the CCG algorithm to it ourselves. We use the whole set of open resolvers (ODNS-2013) we collected in 2013 as clients for CCG. The set of open resolver contain 600,000 open resolver IP addresses from 271,357 distinct /24 prefixes, covering 217 countries/regions and 11,793 ASes. Since it covers a fraction of the 10 million total routable /24 prefixes, we validate the use of CCG with open resolvers and find that it provides similar accuracy to CCG with all routable /24 IP prefixes. Our geolocation is accurate, with 90% of IP addresses having distance error within 500km [10].

CCG does not provide locations for 8% of Google IP addresses and about 16% of Akamai IPs (Table 2). Typically, CCG fails for FE Clusters that see an insufficient number of clients, so these servers may be relatively unimportant.

4   Dynamics of User Redirection

4.1   Are User Prefixes Mapped to Different FE Clusters?

We first examine how many mapping changes and how many FE Clusters each user prefix observes over one month. Figure 1 shows the cumulative distribution. We see that 20% and 70% of prefixes observe more than 60 mapping changes ((A) and (B) in Figure 1) in a month (average 2 a day) for Google and Akamai respectively, suggesting mapping changes are common for many prefixes. (The number of changes we report here is much smaller than prior work [25] because we report the changes between clusters, not just IP addresses.) In addition, we see that most user prefixes have fairly stable mappings for Google, with 92% of them being mapped to at most 4 FE Clusters ((C) in Figure 1). Akamai user prefixes seem to experience more variation, with only around 40% being mapped to 4 FE Clusters or fewer and 14% being mapped to 20 or more FE Clusters ((D) and (E) in Figure 1). This analysis shows that *mappings changes are common*, with some users changing frequently and most occasionally.

4.2   Distances of Mapping Changes

We next examine the distance between the FE Clusters that users switch between. We expect that a user would see little latency change when switched between nearby FE Clusters, while mapping changes between very distant FE Clusters are

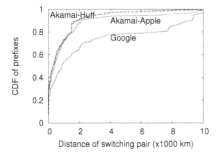

Fig. 2. CDF of distance of switching pairs over all prefixes after a random observation time t

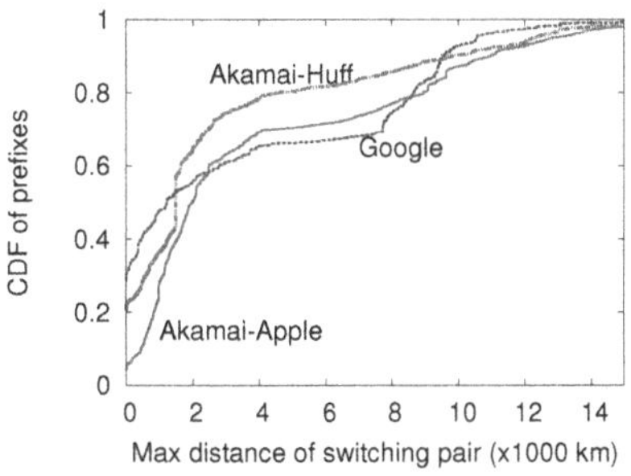

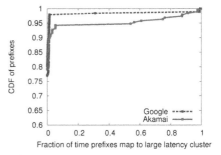

Fig. 3. CDF of maximum distance of switching pair seen in one month over all prefixes

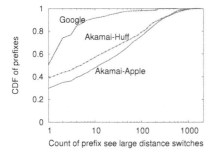

Fig. 4. CDF of the number of times in a month each prefix sees mapping changes of large distances (more than 1000km)

Fig. 5. CDF of fraction of time user prefixes spend on a FE Cluster with large latency (where page-fetch time is 100 ms worse than in the prior/next mapping)

more likely to lead to large latency change. Unless the client is equidistant between the old and new FE Clusters, a large change in FE distance suggests a non-optimal choice of a FE.

We measure distance between the switching pair of a prefix-FE Cluster mapping change. We randomly choose an observation time t, then find the switching pair of the next mapping change (A, B) for each prefix after time t. We then plot the CDF of distance between A and B over all prefixes. We see nearly identical distributions after three trials and so report one case as representative.

Figure 2 shows the CDF of the distance between the switching pair for all prefixes over one randomly chosen observation times for Google and Akamai. While some prefixes switch between FE Clusters that are near each other (about 26–33% are within 100 km), many prefixes change between FE Clusters that are far apart. More than 50% Google changes and 30% of Akamai changes move between switching pairs more than 1000 km apart.

Long-Distance Remapping: Akamai. When measured at a random time We see that many prefixes change between FE Clusters that are distant from each other. We next consider this question for *every* time over a month. Figure 3 plots the distribution of the maximum distance of switching pairs seen by every prefix in one month. Many prefixes experience long-distance changes. For example, 50% of prefixes switch between Google FE Clusters that are at least 1000 km apart, and 60-70% experience such a switch for Akamai servers. Figure 4 shows the distribution of the number of times prefixes experience large distance switching pairs. We see that a few Google prefixes (9%) and many Akamai prefixes (40-50%) move large distances (1000 km) more than 10 times in a single month, suggesting it's not rare for these long distance re-mappings to happen. In § 4.4 we explore reasons why these changes may occur.

4.3   Effects of Mapping Changes on Users

To understand how changes to prefix-FE Cluster mappings affect users, we consider when mapping changes affects (or does not affect) user latency.

Large Distance Leads to Larger Latency. While § 4.2 showed that users are sometimes mapped to FE Clusters in very different places, it does not directly measure performance. While a prefix equidistant between two FE Clusters may see similar performance from both, in most cases we expect that a prefix that is redirected to a very different place will see different user-visible performance.

Here we study measurements taken from 192 prefixes hosting PlanetLab sites since evaluating user performance requires measurements taken from inside each prefix. Although these sites are only a small subset, we verified that they generally are representative of our measurements with 32,871 prefixes [10].

We assess user performance by measuring network latency and application performance. We measure *network* and *application* latencies every DNS TTL, and also immediately after we observe a prefix p has changed its mapping from FE Cluster A to B (prior work measured latency [25,27], but not around mapping changes). We measure network latency with ICMP echo request (ping), observing $RTT_{p,A}$ and $RTT_{p,B}$. We measure application latency by fetching a web page to observe $PFT_{p,A}$ and $PFT_{p,B}$. To avoid noise in individual observations, each observation uses two pings and one page fetch, and analysis uses the second smallest of the 10 most recent observations. For Google we fetch a 75 kB web page corresponding to a search for "USA" (http://www.google.com/search? q=USA). For Akamai we fetch the 9.5 kB home page of Apple (http://www.apple. com). We then evaluate the absolute value of the difference of these metrics: $RTT^{\delta}_{p,A,B} = |RTT_{p,A} - RTT_{p,B}|$ and $PFT^{\delta}_{p,A,B} = |PFT_{p,A} - PFT_{p,B}|$. We use absolute value to judge overall changes, since data shows that at steady state, mapping changes generally alternate between nearer to further FE Clusters.

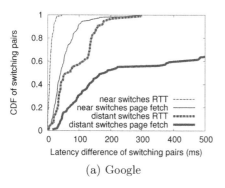

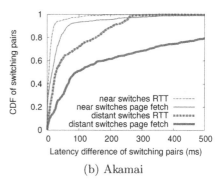

(a) Google   (b) Akamai

Fig. 6. Prefix-FE Cluster latency changes after a mapping change, measured by RTT (dashes) and page fetch time (solid). Left line are near switches, right line are distant switches. (Dataset: PlanetLab-DNS-TTL)

For each prefix, we evaluate all mapping changes over the entire measurement period, giving a set of observations of many $RTT^\delta_{p,A,B}$ and $PFT^\delta_{p,A,B}$. Since changes are generally symmetric, we merge the (A,B) and (B,A) directions and take the median value of all observations to get $RTT^{m\delta}_{p,A,B}$ and $PFT^{m\delta}_{p,A,B}$. Finally, to understand if large distance switches affect performance, we divide observations into *distant switches*, where A and B are 1000 km apart or more, and *near switches* where they are less than 1000 km. We then plot the CDF of $RTT^{m\delta}$ and $PFT^{m\delta}$ for each group.

Figure 6 shows results for Google and Akamai. We first see that the switches between distant FE Clusters (the wider, right-most lines) show much greater performance changes than switches between nearby ones (the thinner, left lines). For Google, near switches show smaller performance changes ($RTT^{m\delta} < 50$ ms and $PFT^{m\delta} < 150$ ms), while for distant switches group, more than 40% have changes more than twice that ($RTT^{m\delta} > 100$ ms and $PFT^{m\delta} > 400$ ms). The results of Akamai are similar, with only 2% of near switches showing $RTT^{m\delta} > 100$ ms, while the number is 28% for distant switches.

To summarize, prefixes that switch between FE Clusters that are far apart tend to also observe large network and page-fetch latency changes.

How Long Do Prefixes Stay On Non-Optimal FE Clusters? Fortunately, we next show that switches that increase user latency are usually brief for most prefixes. We analyze our PlanetLab data to see what fraction of time user prefixes spend in a mapping that has large latency (for this subset of data). We focus on *distant* switching pairs, those with distance larger than 1000 km, and of these, those with *long* differences in page-fetch times ($PFT^{m\delta} > 100$ ms). The resulting subset are all prefixes with large distance switches that raise application

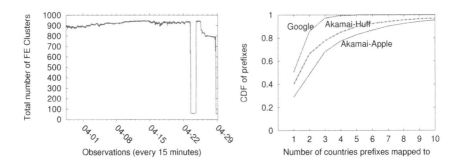

Fig. 7. Total number of Google FE Clusters seen from all prefixes at each observation.

Fig. 8. CDF of the number of different countries to which prefixes are mapped.

latency. Finally, we look at how long each prefix remained at the larger-latency FE Cluster, computing the fraction of observations the prefix spent there.

Figure 5 shows the CDF of fraction of time user prefixes spend on FE Clusters with large latency (where page-fetch time is 100 ms worse than in the prior mapping). Most of these FE Clusters are used only briefly (97% of Google and 93% of Akamai prefixes spend less than 5% of their time at FE Clusters with high application latency). But the tail is long, with 2% of Google and 5% of Akamai prefixes spending more than 60% of time on distant FE Clusters and seeing higher application latencies, even though lower-latency FE Clusters exist.

4.4   Reasons for Mapping Changes

We have shown that mapping changes are common. We next evaluate *why* they occur. Although we cannot categorize every change, we see three general reasons: FE Clusters drain and restore (that is, temporarily shut down), load balancing, user-to-FE Clusters mapping reconfiguration. We cannot completely separate these categories without inside knowledge of each CDN. However, our external observations provide some evidence of each.

FE Clusters Drain and Restoration. CDN sometimes *drain* some of their FE Clusters, assigning no user prefixes to them, in order to, for example, perform maintenance or troubleshoot problems. For example, Facebook recently drained an entire datacenter as part of an infrastructure stress test [30]. As an example drain event, Figure 7 shows the number of active FE Clusters in Google over our Google-15min-EDNS dataset. We see a large drop around April 23rd (from 900 to 60 FE Clusters). Examination of the clusters before and after the drop shows that Google stopped directing clients to all FE Clusters not in Google ASes (the off-net FE Clusters). They restored broader service, then shut off-net FE Clusters again on April 28th.

We checked if these drains biased our previous observations (§ 4.2 and § 4.3). To do so, we re-examined the distance user prefixes switched with and without these days where all off-net FE Clusters drained. We confirmed that overall changes are small, meaning regular changes in mapping dominate our results.

Load Balancing. We observe two patterns of behavior that we believe are due to load-balancing of user prefixes across multiple FE Clusters. First, we sometimes see some prefixes (about 10% for Google and 30% for Akamai) switch between two FE Clusters quite frequently (on average every hour). We sample 10 prefixes from each of these groups, and for each prefix, both FE Clusters they switched between are close to each other (within 200 km). This behavior may indicate that the CDN is spreading the load between FE Clusters at two different PoPs. Second, we see that a few Google FE Clusters (about 10 of 900) display diurnal patterns (as seen in spectral analysis [21]), suggesting some load balancing due to changes in diurnal traffic patterns.

Reconfiguration of User-to-FE Clusters Mapping. Both Google and Akamai strive to optimize performance for users by associating prefixes with nearby FE Clusters [7,18]. Long-term shifts in routing, user population, and FE Cluster deployments may shift this mapping as the CDN re-optimizes. In early data (Google-15min-early dataset), we saw that Google would occasionally shift one-third of user prefixes at the same time [31]. These bulk shifts have diminished in recent observations of Google and never appeared in Akamai, but both CDNs currently have a few percent of user prefixes that have stable mappings for weeks.

Changes also happen at short timescales—Facebook reconfigures their mapping over the course of a day due to changes in observed client latency [16]. We know that Google and Akamai also have short-term changes, but we do not know if they are responses to changes in user latency or responses to changes due to their CDN infrastructure, such as load balancing.

Unknown. We also observe some mapping changes that are not explained by the above reasons. For example, we see Google sometimes map prefixes to very distant Google FE Clusters (across continents) for a single observation.

4.5   Geographic Footprint Seen by User Prefixes

Prefix-FE Cluster mapping changes across long distances, suggesting that users may see FE Clusters in different countries.[2] For some users, traffic leaving a given country may raise concerns about privacy or legal jurisdiction. We next show that some prefixes in many countries are often mapped abroad.

First, we assess how many countries each prefix is mapped to over the course of a month in Figure 8. We see that *more than half* of prefixes are mapped to different countries over time (50% for Google, and 60–70% for Akamai). It is

---

[2] We use the term country generically, sometimes considering smaller or larger regions.

Table 3. Top 10 source countries (with ISO country codes) and their percentage of prefixes that had been mapped to FE Clusters in other countries, and the to three non-domestic countries serving them. Datasets: Google-15min-EDNS and Akamai-Huff-15min-ODNS

source country	Google non-domestic				Akamai-Huff non-domestic			
	%	1st	2nd	3rd	%	1st	2nd	3rd
us (United States)	11%	be (4%)	nl (4%)	de (3%)	98%	ca (38%)	gb (27%)	fr (27%)
kr (S. Korea)	97%	jp (58%)	us (19%)	cn (18%)	99%	tw (99%)	jp (6%)	nl (3%)
ru (Russia)	99%	us (35%)	be (6%)	nl (5%)	96%	se (74%)	no (43%)	de (40)
jp (Japan)	55%	us (30%)	nl (9%)	be (7%)	100%	cn (92%)	us (67%)	vn (9%)
br (Brazil)	48%	nl (18%)	be (17%)	us (14%)	83%	us (78%)	cl (53%)	ar (35%)
tw (Taiwan)	45%	us (24%)	be (9%)	nl (9%)	99%	cn (74%)	us (72%)	vn (48%)
cn (China)	51%	us (27%)	nl (11%)	be (11%)	99%	jp (93%)	us (89%)	gb (67%)
it (Italy)	60%	us (40%)	de (19%)	fr (5%)	–	–	–	–
gb (U. Kingdom)	54%	us (40%)	nl (19%)	be (8%)	–	–	–	–
au (Australia)	52%	us (24%)	nl (18%)	be (11%)	–	–	–	–
hk (Hong Kong)	–	–	–	–	90%	cn (88%)	jp (25%)	vn (12%)
tr (Turkey)	–	–	–	–	91%	it (82%)	se (46%)	de (23%)
fr (France)	–	–	–	–	99%	pl (69%)	gb (57%)	es (56%)

common for a user to be served from multiple countries. We caution that this result reflects two biases in our data: first, our prefix selection under-representing prefixes that are served directly from the provider, as described in § 3.1. Second, because of cluster drain (§ 4.4), we expect many prefixes to shift from off-net FE Clusters, present in many countries, to on-net FE Clusters that operate in only a few countries.

We next consider from where prefixes are served. For each service we select the 10 countries that originate the most user prefixes, then identify from where they are served. (We exclude prefixes that are never served domestically on the assumption that they have no local option or that our geolocation is wrong.) For each country we consider two questions: what portion of prefixes leave the country? Where does their traffic go?

Table 3 shows the results for Google and Akamai. (The top countries differ because the CDNs are different.) For each country, the first column shows how many of that country's prefixes that are sometimes mapped outside its borders. The following three columns show which other countries most often provide service. For Akamai, we show only Akamai-Huff data here for space; we show Akamai-Apple data in [10] and summarize any differences here.

We see that all prefixes but U.S.-ones have many non-domestic mappings— around 50% of user prefixes for Google and more than 90% for Akamai. We see that Google often serves from the U.S., Belgium and Netherlands, perhaps those countreis have good connectivity and host Google datacenters [22]. For Akamai, we see that U.S. FE Clusters serve prefixes from other countries, perhaps because of good U.S. connectivity. Akamai-Huff selection (and also Akamai-Apple) shows a stronger geographic locality than Google, with French and Turkish prefixes remaining in Europe and Hong Kong prefixes in Asia. Surprisingly, most Chinese prefixes are sent abroad in both Akamai datasets.

Both Google and Akamai often map prefixes outside their originating country. Countries that have expressed privacy concerns, such as Brazil [8], or regions with strict privacy laws, such as the European Union, may find traffic leaving their legal jurisdiction weakens their ability to implement some policies. For example, Brazil's exact set of foreign countries varies depending on CDN or service, but in all cases their prefixes are served outside Brazil. In other cases, prefixes in some countries find services in others that have strict limits on domestic handling of some topics. Examples include South Korea and Japan receiving service from China (with limits on Chinese politics), and in Akamai-Apple data where Brazil served from Germany (with limits on Nazi politics). While such issues may not be a concern for Apple or Huffingtonpost's home page, it may be for other services using these CDNs.

5   Related Work

Prior work compared the performance of CDN-selected front-end servers and other servers of the same CDN [17,20,25,27]. Su *et al.* use Akamai's choice of server location to influence their selection to leverage Akamai's network measurements [25]. Triukose *et al.* compare the page download performance difference between Akamai selected server with 80 other randomly selected Akamai servers to study if CDNs enhance performance [27]. Krishnamurthy *et al.* study CDN DNS load balancing performance by using two dozen clients to detect DNS load balancing every 30 minutes and performing file download when observing CDN server changes [17]. Otto *et al.* compare HTTP latency between CDN servers returned by different DNS servers to measure the impact of using remote DNS on CDN performance [20]. Our work differs from this prior work by exploring how CDNs *change* their prefix-FE Cluster mappings over time, and how these changes affect network and application latency for users.

The Ono system uses large set of clients (120,000) to study affinity between users and CDN servers [5]. They use this information to help peer selection in peer-to-peer networks to reduce cross-ISP traffic. Our work also uses a large set of client prefixes to assess user-to-CDN affinity, but we focus on understanding the properties of prefix-FE Cluster mapping changes and their potential impact on both users and previous CDN studies.

Huang *et al.* studied the cache dynamics from users to Facebook Edge Caches as viewed from within Facebook [16]. Facebook optimizes to balance latency, server load, and peering cost, sometimes directed users to caches that are not physically nearest. Our paper complement theirs by looking from the user side.

Torres *et al.* studied mechanism and policy of user to content server mapping of Youtube using video flow data collect from 5 distinct locations over a week [26]. They Geolocate Youtube datacenters using CBG and find that non-negligible fraction of traffic are provided by *non-preferred* datacenter. They find that the reasons of non-preferred datacenter access include load balancing, DNS server variations, limited availability of rarely accessed videos and alleviating hot-spot due to popular videos. Our work differs from theirs by focusing on the effects of user to FE Cluster mapping changes on users, while they focus on understanding the mapping dynamics themselves. We also have a broader coverage on user prefixes and CDN FE Clusters while theirs is deeper from a few vantage points.

Cases *et al.* [4] and Finamore *et al.* [13] each study associations between web services, hosting organizations, content-server IPs, and service provisioning. They use min-RTT estimates to cluster IPs to datacenters. They use measurements from one ISP and observe user/datacenter switches suggesting load balancing. We also cluster IPs to datacenters, but with many vantage points [2]. Both their work and ours identifies load balancing and mapping changes, but they apply their work to provisioning while we study its effects on end-users.

Fiadino *et al.* use a month of HTTP flow data collected from a major European ISP to study the traffic anomaly caused by cache selection dynamics and the impacts on both ISP and users [11,12]. They found Facebook traffic anomaly by identify large amount of flow shift from Akamai to other hosting organization of Facebook. They report the anomaly may increase the transit cost of the users' ISP. They also found Youtube traffic anomaly that shift traffic to different set of /24 subnets of Youtube and found that the shift affect user experienced throughput. Our work differs from them in following ways. First, the methodologies are quite different. They detect synchronized mapping changes for particular web services by watching for large shifts in flow volumes, while we directly measure target FE Clusters with EDNS-client-subnet and direct DNS queries. Their approach is ideal for studying a single ISP when traffic is available, but the second difference is that our approach allows us to provide much broader coverage. We examine 32k user prefixes from hundreds of countries and ASes, while their study focuses only on users of a single ISP. Last, we study how often users traffic changes countries.

6   Conclusions

This work provides the first evaluation of the dynamics of CDN redirection of user's network prefixes to Front-End Clusters from a large range of prefixes. We gather new data about Google and Akamai, and we find that some prefixes switch between FE Clusters that are long distances apart, often seeing large changes in latency and application-level performance. While most of prefixes only stay shortly on FE Clusters that have large application level latency, a few percent of prefixes are mapped to those FE Clusters much of the time. We also find that many user prefixes are directed to multiple countries in a month, complicating questions of jurisdiction.

Acknowledgements and Data Availaility. Our data is publicly available at http://www.isi.edu/ant/traces/mapping_cdns/. This work was identified by the USC IRB (IIR00001412, March 2013) as non-human subject research. We thank Matt Calder for his assistance with CCG.

This research is partially sponsored by the Department of Homeland Security (DHS) Science and Technology Directorate, HSARPA, Cyber Security Division, BAA

11-01-RIKA and Air Force Research Laboratory, Information Directorate under agreement number FA8750-12-2-0344, NSF CNS-1351100, and via SPAWAR Systems Center Pacific under Contract No. N66001-13-C-3001. The U.S. Government is authorized to reproduce and distribute reprints for Governmental purposes notwithstanding any copyright notation thereon. The views contained herein are those of the authors and do not necessarily represent those of DHS or the U.S. Government.

References

1. Ager, B., et al.: Web content cartography. In: ACM IMC (2011)
2. Calder, M., Fan, X., Hu, Z., Katz-Bassett, E., Heidemann, J., Govindan, R.: Mapping the expansion of google's serving infrastructure. In: IMC, October 2013
3. Carter, R.L., Crovella, M.E.: Server selection using dynamic path characterization in wide-area networks. In: IEEE INFOCOM, April 1997
4. Casas, P., Fiadino, P., Bar, A.: Ip mining: extracting knowledge from the dynamics of the internet addressing space. In: ITC (2013)
5. Choffnes, D., Bustamante, F.E.: Taming the torrent: a practical approach to reducing cross-ISP traffic in peer-to-peer systems. In: ACM SIGCOMM (2008)
6. Crovella, M.E., Carter, R.L.: Dynamic server selection in the internet. In: IEEE HPCS, August 1995
7. Dilley, J., Maggs, B., Parikh, J., Prokop, H., Sitaraman, R., Weihl, B.: Globally distributed content delivery. IEEE Internet Comput. 6(5), 50–58 (2002)
8. Edgerton, A.: NSA Spying allegations put google on hot seat in Brazil (2013). http://www.businessweek.com/news/2013-10-28/nsa-spying-allegations-put-google-on-hot-seat-corporate-brazil
9. Fan, X., Heidemann, J., Govindan, R.: Evaluating anycast in the domain name system. In: IEEE INFOCOM (2013)
10. Fan, X., Katz-Bassett, E., Heidemann, J.: Assessing affinity between users and CDN sites (extended). http://www.isi.edu/xunfan/affinity_tech_report.pdf
11. Fiadino, P., D'Alconzo, A., Bar, A., Finamore, A., Casas, P.: On the detection of network traffic anomalies in content delivery network services. In: ITC (2014)
12. Fiadino, P., D'Alconzo, A., Casas, P.: Characterizing web services provisioning via cdns: the case of Facebook. In: TRAC (2014)
13. Finamore, A., Gehlen, V., Mellia, M., Munafò, M., Nicolini, S.: The need for an intelligent measurement plane: the example of time-variant cdn policies. In: IEEE NETWORKS (2012)
14. Guyton, J.D., Schwartz, M.F.: Locating nearby copies of replicated internet servers. In: ACM SIGCOMM, pp. 288–298, August 1995
15. Huang, C., Wang, A., Li, J., Ross, K.W.: Measuring and evaluating large-scale CDNs. Technical Report MSR-TR-2008-106, Microsoft Research, October 2008
16. Huang, Q., Birman, K., van Renesse, R., Lloyd, W., Kumar, S., Li, H.C.: An analysis of facebook photo caching. In: ACM SOSP (2013)
17. Krishnamurthy, B., Wills, C., Zhang, Y.: On the use and performance of content distribution networks. In: ACM IMW, pp. 169–182 (2001)
18. Krishnan, R., et al.: Moving beyond end-to-end path information to optimize CDN performance. In: ACM IMC (2009)
19. Mao, M., et al.: Peer-assisted content distribution in akamai netsession. In: ACM IMC, pp. 31–42 (2013)
20. Otto, J.S., et al.: Content delivery and the natural evolution of dns: remote dns trends, performance issues and alternative solutions. In: ACM IMC (2012)

21. Quan, L., Heidemann, J., Pradkin, Y.: When the Internet sleeps: correlating diurnal networks with external factors. In: ACM IMC (2014)
22. Robinson, F.: Google Sets Big belgian investment, April 2013. `http://blogs.wsj.com/brussels/2013/04/10/google-sets-big-belgian-investment/`
23. Higginbotham, S.: Akamai signs deal with opendns to make the web faster. http://gigaom.com/2014/06/03/akamai-signs-deal-with-opendns-to-make-the-web-faster/
24. Streibelt, F., Böttger, J., Chatzis, N., Smaragdakis, G., Feldmann, A.: Exploring EDNS-client-subnet adopters in your free time. In: ACM IMC (2013)
25. Su, A.-J., Choffnes, D.R., Kuzmanovic, A., Bustamante, F.E.: Drafting behind Akamai (Travelocity-based detouring). In: ACM SIGCOMM (2006)
26. Torres, R., Finamore, A., Kim, J.R., Mellia, M., Munafo, M.M., Rao, S.: Dissecting video server selection strategies in the Youtube CDN. In: ICDCS (2011)
27. Triukose, S., Wen, Z., Rabinovich, M.: Measuring a commercial content delivery network. In: ACM WWW, pp. 467–476 (2011)
28. Wendell, P., Jiang, J.W., Freedman, M.J., Rexford, J.: DONAR: decentralized server selection for cloud services. In: ACM SIGCOMM, August 2010
29. Wikipedia. Internet censorship by country. `http://en.wikipedia.org/wiki/Internet_censorship_by_country`
30. Sverdlik, Y.: Facebook turned off entire data center to test resiliency. http://www.datacenterknowledge.com/archives/2014/09/15/facebook-turned-off-entire-data-center-to-test-resiliency/
31. Zhu, Y., Helsley, B., Rexford, J., Siganporia, A., Srinivasan, S.: LatLong: diagnosing wide-area latency changes for CDNs. IEEE TNSM **9**(1), September 2012

The Online Tracking Horde: A View from Passive Measurements

Hassan Metwalley[1]([⊠]), Stefano Traverso[1], Marco Mellia[1], Stanislav Miskovic[2], and Mario Baldi[1,2]

[1] Politecnico di Torino, Torino, Italy
{metwalley,traverso,mellia}@tlc.polito.it
[2] Symantec Corp., California, USA
{stanislav_miskovic,mario_baldi}@symantec.com

Abstract. During the visit to any website, the average internaut may face scripts that upload personal information to so called online trackers, invisible third party services that collect information about users and profile them. This is no news, and many works in the past tried to measure the extensiveness of this phenomenon. All of them ran active measurement campaigns via crawlers. In this paper, we observe the phenomenon from a passive angle, to naturally factor the diversity of the Internet and of its users. We analyze a large dataset of passively collected traffic summaries to observe how pervasive online tracking is. We see more than 400 tracking services being contacted by unaware users, of which the top 100 are regularly reached by more than 50 % of Internauts, with top three that are practically impossible to escape. Worse, more than 80 % of users gets in touch the first tracker within 1 second after starting navigating. And we see a lot of websites that hosts hundreds of tracking services. Conversely, those popular web extensions that may improve personal protection, e.g., DoNotTrackMe, are actually installed by a handful of users (3.5 %). The resulting picture witnesses how pervasive the phenomenon is, and calls for an increase of the sensibility of people, researchers and regulators toward privacy in the Internet.

1 Introduction

Internet is the revolution that changed our life, allowing us to be informed, buy goods, enjoy shows, play games, keep in touch with friends, and freely express our opinions to potentially very large audiences. People are more and more connected to the Internet, with mobile terminals allowing access to information from anywhere, anytime. Companies see the Internet as a means to stay in contact with their customers, to attract them, and to offer more and more personalized content. Not surprisingly, a large fraction of Internet businesses rely on online advertising, a market that keeps growing year by year, and that generated $42B revenue in 2013 according to the Interactive Advertising Bureau [1].

This work was conducted under the Narus Fellow Research Program.

© IFIP International Federation for Information Processing 2015
M. Steiner et al. (Eds.): TMA 2015, LNCS 9053, pp. 111–125, 2015.
DOI: 10.1007/978-3-319-17172-2_8

Online advertisement – ads for short – enables companies to design very targeted campaigns. The web offers the capability of reaching specific groups of users assembled with very fine granularity, leveraging knowledge of personal interests and taste of individuals. In order to collect such knowledge, companies track the users during their everyday online activity, constantly collecting information for marketing purposes (e.g., products browsed on a shopping website, online newspapers usually read, movies liked). This information is used to profile a user in order to deliver tailored ads, recommend movies to watch, or goods to buy.

Online trackers play a key role in this ecosystem as third-party services that "shadow" users during their browsing activity. Trackers rely on host of solutions to identify a user, ranging from storing a cookie on the user browser or device to exotic tracking techniques that fingerprint users across several web sites [7,14, 18]. The tracker business models also vary greatly. Some offer customized ads, while others sells user information to ads companies, acting as data brokers. Google's DoubleClick and Yahoo's YieldManager are notable tracker examples. However, the full list of companies that build their business around information collection includes several hundreds.

The mechanisms associated to tracking users can be beneficial for both companies and consumers. But they also raise many privacy concerns among the regulators and researchers. Ultimately, the consciousness of the people about their privacy being violated in the Internet is growing day by day.

Several works in the literature study the latest advances in online tracking, unveiling new and more subtle mechanisms [7,13,16,17], and proposing countermeasures to be protect users'privacy, typically in the form of browser plugins [2–6]. Some works studied the pervasiveness of online tracking by running active measurement campaigns and by crawling the web [8,12,15]. This paper falls in this second class: we aim at quantifying the pervasiveness and extensiveness of online tracking. Differently to any previous work, we are the first, to the best of our knowledge, to leverage passive measurements, which have the major advantage to naturally factor the users into the picture. We address questions as how many tracking services an internaut would normally face during her activity? How different is the picture from past years, or from different vantage points? How invasive are tracking services?

For our study, we rely on an extensive dataset composed by (anonymized) traces we collect by passively observing normal users from four different probes installed in two ISPs in two different countries. We use this data to pinpoint the traffic exchanged with a list of online trackers that we manually built from various sources. We then collect statistics to characterize such traffic.

Results confirm what is known from the literature: online tracking is ubiquitous. We count more than 400 active online tracking services, with 100 of them being regularly contacted by more than 50% of users, and the most pervasive ones that are impossible to avoid. Results confirm observations shown in other works based on active campaigns [12,16], but our passive approach naturally factors the user browsing behavior, and allows us to obtain a very detailed and fine-grained picture that quantifies the pervasiveness of tracking services in real life.

For instance, 77% of users face the first tracker just 1 s after starting their online activity. We observe websites that nowadays embed more than 50-100 third-party trackers, attracted by the chance to monetize visits, and in practice contributing to collect personal information. Notably, most of these services are not popular to enter in the top list of websites (and thus have never being considered by active studies). Yet, those are popular enough to collect a sizable number of users. Our unique vantage point allows us to measure things that active campaigns can not gauge. We are the first at quantifying the popularity of privacy-enhancer browser plugins. Surprisingly this is limited, with DoNot-TrackMe installed by a mere 3.5% of users. This testifies the small consciousness and sensibility of internauts versus their privacy. Similarly, by splitting statistics by type of user device, we highlight how Android devices are more prone to interact with tracking services than iOS devices and regular Windows PCs. Finally, our measurements highlight another phenomenon: the increase adoption of HTTPS as the means to collect data. This exacerbate the tension on the need to protect users privacy, since for instance this mines the possibility to develop in-network solutions to control and limit online tracking services.

We hope the picture we draw can contribute to increase the sensibility of people, researchers and regulators towards privacy in the Internet. We do not believe in an "arms race" as a possible solution, but rather in a solution in which people is offered the means to take informed choices.

The remainder of the paper is structured as follows. Sec. 2 introduces the related work, Sec. 3 details the dataset we employ in this study, Sec. 4 presents the results, and, finally, Sec. 5 concludes the paper.

2   Related Work

Our work is related to recent literature in the area of web measurement driven studies about web tracking and online advertisement. We can divide most of the notable works in this area in three branches. The first branch is mostly oriented to understand which identifiers and techniques online tracking services exploit to record users' browsing activities. Yen et al. [18] examine the common identifiers trackers can leverage to identifying users, and the authors of [16] and [11] describe the techniques third party trackers and online social networks use to monitor the activity of their users. The second branch is mostly oriented to understand the leakage of personal information due to web trackers. For instance, Balachander et al. [15] studies privacy leakage and evolution of third party trackers over four years from 2005 to 2008 using DNS logs. Another notable example is [14], which analyzes how popular websites share users' private information with tracking services, remarking that this trend is worryingly diffused. The last branch focuses about the analysis of the mechanisms which drive online advertisement. Vallina et al. [17] specifically examine ads in mobile terminals. Our aim is different as we address the problem of understanding how pervasive tracking services are by leveraging a large set of passive measurements. And to the best of our knowledge, we are the first to perform this analysis following a passive approach.

Table 1. The sets of traces we consider in this study.

Trace	Probe	Period	IP addr	Services
ISP1-Vp1-1d-05/12	ISP1-Vp1	09/05/2012	11660	200320
ISP1-Vp1-1d-05/13	ISP1-Vp1	08/05/2013	12218	239230
ISP1-Vp1-1d-05/14	ISP1-Vp1	07/05/2014	10458	238617
ISP1-Vp1-1d-02/14	ISP1-Vp1	26/02/2014	11027	247797
ISP1-Vp2-1d-02/14	ISP1-Vp2	26/02/2014	11927	297488
ISP2-Vp1-1d-02/14	ISP2-Vp1	26/02/2014	4911	113648

(a) One-day long traces.

Trace	Probe	Period	IP addr	Services
ISP1-Vp1-10d-10/14	ISP1-Vp1	13-23/10/2014	13408	1046339
ISP1-Vp2-10d-10/14	ISP1-Vp2	13-23/10/2014	11149	1306612
ISP1-Vp3-10d-10/14	ISP1-Vp3	13-23/10/2014	1321	415550

(b) Ten-day long traces.

Our study shares some common points with other works. We discuss in the following the differences which distinguish our work. Barford et al. [8] build their analysis around a dataset they collect thanks to a web crawler they develop. Web crawling lets the authors infer detailed information about the online ads which populate webpages. They specifically focus on the analysis of online ads, while our study addresses online tracking services in general, and from users' perspective.

The work which mostly approaches this study is Gomer et al. [13], where authors propose a methodology to identify tracking services from the analysis of pages returned by search queries. Specifically, using Google, Bing and Baidu, they run popular queries (extracted from the 2005 KDD dataset). They then crawl the top 10 returned pages, and check for the presence of trackers embedded in each page.

Similarly, [10] and [12] offer a global point of view of this phenomenon. In first case, Castelluccia et al. [10] analyze the provenance of most important third party tracking services using two popular browser extensions, AdBlock Plus and Ghostery, for the geographical classification. In second case, Falahrastegar et al. [12] crawl the top websites in Alexa rank for different countries, and measure the per-country pervasiveness of third party trackers. Despite our study share the same aim, as said, we rely on passive traces. This allows us to naturally factor the interactions with third-party trackers and real internauts during their daily activities, and check the impact of multiple devices, or browsers, or even malware eventually being installed on end-users' terminals.

Finally, we are the first to analyze in a real scenario the adoption of those do-not-tracking extensions as AdBlock Plus or DoNotTrackMe which are expected to protect users' privacy. Thanks to our vantage point, we show the breadth of the most invasive trackers, considering both the services hosting them, and the users' chances to contact them.

3   Dataset

In this work, we employ four different passive probes running Tstat[1] that we installed in Points-of-Presences (PoPs) in the operational networks of two different ISPs (ISP1 and ISP2) in Europe. Tstat observes all packets flowing on the links connecting the PoP to the ISP backbone network. It rebuilds each TCP

---

[1] http://tstat.polito.it

flow, tracks it, and at the end of the flow, logs more than 100 detailed statistics in a simple text format. For instance, for each TCP flow, Tstat logs the anonymized client IP address, the server IP address, the application (L7) protocol type, L7-bytes sent and received, etc. Tstat also implements DN-Hunter, an advanced mechanism that allows to annotate each TCP flow with the server hostname the client resolved via DNS before actually contacting the server IP address [9]. For TCP connections carrying HTTP and HTTPS data, DN-Hunter has been proved to unveil the *service* being contacted, e.g., *www.acme.com* or *mail.acme.com*. For HTTP traffic, Tstat produces a separate log which details most relevant HTTP fields: the HTTP method (GET, POST, etc.), the server hostname, the URL path, the referer, the client user-agent, etc.[2]

We have been collecting TCP and HTTP logs since May 2012. In this work, we focus on a subset of the data. Specifically, we consider three probes (ISP1-Vp1, ISP1-Vp2 and ISP1-Vp3) that are located in PoPs of the same ISP (ISP1), in two different cities of the same country. A fourth probe (ISP2-Vp1) is installed in a different ISP (ISP2), in a second country. Tab. 1 describes, for each trace, the name used throughout the paper, the location, the period, the number of households (identified by the IP address of the access gateway, see next section), and the total number of different services, i.e., server hostnames. Tab. 2(a) refers to traces which are one-day long, from the same probe, collected on the second Wednesday of May 2012, 2013 and 2014. We complement them with three traces we collected in the same day (February 26th, 2014), but from three different PoPs and countries. Tab. 2(b) refers to ten-day long traces that we collected from three different PoPs of ISP1, during the same period in October 2014.

Among the details, Tab. 1 shows that the dataset we use covers several thousands of regular users, which browse some millions of hostnames. Results we present are as such generic, even if specific to the country where the vantage points are located.

3.1   Identifying Active Users and Number of Connected Devices

Notice that the client IP address field in our logs refer to the access gateway (ADSL/FTTH modem) customers are given by the ISP. As such, the IP address can be considered as an identifier of the household, which may hide several actual devices and users that connect to the Internet using NAT at the access gateway. This includes possible households in which no actual user is present, but in which some device generates some traffic. In particular, ISP1 offers native VoIP communications. The access gateway acts also as VoIP gateway, thus we

---

[2] The traffic logs Tstat generates do not contain information which may offend ISP users privacy. Indeed, Tstat processes IP packets (and their payload) in real time and generates transport- and HTTP-level logs in which we take care of obfuscating any privacy sensitive information (e.g., IP addresses are anonymised using irreversible hashing functions, all URLs are truncated, etc.). Second, Tstat has no visibility on encrypted traffic (HTTPS), where the sensitive information concentrates. Furthermore, we report that our traffic monitoring activity is approved by the Security Office of the ISP in which we deploy our probes.

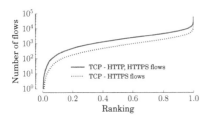
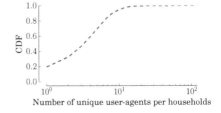

(a) Number of flows per household. Trace ISP1-Vp1-1d-05/14.

(b) CDF of user-agents seen behind a single household. Trace ISP1-Vp1-10d-10/14.

Fig. 1. Per-household statistics.

expect some households to appear as "active" (IP address is used) even if no terminal is present (we observe VoIP data only).

Fig. 1(a) shows the number of total HTTP and HTTPS flows per each IP address, sorted for increasing number. Notice the log scale on y-axis. Plot refers to trace ISP1-Vp1-1d-05/14. It shows the bias induced in ISP1 by the presence of VoIP gateways at the modem. They indeed generate some signalling HTTP and HTTPS traffic to report VoIP usage statistics to the operator. The presence of the sharp knee in the figure suggests that a simple threshold based filter is sufficient to identify "active" households.[3] In the remainder of the paper, we take a conservative choice, by considering active only those IP addresses for which we see at least one HTTPS flow, and at least 100 HTTP or HTTPS total flows for the 1-day long dataset (1000 flows for the 10-day long traces). This filters out those sources of traffic we are not interested in (e.g., smart TVs, VoIP gateways, or pure P2P clients). Most active households reach 100,000 flows per day.

To quantify the presence of multiple clients that are hidden behind the NAT at the ADSL router, Fig. 1(b) shows the CDF of the number of different user-agents seen for a given active IP address. We consider only user-agents associated to actual browsers, for PC and mobile terminals. We leverage the User-agents 0.3.1 Python library for this.[4] Results show that only 20% of households have only one terminal, with 75% of them showing between 2 to 10 different user-agents. Manually checking this, we observe a lot of smartphones and tablets, with some cases showing multiple browsers being normally used. Surprisingly, in few cases we see more than 10 user-agents. A manual check shows the presence of suspicious behavior with possibly a malware generating lots of HTTP requests toward few IP addresses serving advertisements. HTTP requests contain a rotating set of legitimate browsers user-agents. We suspect this to be related to some click fraud activity, i.e., a malicious user artificially generating clicks on

---

[3] We use the term "household" and "user" interchangeably in the paper.

[4] https://pypi.python.org/pypi/user-agents

ads servers by forging user-agents. We noted the presence of these outliers, and check their presence is not affecting our statistics in the remainder of the paper.

3.2 Identifying Online Tracking Services

We build a list of online tracking services by merging together data we obtain from different sources. First, inspired by the approach used by the authors of [12], we instrument a browser to visit the top 500 websites of the global Alexa rank. For each page, we visit it and use the Ghostery plugin [2] to pinpoint the presence of trackers. Given then the hostname of the tracker server, we extract only the second-level domain name to reduce the list. For instance from *cnt2.acmetracksyou.com* and *srv1.acmetracksyou.com* we consider *acmetracksyou* only. We repeat the procedure using the top 500 websites in the general Alexa rank, and of countries where ISP1 and ISP2 are located. By merging the resulting lists we obtain more than 350 distinct online tracker services. Then, we complement this list with the one obtained from the developers of Abine[5], and with some specific trackers we manually identify. This list also includes hostnames referring to trackers specifically tailored to track mobile clients. The final list consists of 443 distinct online tracking services. The list includes only services that we classify as third party sites that collect users' information, and eventually serve advertisements. This includes tracking services that profile users explicitly (e.g., Doubleclick) or that track users when on a website (e.g., Google Analytics). We do not consider social network buttons, plugins, and active code.

In the remainder of the paper, we rely on this list to pinpoint connections that clients establish with tracker servers. When analyzing the TCP logs, we use the DN-Hunter hostname to identify traffic to trackers. For HTTP logs instead we use the server hostname in the HTTP request.

4 Results

4.1 Penetration of Online Tracking Services

We start our analysis by measuring the "penetration" of each online tracker that appears in our list. We consider the trace ISP1-Vp1-10d-10/14. Fig. 2 reports the percentage of users that contacted at least one time a given tracker with respect to users that we find active considering the entire 10 days. The results are shocking: the top online tracking services – DoubleClick, Google Analytics, and Google Syndication – track 98.8%, 98.7% and 97.4% of users, i.e., as soon as a user goes online, sooner or later she/he will contact one of Google tracking services. While they might be known to some users, the list of trackers includes a vast majority of players that are mostly unknown even to experts internauts. Fig. 2 reports some of the names. Observe the solid blue curve which refer to the ten-day long period. More than 50% of users contacts 120 distinct trackers, with 429 out of 443 trackers that have being contacted by at least one user.

---

[5] https://www.abine.com/

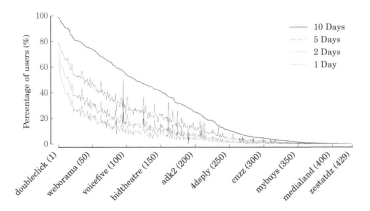

Fig. 2. Penetration of online trackers in ISP1-Vp1-10d-10/14.

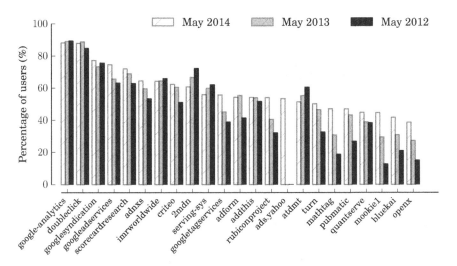

Fig. 3. Penetration of online trackers compared for different years in ISP1-Vp1-1d-05/*.

When considering shorter periods of time, e.g., one, two, five days (red, green and black curves), the number of users seen by trackers decreases. Yet, the top 20 trackers can observe more than 35% of internauts active during the first day of the trace.

Next, we compare penetration of trackers over years. Fig. 3 shows the results. This time we are considering one-day long traces during October 2012, 2013 and 2014, and we focus on the top 23 trackers. Penetration is higher in this case as we compute it over the active population of a single day. Top trackers show marginal changes over year, reflecting the fact that they have saturated the coverage. Going down in the list, we see that most of trackers shows an increase

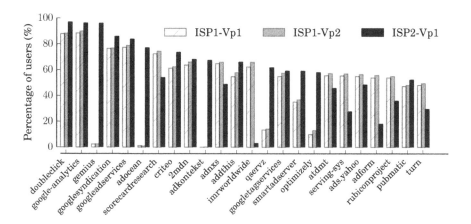

Fig. 4. Penetration of online trackers compared for different years in ISP1-Vp1-1d-02/14, ISP1-Vp2-1d-02/14 and ISP2-Vp1-1d-02/14.

in the penetration, with only few exceptions. Some new players shows up, i.e., *ads.yahoo*. No service went out of business (or disappeared).

We next compare the penetration from different vantage points. Fig. 4 show results considering the top-30 most popular trackers seen in the merged list of ISP1 and ISP2. Again, one-day long traces (in February 2014) are considered. Two observation holds: ISP1-Vp1 and ISP1-Vp2 show practically the same results. Despite being in two different cities, the population interest and habits is very similar, being in the same country. Conversely, comparing ISP1 and ISP2 results, we observe a very different penetration for some trackers, which reflects a localized service. This confirms the finding in [12] which highlighted the different coverage of online tracking services. For instance, Google tracking services present a higher penetration in Country 2 than in Country 1, while some trackers do not cover ISP2 market, e.g., *imrworldwide*, and viceversa, e.g., *adocean*.

To gauge the amount of data trackers collect, we compute the distribution of the fraction of TCP flows to trackers (not reported for the sake of brevity). We observe that 60% of users exchange from 10% to 30% of flows with trackers. We also see few cases in which more than 95% of flows are sent to trackers. Investigating, we observe i) click fraud activity of some users infected by some ad-malware, and ii) some mobile application that keeps downloading tens of ad-banners per minute, for hours. Both are likely illicit behaviors caused by malicious attackers that abuse of unaware users to game the ads market.

At last, we measure to which extent the top trackers rely on encrypted channels, i.e., HTTPS, to collect information about the users. To this end, we measure how many TCP flows the users exchange with the trackers, and how many of these flows are HTTPS. We consider again the one-day long traces we collected

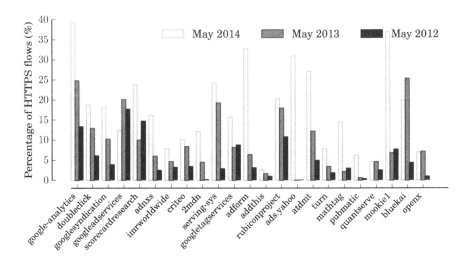

Fig. 5. Percentages of HTTPS transactions users establish with third party tracking services for different years in ISP1-Vp1-1d-02/1*.

in 2012, 2013 and 2014. Fig. 5 reports the percentages of connections carrying HTTPS traffic for the top 23 most popular trackers. We observe some trackers do use encryption to collect users' information: in 2014, *google-analytics* (39%), *adform* (33%), *ads.yahoo* (31%) and *mookie1* (36%). In general almost all the top 23 tracker has consistently increased the usage of HTTPS over the last three years. This is also mandated by the general increase of HTTPS-enabled websites that enforce HTTPS for all third party content too.

4.2   Popularity of Privacy Enhancer Plugins

We now investigate the popularity of plugins that can enhance and customize the browsing experience. We focus on those well-know plugins which i) block Javascript code commonly used by advertisers (NoScript), ii) warn about the presence of online tracking service (Ghostery, WordOfTrust, DoNotTrackMe), and iii) block advertisement traffic (AdBlock, AdBlockPlus). We count how many users run these plugins. For each plugin, we perform some active experiments to understand which hostnames it has to contact to check if updates are available[6] We then compute the fraction of users that contact such hostnames in our traces.

We report in Fig. 6 the shares of households that have installed a given plugin in at least one device, together with the percentage of those which did not

---

[6] We observe that each plugin contacts its update server with a fairly large frequency (e.g., at any browser bootstrap or once a day) with respect to the considered observation window.

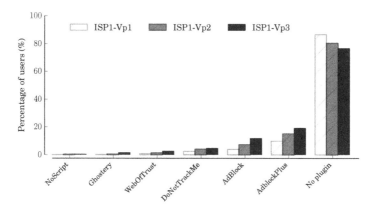

Fig. 6. Percentage of households installing the most popular do-not-tracking plugins. Results from traces ISP1-Vp*-10d-10/14.

install any plugin in any device. We compute these statistics for all our ten-day long traces. As shown, the share of users installing a plugin is in general rather small, and it seems that users are more interested in blocking the ads they encounter while browsing the web, rather than trackers. Indeed the popularity of AdBlockPlus is between 10% to 18%. Less than 3.5% of users run DoNotTrackMe. Moreover, we observe that more than 80% of the users do not install any of the considered plugins, thus offering the trackers the capability of easily following their surfing activity.

4.3   Trackers Penetration among Services

Next, we investigate the penetration of the online trackers among different services (e.g., websites) that users contact during their everyday online activity. To this end, we consider the HTTP trace. From each URL where the `hostname` is a given tracker, we check the `Referer` field to observe which service was embedding it. As before, we consider only the second level domain name as the name of the service. We count more than 25,000 services that host third party trackers. For each of them, we count how many users contacted them, i.e., how popular they are, and how many and which trackers they embed. In the scatter plot in Fig. 7, each black dot represents a service; the x-axis (in log scale) reports the number of distinct users accessing it; the y-axis reports the number of embedded trackers. Data refers to ISP1-Vp1-1d-5/14. The scenario is rather heterogeneous, with many services embedding several tens of tracking services. We observe both unpopular services hosting many trackers – e.g., the few services contacted by one or two users only, but hosting more than 50 trackers – and popular services hosting a few trackers – e.g., the rightmost bottom corner of the plot. In general the number of trackers per service tends to increase with the popularity of the service.

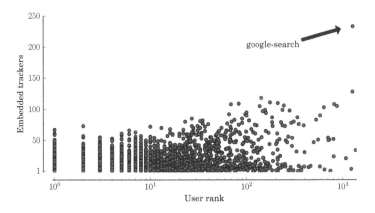

Fig. 7. Scatter plot of the number of users contacting a service, and the number of trackers embedded by the same service. ISP1-Vp1-1d-5/14.

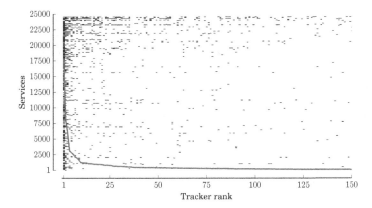

Fig. 8. Trackers embedded by the services users visited (black dots), and the number of services covered by each tracker (red curve). trace ISP1-Vp1-1d-5/14.

When checking the results we noticed that *www.google.com*, the most popular service, apparently embeds 222 trackers. By manually digging in our traces we observe that such large number of trackers is due to a bug in the *google-search* widget installed in version 4 of Android devices which affect our (and possible other datasets). Indeed, when an Android user performs a search query using the widget, and then visit a webpage by tapping on a link in the returned page, the Android browser keeps using http://www.google.com as `Referer` field for all objects that actually refer to the visited page. Besides affecting our results, this bug can possibly also poison the counters that trackers use to share their revenues with services.

To complement the above observations, we analyze tracker's "breadth", i.e., the number of services that embed each tracker. We report the results in Fig. 8.

The x-axis reports the rank of the 150 most popular trackers in our lists, and the y-axis reports all the services present in ISP1-Vp1-1d-05/14. Each dot represents the association of tracker x with the service y. We sort the services by considering their popularity among the users, from the most popular (top) to the least popular (bottom). First, most popular services embeds a large variety of trackers (observe the dense area in the top part of the plot). This confirms the trend of Fig. 7. Second, the dense vertical area in the leftmost part of the plot indicates that trackers with the highest penetration are also associated to many services (and vice-versa). To ease the visualization, the red solid curve shows the number of services associated to each tracker in the rank. The curve is very steep, with less than 10 trackers are associated to more than 1000 services. In particular, the three trackers with the largest service coverage belong to Google: *google-analytics*, *doubleclick* and *googlesyndication*, embedded by $17,814$, $8,176$, and $5,921$ services, corresponding to 71%, 32%, and 24% of the total number of active services, respectively. The first tracker not belonging to Google in the rank, *addthis* takes the fourth place with $3,080$ (12%) covered services. Despite this, it sees more than 50% of population (see Fig. 3). This reflect a market dominated by Google, in which a lot of other small players are present. The ones that are hosted in popular domains are able to still track a lot of users.

4.4   Time to Be Tracked

In this section, we investigate how invasive trackers are at getting in touch with users. We measure how much time a user spends online before encountering the first tracker. Let $T0$ be the time of the first HTTP or HTTPS TCP flow generated by a user, and let $T1$ be the time of the first TCP flow to a tracker. We measure the Time-To-Tracker as $TTT = T1 - T0$. For this analysis, we leverage the TCP trace in ISP1-Vp1-1d-5/14. We consider only those households for which we know just PC-based terminals are used, i.e., only one single PC-based user-agent is seen. Results are astonishing: TTT is smaller than 1 s in 77% of PC users, i.e., as soon as a users goes online, she/he hits the first tracker in less than a second. Even worse, 100% of users have a TTT smaller than 100 s. When considering all households, we observe even shorter TTT.

To give the intuition behind this, we detail the number of HTTP connections needed to hit a tracker using the HTTP traces. We split the dataset according to the user-agent field in three categories: PC-based, Android-based and iOS-based. For each category, we compute the distribution of the number of HTTP requests a user generates before contacting a tracker. Fig. 9 plots the results. Independently on the device, in about 10% of the cases, the first HTTP transaction of the day goes to a tracker[7], and within the first 100 (1000) requests in about 60% (97%) of the cases. Interestingly, users with an Android device contact a tracker earlier on than users with a PC or an iOS-based device.

---

[7] The reason why the first HTTP request goes to a tracker is due to the user browsing on HTTPS before moving to HTTP, thus becoming visible for this measure.

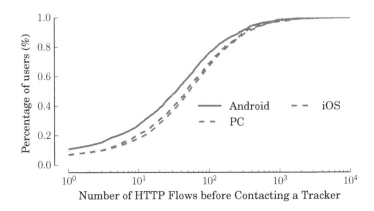

Fig. 9. CDF of number of HTTP requests before contacting a tracker. Trace ISP1-Vp1-1d-5/14.

5   Conclusions

Motivated by the privacy concerns that online tracking services have recently raised, we presented in this paper a passive characterization of this phenomenon. We leveraged a large dataset of traffic summaries we collected from ISPs located in two different countries to passively quantify the pervasiveness and the intrusiveness of online tracking services in our life. To the best of our knowledge, we are the first to passively analyze the behavior of trackers in a real scenario, where the users are naturally factored.

The results presented in this paper are boggling. We observed that top 100 trackers collect information from 50% of the users on a regular basis. Plus, some of these being able of tracking 98% of the Internauts. They are embedded into more than 70% of websites, including the most popular ones, but also those that are visited by few users. Similarly, trackers' intrusiveness is astonishing, with 77% of users that contacts a tracker within 1 second after she/he starts browsing the web. We also observe that trackers are increasingly embracing HTTPS to collect data. While this is possibly driven by the increase of HTTPS usage, this increases the warning level since is becomes more and more complicated to control and limit the information they can collect.

Our results show that the consciousness of the users about their activity being monitored by trackers is limited. Indeed, only a small fraction of users rely on privacy-enhancer browser plugins as DoNotTrackMe, and they appear to be more interested in ad-blocking extensions such as AdBlockPlus.

We believe that the information contained in this paper can contribute to increase the consciousness of people about the fragility of their privacy in modern web. We hope that our findings may be of stimulus for regulators, researchers and practitioners who aim at designing solutions to let the users take control of the information they exchange with the Internet.

References

1. IAB internet advertising revenue report, 2013 full year results. http://www.iab. net/media/file/IAB_Internet_Advertising_Revenue_Report_FY_2013.pdf
2. Ghostery. https://www.ghostery.com/en/
3. DoNotTrackMe. http://www.abine.com/donottrackme.html
4. Privacy Badger. https://www.eff.org/privacybadger
5. AdBlockPlus. http://adblockplus.org/
6. WoT. https://www.mywot.com/
7. Acar, G., Eubank, C., Englehardt, S., Juarez, M., Narayanan, A., Diaz, C.: The web never forgets: persistent tracking mechanisms in the wild. In: ACM SIGSAC (2014)
8. Barford, P., Canadi, I., Krushevskaja, D., Ma, Q., Muthukrishnan, S.: Adscape: harvesting and analyzing online display ads. In: WWW (2014)
9. Bermudez, I.N., Mellia, M., Munafo, M.M., Keralapura, R., Nucci, A.: DNS to the rescue: discerning content and services in a tangled web. In: ACM IMC (2012)
10. Castelluccia, C., Grumbach, S., Olejnik, L.: Data harvesting 2.0: from the visible to the invisible web. In: WEIS (2013)
11. Chaabane, A., Kaafar, M.A., Boreli, R.: Big friend is watching you: analyzing online social networks tracking capabilities. In: ACM WOSN (2012)
12. Falahrastegar, M., Haddadi, H., Uhlig, S., Mortier, R.: The rise of panopticons: examining region-specific third-party web tracking. In: Dainotti, A., Mahanti, A., Uhlig, S. (eds.) TMA 2014. LNCS, vol. 8406, pp. 104–114. Springer, Heidelberg (2014)
13. Gomer, R., Mendes Rodrigues, E., Milic-Frayling, N., Schraefel, M.: Network analysis of third party tracking: User exposure to tracking cookies through search. In: ACM WI-IAT (2013)
14. Krishnamurthy, B., Naryshkin, K., Wills, C.E.: Privacy leakage vs. Protection measures: the growing disconnect. In: W2SP (2011)
15. Krishnamurthy, B., Wills, C.: Privacy diffusion on the web: a longitudinal perspective. In: WWW (2009)
16. Roesner, F., Kohno, T., Wetherall, D.: Detecting and defending against third-party tracking on the web. In: USENIX NSDI (2012)
17. Vallina-Rodriguez, N., Shah, J., Finamore, A., Grunenberger, Y., Papagiannaki, K., Haddadi, H., Crowcroft, J.: Breaking for commercials: characterizing mobile advertising. In: ACM IMC (2012)
18. Yen, T.F., Xie, Y., Yu, F., Yu, R.P., Abadi, M.: Host fingerprinting and tracking on the web: privacy and security implications. In: NDSS (2012)

SFMap: Inferring Services over Encrypted Web Flows Using Dynamical Domain Name Graphs

Tatsuya Mori[1]([✉]), Takeru Inoue[2], Akihiro Shimoda[3], Kazumichi Sato[3], Keisuke Ishibashi[3], and Shigeki Goto[1]

[1] Department of Computer Science and Communications Engineering, Waseda University, Tokyo, Japan
mori@nsl.cs.waseda.ac.jp
[2] NTT Network Innovation Laboratories, NTT Corporation, Tokyo, Japan
[3] NTT Network Technology Laboratories, NTT Corporation,Tokyo, Japan

Abstract. Most modern Internet services are carried over the web. A significant amount of web transactions is now encrypted and the transition to encryption has made it difficult for network operators to understand traffic mix. The goal of this study is to enable network operators to infer hostnames within HTTPS traffic because hostname information is useful to understand the breakdown of encrypted web traffic. The proposed approach correlates HTTPS flows and DNS queries/responses. Although this approach may appear trivial, recent deployment and implementation of DNS ecosystems have made it a challenging research problem; i.e., canonical name tricks used by CDNs, the dynamic and diverse nature of DNS TTL settings, and incomplete measurements due to the existence of various caching mechanisms. To tackle these challenges, we introduce domain name graph (DNG), which is a formal expression that characterizes the highly dynamic and diverse nature of DNS mechanisms. Furthermore, we have developed a framework called Service-Flow map (SFMap) that works on top of the DNG. SFMap statistically estimates the hostname of an HTTPS server, given a pair of client and server IP addresses. We evaluate the performance of SFMap through extensive analysis using real packet traces collected from two locations with different scales. We demonstrate that SFMap establishes good estimation accuracies and outperforms a state-of-the-art approach.

1 Introduction

Background:
Monitoring and understanding traffic mix is crucial for network operators. Port number conventions and deep packet inspection (DPI) are widely used to understand the breakdown of traffic mix. However, these techniques have become less effective for the following reasons. First, the majority of modern services, such as social networking service, video, and messaging services, are all performed over web traffic [9], and port number information is too coarse-grained to distinguish such services from each other. Second, the encryption of communication channels has disabled inspection of HTTP headers, which include useful information such as uniform resource identifiers (URIs). Modern protocols for accelerating the web such

© IFIP International Federation for Information Processing 2015
M. Steiner et al. (Eds.): TMA 2015, LNCS 9053, pp. 126–139, 2015.
DOI: 10.1007/978-3-319-17172-2_9

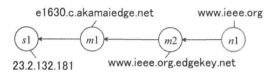

Fig. 1. Example of a CNAME chain

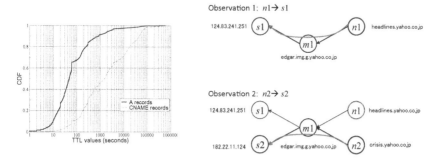

Fig. 2. CDFs of TTL values

Fig. 3. An example of CNAME ambiguity

as SPDY and Websocket employ mandatory encryption of HTTP with SSL/TLS (secure socket layer/transport layer security), i.e., HTTPS. Naylor et al. [7] recently reported that fraction of HTTPS traffic volume measured at a large-scale ISP has significantly increased over these 2+ years (from April 2012 to July 2014). They also found that their meausrement study suggests that cost of deploying HTTPS is decreasing. Hence, the increasing adoption of HTTPS brings new research challenges to traffic classification problems [2,5][1].

Goal and Challenges:
Based on the aforementioned information, this work aims to enable network operators to infer the hostnames of HTTPS traffic. Hostname information is useful for network operators to understand what types of services are carried over HTTPS flows. Although the IP address property of an HTTPS server may reveal that the server is used by a particular company such as Google, this information often fails to provide us with information about the services that are used over the flow, such as web searches, blogs, and videos. Such services are associated with distinct hostnames such as www.google.com, www.blogspot.com, and www.youtube.com. Bermudez et al. [2] revealed that simple reverse DNS lookup does not return accurate domain

---

[1] We note that server name indication (SNI) extention of TLS can be used to obtain hostname of HTTPS server. However, there are many client/server implementations that do not adopt SNI. In fact, in our dataset, roughly half of HTTPS clients did not use the SNI extention.

information used by HTTPS servers. Thus, to understand the traffic mix of HTTPS flows, we need to infer server hostnames.

The main idea of our approach is to correlate HTTPS flows and DNS queries/responses. The basic assumption is that prior to requesting an HTTPS flow, a web application should resolve the IP address of the HTTPS server by querying a DNS query. Therefore, by monitoring prior DNS queries/responses, we can estimate the hostname that is associated with IP address of the HTTPS server. Although this approach might look trivial, there are three practical challenges.

(**Challenge 1**) *Canonical name (CNAME) tricks used by CDNs*

First, modern CDN providers leverage CNAME tricks to accelerate the efficiency of content delivery [10]. Figure 1 shows an example of a CNAME chain used by a CDN provider. Here, assume that we know that the IP address of an observed HTTPS server is $s1 = 23.2.132.181$. Now, our task is to associate $s1$ with the original hostname, $n1 = $ www.ieee.org. However, as is shown in Fig. 1, $n1$ is not directly resolved to $s1$ due to the existence of the CNAME chain. Using this chain structure, a CDN provider can provide the optimal server IP address $s1$ to serve the content of $n1$ to client $c1$. Thus, to associate $s1$ and $n1$, we need to keep track of the CNAME chain, which exhibits dynamic and complex behavior as we shall see soon.

(**Challenge 2**) *Incomplete measurements*

A DNS record can be cached by several mechanisms such as local DNS resolvers, DNS caching within operating systems, and DNS caching within applications such as web browsers. The implementations of these caching mechanisms are diverse. Some recent implementations used in web browsers store DNS records aggressively to improve response time, thereby ignoring DNS TTL settings [4]. Even though such implementations violate the rule of DNS TTL, they can work because even if a selected server IP address is no longer an optimal one, the server IP address generally continues to be valid. Thus, due to the standard and illicit caching mechanisms, a DNS query, which should have appeared prior to an HTTP request, is often invisible. The absence of DNS queries suggests that we require estimation techniques to recover incomplete measurements.

(**Challenge 3**) *Dynamicity, diversity, and ambiguity*

Every hostname used in DNS is assigned a time-to-live (TTL), which defines the lifetime of the hostname within a stub DNS resolver. If the hostname is not queried again before the TTL has expired, the DNS record of the hostname will be removed from a stub DNS resolver. In general, the hostnames in a CNAME chain have different TTL values. Figure 2 presents an example of cumulative distributive function (CDF) of TTL values for hostnames that are resolved to IP addresses (A record) and hostnames that are resolved to CNAMEs (CNAME record). Note that the data was taken from a mid-sized production network, and the characteristics of CDF were the same for other dataset. The graph clearly shows that A record hostnames have shorter TTLs than CNAME hostnames. For example, more than 50% of A record hostnames have TTL values that are less than 60 seconds. This indicates that the association between hostnames and IP addresses is highly dynamic. These hostnames have shorter TTLs because CDN providers tend to control traffic at a fine granularity [4].

The diversity of TTL values and DNS caching mechanisms leads to ambiguity of CNAME association behavior. We illustrate an actual sample in Fig. 3, which presents DNS resolutions for a client, $c1$. The first observation generates the relationship between $s1$ and $n1$ for client $c1$. The second observation generates the relationship between $s2$ and $n2$ for client $c1$. Now, assume an estimation problem. If we observe the pair $(c1, s1)$, which hostname should it be associated with? If we simply keep the relationships shown above, the answer is $n1$. However, due to the existence of intermediate CNAME node $m1$, the actual answer is $n2$ because $m1$ is now associated with $s2$ by a query of $n2$, and $n1$ is associated with $m1$ due to a caching mechanism. Note that this behavior depends on the implementation of the stub DNS resolver used by the client $c1$. If the implementation ignores intermediate CNAME nodes, the answer could be $n1$. Thus, there is an intrinsic ambiguity in CNAME associations.

Contributions:
In this work, we present a novel methodology that aims to infer the hostnames of HTTPS flows, given the three research challenges shown above. The key contributions of this work are summarized as follows.

– We present domain name graph (DNG), which is a formal expression that can keep track of CNAME chains (Challenge 1) and characterize the dynamic and diverse nature of DNS mechanisms and deployments (Challenge 3).
– We develop a framework called Service-Flow map (SFMap) that works on top of the DNG. SFMap estimates the hostname of an HTTPS server given a pair of client and server IP addresses. It can statistically estimate the hostname even when associating DNS queries are unobserved due to caching mechanisms, etc. (Challenge 2).
– Through extensive analysis using real packet traces, we validate the performance of SFMap in terms of accuracy and resource consumption.

The remainder of this paper is organized as follows. Section 2 summarizes the related work. Section 3 describes the proposed SFMap framework in detail. We evaluate the performance of SFMap in Section 4. Section 5 discusses the limitations of SFMap and future research directions. We conclude our work in Section 6.

2   Related Work

Many studies have examined the Internet traffic classification problem. Ref. [3] lists 68 studies on the topic. Here, we focus our attention on the studies that make use of DNS information to the traffic classification problem [2,6,8]. Mori et al. [6] proposed a method to identify traffic originating from large-scale video-sharing services such as YouTube. The key idea was to extract the rules of IP address numbering and naming conventions of fully qualified domain names (FQDNs) used for the services. Although their approach may work for a limited scope, it cannot be used to solve more generic web traffic classification problems. Plonka et al. [8] presented a traffic classification method that uses DNS traffic. They developed a method that stores per client DNS *rendezvous* state information in a tree-like data structure. Although their results demonstrated that the DNS rendezvous-based method performs well, even for encrypted traffic, their goal was different from ours because they assumed that DNS traffic implies the ground truth. In contrast, our goal is to estimate the hostnames of HTTPS traffic from the observations of DNS traffic. Bermudez et al.[2] developed a framework called DN-Hunter, which aims to classify traffic flows using DNS traffic. DN-Hunter uses a FIFO (first-in first-out) circular list to store the relationships among FQDN information and client-server pairs. Since the scope of DN-Hunter is mostly similar to ours, this work compares the performance of SFMap with DN-Hunter.

3   SFMap Framework

This section describes SFMap in detail. Section 3.1 presents the overview of the SFMap framework. Section 3.2 describes DNG, which is a key component of the SFMap framework. Section 3.3 details how SFMap estimates hostnames. Lastly, Section 3.4 explains how SFMap updates DNG and statistics that are used for the estimation.

3.1   Overview

The goal of SFMap is to infer a hostname n of an HTTPS flow by associating preceding DNS responses with a flow key, which is defined with a pair of server IP address s and client IP address c. To this end, SFMap needs to address the research challenges discussed in Section 1. To tackle the research challenges, the SFMap framework works on top of DNG, which will be detailed in the next subsection. A DNG keeps track of the structure of DNS records; thus, it can deal with CNAME chains (Challenge 1). Next, by relaxing the constraints of the DNG, the SFMap framework can handle cases wherein there are no preceding DNS responses that are associated with the client-server pair (challenge 2). The details of the hostname estimation will be described in Section 3.3. Finally, by adequately maintaining the DNG and using the observed TTL values, the SFMap framework can deal with the dynamic nature of DNS mechanisms (Challenge 3). The updating mechanism for the DNG will be discussed in Section 3.4.

Figure 4 summarizes the components of the SFMap framework. SFMap has three main functions, i.e., Learner, Estimator, and Updater. Learner consists of two components: the DNG and the Frequency counter. Learner component reads DNS queries/responses and builds and keeps the DNG and Frequency counter. Estimator performs host estimation; i.e., given a pair of client-server IP addresses (c, s) for an HTTPS flow, estimator returns the most plausible hostname(s) using the information collected from DNG and Frequency counters. Updater reads DNS queries/responses and updates the status of the DNG and the Frequency counter.

Given these primitives, our problem can be formulated as maximum likelihood estimation (MLE) under the constraints of a DNG. Given c and s in an HTTPS flow,

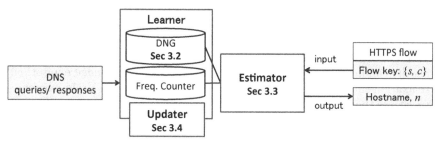

Fig. 4. Components of SFMap

the MLE is formulated as follows.

$$\hat{n}(c, s) = \operatorname*{argmax}_{n \in N} \Pr(n, c, s) \tag{1}$$

$$\text{s.t.} \quad N = \{n \in V_c : n \underset{G_c}{\to} s\}, \tag{2}$$

where $G_c = (V_c, E_c)$ denotes a DNG built for c, and binary operator $x \underset{G}{\to} y$ represents whether vertex x can reach to vertex y on graph G. In the following, we describe how we build and update G_c, how we extract N, how we compute the likelihood probability $\Pr(n, c, s)$, and how we get the final estimation $\hat{n}$.

3.2 DNG

A DNG, G_c, is a directed graph used to keep A and CNAME records observed in DNS responses queried by client c. DNGs can be built separately for each client c. A vertex, $v \in V_c$, is a server IP address or a hostname, while an edge, $e \in E_c$, represents an A or CNAME record that links a vertex to another vertex. Each edge is grafted by a corresponding A or CNAME record observed in a DNS response, and is associated with its expire time determined by observed TTL. If an edge, $e \in E_c$, is expired, it will be removed from G_c.

Here, we examine how the DNG expression naturally represents the behavior of DNS resolution. Assume that clients obtain a server address via DNS responses only and that we have never missed any DNS response for the clients; i.e., DNG G_c represents all name resolutions requested by a client c. When a client c sends an HTTP request to a server n, the server n's IP address s should have been resolved by DNS. This association of n and s obtained through the DNS mechanism can be expressed as a path from n to s on the DNG G_c. Note that there are cases where we cannot find such a path due to the caching mechanisms. In such cases, we need to employ several techniques that will be described soon.

3.3 Estimator

In the estimation phase, we must first select candidate hostnames that are likely the original hostname for a given client-server pair (c, s). We extract a set of candidate hostnames N from DNG G_c, using Eq. 2. If $|N| \geq 1$, we estimate the hostname with the MLE shown in Eq. 1. A method to calculate the likelihood probability $\Pr(n, c, s)$ will be shown later.

As we mentioned in Section 1, N can be an empty set due to the standard and illicit DNS caching mechanisms. In such cases, we cannot directly associate an HTTPS flow with preceding DNS responses. To deal with these cases, SFMap extends the candidate hostnames by relaxing the constraint of edge expiration. This relaxation enables us to select hostnames that are missed due to the existence of DNS clients that ignore DNS TTL for improving the user experience. Now, N is obtained as

$$N = \{n \in V_c : n \underset{\tilde{G}_c}{\rightarrow} s\}, \tag{3}$$

where $\tilde{G}_c = (V_c, \tilde{E}_c)$ and $\tilde{E}_c$ include both valid and expired edges.

Finally, if we do not have any candidate hostnames at this stage, we use the union of all clients' DNGs (union DNG). In other words, we use the observations of other clients as a hint to estimate the most plausible hostname. Let C denote a set of all clients. The union DNG is defined as $G = (V = \bigcup_{c \in C} V_c, E = \bigcup_{c \in C} E_c)$. Using the union DNG G, the candidate hostnames can be selected as

$$N = \{n \in V : n \underset{G}{\rightarrow} s\}. \tag{4}$$

It then estimates the hostname with the following MLE formulation:

$$\hat{n} = \underset{n \in N}{\operatorname{argmax}} \Pr(n, s). \tag{5}$$

Like Eq. 3, we can further relax the constraint of expiration for the union DNG G; i.e.,

$$N = \{n \in V : n \underset{\tilde{G}}{\rightarrow} s\}, \tag{6}$$

where $\tilde{G} = (V, \tilde{E})$ and $\tilde{E}$ include both valid and expired edges.

To recap, the Estimator runs the combinations below from top to bottom in a step-by-step manner until a plausible hostname is found. For future reference, we give names to these steps, where LE and UE refer to Local and Union Estimators, and NTE refers to "No TTL Expiration". For instance, the estimator LE-NTE (Local Estimator with No TTL Expiration) starts with the first step and continues to the second step until at least one candidate hostname is found, but will not proceed to the third and fourth steps. We will examine the accuracies of these estimators to study the factors that contribute to improve the estimation accuracies.

Step	MLE	constraint	Name
1st	Eq. (1)	Eq. (2)	LE
2nd	Eq. (1)	Eq. (3)	LE-NTE
3rd	Eq. (5)	Eq. (4)	UE
4th	Eq. (5)	Eq. (6)	UE-NTE

Finally, we note the time complexity of the Union Estimators. In the Union DNG, a single-source path search from s with reverse edges requires $O(|E|)$ on a directed acyclic graph with topological sort, and frequency lookups are executed for $n \in N \subseteq V$. Therefore, the time complexity of Union Estimators is $O(|V| + |E|)$. However, we empirically revealed that the actual mean time complexity is much smaller than this worst-case upper bound, and is close to $O(|V_c| + |E_c|)$ because majority of hostnames can be estimated with LE and LE-NTE as we shall show in Section 4. The details are omitted due to the space limitation.

Calculation of the Likelihood Probabilities. To calculate the likelihood probabilities, we make use of empirical data. Let $F_c(n, s)$ denote the frequency of DNS messages queried by client c for hostname n with resolved address s. Using $F_c(n, s)$, Eq. 1 can be calculated as

$$\underset{n \in N}{\operatorname{argmax}} \Pr(n, c, s) = \underset{n \in N}{\operatorname{argmax}} F_c(n, s).$$

Similarly, Eq. 5 can be calculated as

$$\underset{n \in N}{\operatorname{argmax}} \Pr(n, s) = \underset{n \in N}{\operatorname{argmax}} F(n, s),$$

where $F(n, s) = \sum_{c \in C} F_c(n, s)$. The method to update the frequency will be shown in the next subsection.

3.4 Updater

The Updater updates DNG G_c and frequency F_c when it receives a DNS response. A DNS response is associated with client c and queried hostname $n^\star$. The response also includes a set of A records and another set of CNAME records. Let these sets be A and M, respectively. An A record associates hostname n and server address s, while a CNAME record associates two hostnames n' and n. Let these records be $(n, s) \in A$ and $(n', n) \in M$, respectively.

Due to the existence of short TTL value set for an A record, a client often resolves an intermediate hostname (i.e., CNAME) instead of the original one. In such a case, the frequency of an original hostname is undervalued. To cope with such a case, SFMap increments the frequencies of all original hostnames that can reach to the queried hostname. Let a set of edges be $E_c = \{(n'', n), (n', n), (n, s)\}$, where n is a CNAME of n'' or n'. If $n^\star = n$ is queried, the Updater increments $F_c(n'', s)$ and $F_c(n', s)$, instead of $F_c(n, s)$. Note that we assume that original hostnames should be leaf vertices on a DNG (a leaf is a vertex without incoming edge). In fact, more than 99.7% of requested hostnames are leaf vertices in our observations.

Algorithm 1 presents an algorithm that updates G_c and F_c upon receiving a DNS response, $(c, n^\star, A, M)$. We discount the incremental value by the number of (n', s) pairs at Line 7, because the algorithm increments F_c for all $n' \in V$ reachable to $n^\star$ and for all s in A. At Line 3, we update the expiration time of edge (u, v). In addition to Algorithm 1, the Updater periodically checks the TTL expiration for

Algorithm 1. Updater

Input: $c, n^{\star}, A, M$ // DNS response
1 **for** $(u, v) \in A \cup M$ **do**
2    $\quad E_c = E_c \cup \{(u, v)\}$ // to add edge
3    $\quad$ update expire time of edge (u, v)
4 $N' = \{n' \in V_c : (*, n') \notin E_c,\ n' \underset{G_c}{\rightarrow} n^{\star}\}$ // leaf vertices reachable to $n^{\star}$
5 **for** $n' \in N'$ **do**
6    $\quad$ **for** $(*, s) \in A$ **do**
7    $\quad\quad F_c(n', s) = F_c(n', s) + \frac{1}{|N'| \cdot |A|}$ // to increment frequency
8 **return** G_c, F_c

---

all edges. If the DNS TTL expires for an edge (u, v), the edge will be removed. The time complexity of maintenance is $O(|V_c|)$ for the loop at Line 5, assuming $O(|A|) = O(|M|) = O(1)$.

4   Evaluation

Here, we first describe the datasets used and present some basic statistics derived from the data. We then evaluate the estimation accuracy of SFMap. For reference, we compare the performance of SFMap with DN-Hunter [2]. Finally, we examine the resource consumption of SFMap, which was implemented with Python.

4.1   Datasets and Statistics

To investigate the effectiveness of SFMap, we used the two datasets, LAB and PROD, which are the packet traces collected from a gateway router of local area network used by a research group and a gateway router of middle-scale production network, respectively. The basic statistics of the datasets are summarized in Table 1. As is shown in Table 1, the datasets cover two different scales, small and middle. Both datasets have same time length, twelve hours. Of the twelve hours, the last two hours are used to examine the accuracy; i.e., the first 10 hours are used for *warm-up* phase. We adopted the length of warm-up from the observation of TTL distribution shown in Fig. 2; i.e., majority of the DNS resource records had TTL values less than 10 hours.

Here, we present the characteristics of DNGs derived from our datasets. Table 2 presents the statistics of the DNGs. For brevity, we omit DNGs with TTL expiration because these DNGs should be smaller than those without TTL expiration. As is shown in the table, Union DNGs have fewer nodes and edges. For instance, since the number of clients for the LAB dataset is 10 (see Table 1), the total number of nodes in the Local DNGs should be $10 \times 460 = 4600$. Thus, the number of total nodes in the Union DNG (=2849) is less than the number of total nodes in the Local DNGs. This observation implies that (1) each client-server pair in the Local DNGs

Table 1. Basic statistics of the datasets

	learning time	# of clients	# of DNS responses	estimating time	# of servers	# of HTTP requests	# of hostnames
LAB	0 ∼ 12 h	10	5,226	10 ∼ 12 h	1,705	542	1,135
PROD	0 ∼ 12 h	4,250	86,854	10 ∼ 12 h	10,785	55,091	10,534

Table 2. Statistics of the DNGs at the end of measurement period

	Local DNG w/o TTL expiration		Union DNG w/o TTL expiration	
	mean # of nodes	mean # of edges	total # of nodes	total # of edges
LAB	460	755	2,849	5,979
PROD	56	80	25,403	172,974

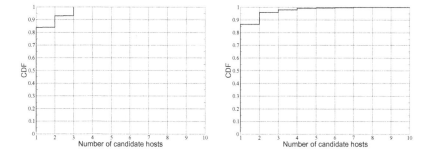

Fig. 5. CDFs of the number of candidate hostnames for each HTTP request: LAB (left) and PROD (right)

has duplicate nodes and edges, and (2) the Union DNGs can be maintained with less memory. Figure 5 shows the CDF of the number of candidate hostnames for each HTTP request. The results suggest that roughly 15% of the HTTP requests have multiple candidates; i.e., we must statistically estimate the original hostname from these candidates.

4.2 Estimation Accuracy

Our methodology was evaluated using the two datasets. We make use of HTTP as a means to evaluate the accuracy of our methodologies. The ground truth was obtained from HTTP request headers, which contain hostname information. We note that although the distributions of hostnames could be different between HTTP and HTTPS, the fundamental mechanism of resolving hostname before starting HTTP/HTTPS communication should be identical. From the packet traces, we

Table 3. Accuracies of the estimators (exact matching)

	LE	LE-NTE	UE	UE-NTE	DN-Hunter
LAB	54.98%	68.08%	71.59%	92.25%	67.90%
PROD	79.90%	88.29%	90.88%	90.88%	85.40%

Table 4. Accuracies of the estimators (public suffix matching)

	LE	LE-NTE	UE	UE-NTE	DN-Hunter
LAB	57.20%	70.30%	73.80%	94.46%	73.43%
PROD	83.20%	92.12%	94.52%	94.98%	89.98%

Table 5. Accuracies of the Top-3 estimations (UE-NTE)

	Exact matching			Public suffix		
	Hit in 1	Hit in 2	Hit in 3	Hit in 1	Hit in 2	Hit in 3
LAB	92.25	97.23	98.16	94.46	98.16	98.16
PROD	90.88	95.77	96.71	94.98	97.01	97.43

read DNS packets to build and update the DNGs. For each HTTP request pair (c, s), we estimate the hostname and compare it against the ground truth. For comparison purposes, we implemented DN-Hunter [2]. DN-Hunter has a single parameter that determines the size of memory, which keeps track of tuples of (c, s, N), where N is a hostname. To obtain the highest performance of DN-Hunter, we set infinite amount of memory size. We note that this configuration did not overflow physical memory we used in our experiments.

Table 3 and Table 4 summarize the results, where we use the notations introduced in Section 3.3. Table 3 shows the estimation accuracies in the context of exact matching, and Table 4 relaxes matching using a public suffix [1]; i.e., we can see that aaa.example.com and bbb.example.com are matched in the context of the public suffix. Using the public suffix matching allows us to distinguish hostnames with different domains, e.g., youtube.com and google.com.

First, the accuracies were improved for estimators with no TTL expiration (NTE). This observation suggests that there are a non-negligible number of DNS implementations that ignore TTL settings, which agrees with a previous report [4]. Second, the Union DNG also contributed to improve the accuracy. This observation suggests that using other clients' information is useful in improving the accuracy when no other hint is available. Third, if we allow public suffix matching, accuracies are further improved for all the estimators. The UE-NTE achieved roughly 95% of accuracy for both datasets. Finally, the UE-NTE outperformed DN-Hunter. For the exact matching experiments, while the estimation error rates of DN-Hunter were 15-32%, the estimation error rates of UE-NTE were 8–9%. Thus, UE-NTE successfully reduced the error rates by 50-70%.

DN-hunter returns a single hostname given a client-server pair; however, if there are multiple candidate hostnames, SFMap can return several hostnames with the highest likelihood probabilities. Table 5 shows the results where we accept the top

Table 6. Memory usage of RAM and processing time for UE-NTE

	memory (MB)	time (s)
LAB	35.1	0.8
PROD	686.2	20.6

three hostnames as estimation. Notably, accuracies exceed 96-98% for exact matching if we pick up the top three hostnames. We note that in most cases, the hostnames ranked in the top three look similar. For instance, the top three hostnames are: pagead2.googlesyndication.com, pubads.g.doubleclick.net, and googleads.g. doubleclick.net, which are all attributed to Ad Network services. Thus, by extending the candidate hostnames, we can establish better estimations that work in practice. This extension is acceptable for our original motivation; i.e., understanding the mix of HTTPS traffic.

4.3 Resource Consumption

We study the resource consumption of SFMap, using its implementation with Python. We note that the implementation has a much room for improvement in terms of optimizing resource management. Table 6 shows the amount of memory consumed and the amount of time to process the entire data, including data for warm-up. The results demonstrate that our implementation of SFMap works within a reasonable amount of memory, i.e., less than 40 MB for LAB and less than 700 MB for PROD. Also, processing time is much shorter than the actual measurement length, 12 hours. Thus, SFMap should work in a real-time fashion. We will further discuss the scalability of SFMap in the next section.

5 Discussion

Here, we discuss the limitations of the proposed SFMap framework. We also outline several future research directions that can help extend our framework.

5.1 Sources of Misclassification

By carefully examining the estimation results, we found several intrinsic sources of misclassification. There are several factors that are associated with the incomplete measurements. As we mentioned before, the first factor is the existence of aggressive DNS caching mechanisms that ignore DNS TTL setting. The second factor we found through this study was mobility of terminals; i.e., an IP address had already been resolved in other network before the terminal arrived to the vantage point. The third factor we found was the use of an IP address in the URI. We found a non-negligible number of HTTP requests had such URIs. We manually inspected the cases and found that there are several applications that likely hard-coded an IP address; thus, they never send DNS queries. Although these are not the controlling factors today, we may need to address them if such deployments become popular in future.

5.2   Scalability

As shown in Section 4.3, our SFMap implementation processed traffic collected at middle-scale production network within a reasonable amount of memory; i.e., less than 700 MB. Then, we may want to ask whether SFMap works for large-scale networks. First, because SFMap does not require per-packet processing, we believe that the processing time does not matter in practice. It just processes DNS response packets and the first packets of HTTPS flows, ignoring remaining packets. Furthermore, as we discussed in Section 3.3, empirical studies revealed that time complexity of estimation is close to $O(|V_c| + |E_c|)$, which is fairly small as shown in Table 2. We also note that estimation processes can be parallelized if we need it. Second, it is clear that the size of DNGs increases as the number of observed client increases. If the size of DNG becomes large enough to press the capacity of memory, we need to eliminate old records. Instead of keeping all the records for a certain amount of time, e.g., 12 hours, we may want to quickly delete old records that are less-likely to be reused in future. More sophisticated way to manage the elements in DNGs is left for the future study. Another possible solution would be to build a new algorithm that can maintain and update DNGs in a more compact data structure. The topic is also left for the future study.

6   Summary

The SFMap hostname estimation framework was presented. SFMap enables network operators to estimate the hostnames of HTTPS traffic by observing DNS queries/responses. To tackle the challenges that arise from the recent dynamic deployment and diverse implementations of DNS ecosystems, the proposed SFMap framework runs on top of a single key component; i.e., a DNG, which is a formal expression that characterizes the highly dynamic and diverse nature of DNS mechanisms. From extensive analyses using real packet traces collected from two distinct locations with different network scales, we have demonstrated that SFMap has good estimation accuracy and can outperform DN-Hunter, which is a state-of-the-art estimation technique. Our experiments using middle-scale network traffic with thousands of clients demonstrated that SFMap can be run on a standard commodity PC, using less than 700 MB of memory space. In future, we plan to enhance the scalability of SFMap.

Acknowledgments. This work was supported by JSPS KAKENHI Grant Number 25880020.

References

1. Public suffix list. https://publicsuffix.org/
2. Bermudez, I.N., Mellia, M., Munafo, M.M., Keralapura, R., Nucci, A.: DNS to the rescue: discerning content and services in a tangled web. In: Proc. of IMC, pp. 413–426 (2012)

3. CAIDA. Internet traffic classification. http://www.caida.org/research/traffic-analysis/classification-overview/
4. Callahan, T., Allman, M., Rabinovich, M.: On Modern DNS Behavior and Properties. SIGCOMM Comput. Commun. Rev. **43**(3), 7–15 (2013)
5. Korczynski, M., Duda, A.: Markov chain fingerprinting to classify encrypted traffic. In: Proc. of INFOCOM, pp. 781–789 (2014)
6. Mori, T., Kawahara, R., Hasegawa, H., Shimogawa, S.: Characterizing traffic flows originating from large-scale video sharing services. In: Ricciato, F., Mellia, M., Biersack, E. (eds.) TMA 2010. LNCS, vol. 6003, pp. 17–31. Springer, Heidelberg (2010)
7. Naylor, D., Finamore, A., Leontiadis, I., Grunenberger, Y., Mellia, M., Munafo, M., Papagiannaki, K., Steenkiste, P.: The cost of the "S" in HTTP. In: Proc. of CoNext (2014)
8. Plonka, D., Barford, P.: Flexible traffic and host profiling via DNS rendezvous. In: Proc. of SATIN (2011)
9. Sandvine. Global internet phenomena report: 1H 2014. http://bit.ly/1jHpsW5
10. Su, A.-J., Choffnes, D.R., Kuzmanovic, A., Bustamante, F.E.: Drafting behind akamai (travelocity-based detouring). In: Proc. of SIGCOMM, pp. 435–446 (2006)

Security

Monitoring Internet Censorship with UBICA

Giuseppe Aceto[1]([✉]), Alessio Botta[1], Antonio Pescapè [1], Nick Feamster [2],
M. Faheem Awan[3], Tahir Ahmad[3], and Saad Qaisar[3]

[1] University of Napoli Federico II, Napoli, Italy
{giuseppe.aceto,a.botta,pescape}@unina.it
[2] Georgia Institute of Technology, GA, USA
feamster@cc.gatech.edu
[3] NUST SEECS, Islamabad, Pakistan
{10mscsemawan,11msccstahmad,saad.qaisar}@seecs.edu.pk

Abstract. Censorship is becoming increasingly pervasive on the Internet, with the Open Net Initiative reporting nearly 50 countries practicing some form of censorship. Previous work has reported the existence of many forms of Internet censorship (e.g., DNS tampering, packet filtering, connection reset, content filtering), each of which may be composed to build a more comprehensive censorship system. Automated monitoring of censorship represents an important and challenging research problem, due to the continually evolving nature of the content that is censored and the means by which censorship is implemented. UBICA, User-based Internet Censorship Analysis, is a platform we implemented to solve this task leveraging crowdsourced data collection. By adopting an integrated and multi-step analysis, UBICA provides simple but effective means of revealing censorship events over time. UBICA has revealed the effect of several censorship techniques including DNS tampering and content filtering. Using UBICA, we demonstrate evidence of censorship in several selected countries (Italy, Pakistan, and South Korea), for which we obtained help from local users and manually validated the automated analysis.

1 Introduction

Akin to network monitoring for faults, attacks, and performance variations, Internet censorship monitoring is a relatively new field of research with methodologies, tools and practices still in course of definition. We consider Internet censorship *detection* as *"the process that, analyzing network data, reveals impairments in the access to content and services caused by a third party (neither the client system nor the server hosting the resource or service) and not justifiable as an outage"*. In turn, Internet censorship monitoring is the automated and continuous process of detecting Internet censorship over time, with the aim of revealing status changes in terms of the affected targets or the adopted censoring techniques. Regardless of the ethical and political positions regarding censorship, the interference with Internet protocols standard and intended behavior

---

This work has been carried out thanks to a *Google Faculty Research Award* for the project UBICA (User-Based Internet Censorship Analysis).

M. Steiner et al. (Eds.): TMA 2015, LNCS 9053, pp. 143–157, 2015.
DOI: 10.1007/978-3-319-17172-2_10

has practical implications. Moreover significant aspects of censorship, such as its enforceability, its transparency, and the accountability of the censors to the affected population, strongly depend on the technical details of the censorship technique adopted and thus evolve with both the technology and its application in practice. Collection of the appropriate network measurements for monitoring censorship is thus a fundamental part of understanding the existence, prevalence and evolution of censorship [3,12], and to tell it from unintentional network outages or performance issues. Although tools for monitoring censorship abound, most of them do not base their analysis or conclusions on widespread, scalable, continuous network measurement. One well-known censorship monitoring tool is Herdict [1], a crowd-sourced platform. Its main interface is a website allowing users to report about "accessibility" of URLs from within their browser; this way the platform leverages crowdsourcing both for the collection of *targets* of interest for the users, and by having the users to perform an application-level censorship test. A browser plugin also allows users to submit reports without accessing the web interface. Another tool called *CensMon* is specifically designed for censorship monitoring [16]. It is designed for continuous and automatic functioning, and addresses the "needle in a haystack" problem of selecting *targets* worth checking by feeding the system with URLs automatically harvested from a variety of online sources. The most complete and wide-ranging tool for censorship detection is provided by the OONI project [10]. It is a Free Software project, part of the wider *Tor project* with which it is tightly integrated. The main component is a Python script offering a list of censorship detection tests to be performed using Tor. In addition to platforms or tools for censorship detection and monitoring, previous work has performed many studies of various censoring systems and techniques [8,18], often focused on the Great Chinese Firewall [5,15,19], or investigate outage-like censorship events [2,7].

In this paper we discuss results obtained by means of a platform for censorship monitoring called UBICA, standing for User-based Internet Censorship Analysis. Due to space constraints, we focus on the results and on the analyses allowed by the platform, and describe the platform at a functional level, referring to future works for a more in-depth discussion. UBICA adopts an integrated and multi-step analysis and provides a simple but effective dashboard thanks to which censorship events are easily spotted and described also in their temporal evolution. UBICA integrates an algorithm for detecting censorship based on Internet measurements: if the test finds evidence of blocking, additional tests attempt to identify possible mechanisms, including DNS blocking, IP blocking, No HTTP Reply, RST (TCP-level tampering), Infinite HTTP Redirect, and Block page. Using UBICA for several months on selected targets, we found evidence of several censorship techniques, such as DNS tampering and content filtering. We validated the accuracy of UBICA with the help of users in selected countries and also show evidence of censorship in several countries (Italy, Pakistan, and South Korea).

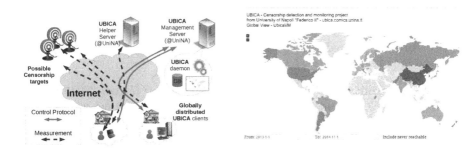

(a) Architecture diagram   (b) Report interface (detail: global map)

Fig. 1. The UBICA platform

2   UBICA

The main objective of UBICA is to provide users with a *censorship monitoring* system that presents both a report on world-wide Internet censorship status and a quick view of censorship from users' perspectives. To gather data, the platform leverages a distributed deployment of probes belonging to different kinds (router-based, headless client, GUI-client) that are orchestrated by a central management server. The platform provides: (i) dynamically updated censorship tests; (ii) dynamically updated targets to be verified; (iii) support for different types of probing clients; (iv) automatic censorship detection and censorship technique identification. Fig. 1a shows the UBICA architecture. An example of monitoring report is shown in fig. 1b.

Monitoring Control Flow. The collection of evidences of censorship is performed through *active measurements* from the probes, that periodically retrieve from the Management Server a list of test requirements (eventually updating the necessary targets lists and code). The target lists are build from up-to-date reports from Herdict [1], a list of worldwide top accessed websites, and lists suggested from in-country volunteers; they are distributed to probes based on the country the probe is located at. After the evidence collection each probe packs all the results in a report file and uploads it back to the Management Server. Such server asynchronously parses the reports and inserts the relevant information into an SQL Database. The *Analysis Engine* periodically processes data in the database, performing the censorship detection analyses described in the *Experimental results* section. The different types of measurements performed are described in the following.

DNS Resolution. To collect clues about this phase, a name resolution is elicited: given a fully qualified domain name, a DNS request of `type A` is issued from the probe towards its default resolver. The tool used to issue the request is nslookup. To distinguish among different DNS tampering techniques, the same request is issued also towards a list of open resolvers, used as *control* resolvers from inside the censored network. The list of open resolvers is the same as the one used in [14].

TCP Reachability. To check for filtering triggered by *IP:port*, this test tries to establish a TCP connection, starting a three-way handshake with a given timeout. The tests takes as parameters *targetIP:port* and a timeout value in seconds, that has been set by default to 15s.

HTTP Reachability. This test issues an HTTP GET request: the response (or lack of it) from the server is collected, along with application level values. The HTTP header field User-Agent is chosen randomly from a list of the most common user agent strings, according to [9]. The tool used to issue the request and collect application level information is curl. The report from this test includes several values, such as content type, HTTP response code, number of redirects, etc., not reported for the sake of brevity.

3   Experimental Results

With the help of professional and personal contacts, a number of software probes have been deployed in different countries worldwide, plus more than a dozen BISmark routers [17] from an experimental deployment in Pakistan, one in Italy and another one in USA. The distributed platform PlanetLab [4] has also been employed, deploying UBICA probes in the most diverse set of countries available at the time of the experiments. The measurement campaigns have been conducted using more than 200 probes, constituted by: 47 clients with GUI (run by volunteers both in Italy and abroad); 188 headless clients (of which 19 run by volunteers worldwide and 169 in PlanetLab nodes); and 16 BISmark home routers run by volunteers (mostly in Pakistan). The target lists for each country included Herdict reports for the country, a list of worldwide top accessed websites, and URLs suggested by local volunteers. Measurements have been made from 31 different countries, testing more than $16K$ different *targets* (about $15K$ different hostnames) on a timespan of 4 months.

The application of the UBICA detection algorithm to data collected in this experimental campaign and the time analysis of the related outcomes have tested the functionalities of the platform. In the following we report an extract of the most interesting results, concentrating on those for which we had a ground truth.

3.1   Censorship in Pakistan

In *ONI* country profiles, Pakistan (PK) is classified as applying "selective filtering", showing a consistent level of censorship and tight control on Internet communications across the national border. The government body Pakistan Telecommunication Authority (PTA) is in charge of the management of the Pakistan Internet Exchange, the exchange point connecting the country to the rest of the Internet, and maintains a blacklist of URLs to be censored [14]. According to the last report from *The OpenNet Initiative*, blocked resources belong to the classes: religion, sex, and politics.

A General View. Our experimental campaigns performed through UBICA probes in Pakistan evidenced that many resources were actually censored in this country. The censorship detection algorithm reported that the techniques used were mainly two: DNS injection and HTTP tampering. To understand what happened and to confirm these results we analyzed the intermediate data, comprising the results of the different tests performed by UBICA. We describe the overall results and the details about the intermediate ones in the following.

As for DNS, 68% of the resources are identically resolved from inside PK and USA (USA has been used for comparison purposes). Thus the algorithm for censorship detection excluded the occurrence of DNS-based censorship for the related resources. Therefore, for the remaining resources, the analysis has exploited information about the size of the resource (the *content size* tests). Similar analysis based on content size has been recently published in [11], but it leverages the availability of a ground truth, i.e., a copy of the content known to be uncensored, to compare with. Our algorithm, described hereafter, does not need such knowledge.

Considering the size of the resource (webpage) that has been retrieved, and averaging on all measurements from within a country, we expect to find a significant difference between different countries if one of the two is censoring the content by means of a "blocking page". For each URL u, the average resource size per country $s_{u,PK} = \frac{\sum_{u \, in \, PK} size(u)}{|PK|}$ is calculated and divided by the corresponding size averaged on all the other countries; as an example, we show the ratio with USA in this case, but in the following reports the more general setup is adopted. Considering the empirical CDF of such ratio (Fig. 2a), we can see that while most of URLs show a comparable average size, there is an interesting fraction of them whose size is much smaller in Pakistan than in USA. The empirical probability mass function distribution reported in Fig. 2b clearly shows two modes: one centered in 1 and a smaller one close to 0. The variability around 1 can be considered as due to differences in parts of the HTML code that are updated in the dynamic generation of the resource. The relatively big variations that lead to the mode close to zero hint to a different phenomenon, on which we will focus to find evidence of censorship. To differentiate between the two modes, we choose a threshold of 0.3, which is halfway between the two modes minus a guard interval of 0.2 to account for variability across multiple countries and coherently with the design principles of the detection algorithm. An excerpt of some URLs whose size ratio falls below this threshold (in total 56, of which 28 are *youtube* videos) are reported in Tab. 1. We took one of the URLs selected through the *average content size ratio* test, namely *ninjaproxy.com* (accounting for $343 Bytes$ in Pakistan and $14753 Bytes$ from USA) and looked at the HTML code received by the client in Pakistan. The inspection confirmed that the page is completely different from the one retrieved from outside Pakistan (not shown for space constraints). Indeed censorship has been enacted providing a webpage

Table 1. Selection of URLs whose content size ratio (size PK divided by size USA) is smaller than 0.3; URL path is truncated for presentation constraints

URL	size PK	size USA	Ratio
barenakedislam.wordpress.com	453.0	49095.63	0.01
ninjaproxy.com	342.45	14085.42	0.02
NinjaProxy.com	342.39	13154.06	0.03
www.similarsites.com	375.33	13701.44	0.03
www.youtube.com	4183.91	144177.2	0.03
www.freefacebookproxies.com	9041.17	241485.33	0.04
friendlyatheist.com	7881.34	205294.23	0.04
www.loonwatch.com	2661.73	65075.19	0.04
www.sodahead.com	3575.67	73969.7	0.05
www.hotspotshield.com	731.8	10789.91	0.07
face-of-muhammed.blogspot.com	6208.7	85342.93	0.07
www.foxnews.com	4705.53	63425.26	0.07
www.buzzfeed.com	22097.93	287001.77	0.08
www.freefacebookproxies.com	18245.93	233254.73	0.08
www.hotspotshield.com	870.1	10632.97	0.08
www.cagle.com/news/muhammad	3594.5	40974.12	0.09
www.smugbox.com/facebook/...	1883.93	21455.95	0.09
www.faithfreedom.org/Gallery/...	1438.93	15423.32	0.09
www.turbohide.com/	896.91	8744.12	0.1
www.unblockbook.net	812.48	6348.47	0.13
www.thesecretninjaproxy.info	469.79	3416.17	0.14
www.kproxy.com.	647.47	4694.55	0.14
www.kproxy.com	666.39	4618.71	0.14
www.unblock-facebook.net	840.26	5783.3	0.15
www.blockedsiteaccess.com	1271.46	7780.19	0.16

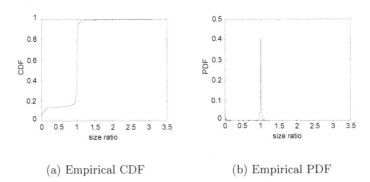

(a) Empirical CDF   (b) Empirical PDF

Fig. 2. Distribution of content size ratios (size PK divided by size USA) for each URL, tested URLs are from [14] (468 URLs)

with iframe redirection to a blocking page. These results are consistent with [14], and the analysis in the report by *The Citizen Lab* on this country. More details on reports generated by UBICA are described in the following for specific *targets* that better expose the detection algorithm inner working.

The Case of YouTube. One of the final results of the UBICA detection algorithm is the summary of the censorship techniques detected for a given *target* as accessed from different ISPs. This report shows an evaluation of censorship conditions and technologies in the considered country for the specified resource. An example of blocked URL showing interesting differences among ISPs is the streaming video platform - with content and comment sharing from users - *YouTube* (www.youtube.com), integrated with the social network *google plus* and the search engine google). The report that UBICA generated for the URL

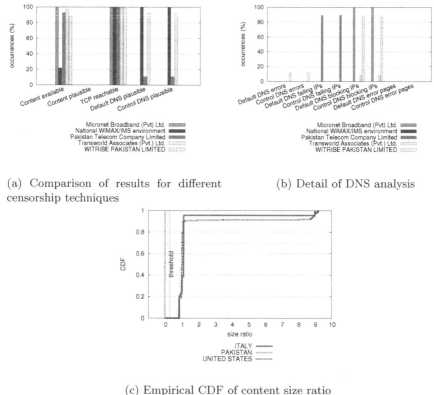

(a) Comparison of results for different censorship techniques

(b) Detail of DNS analysis

(c) Empirical CDF of content size ratio

Fig. 3. Censorship in Pakistan: the case of YouTube

of a resource on *YouTube*, as tested from different ISPs in Pakistan, is shown in form of a bar chart in Fig. 3a. The lack of bars in the second aggregate (with label "Content plausible") means that this resource is never reachable, even though for all but one ISP, a resource is returned when performing an HTTP request (first aggregate of bars, labeled "Content available"). We recall that "Content plausible" is the percentage of URLs that passed the *size ratio* censorship test, and thus present a content size comparable to the average on all countries. The outcome of this test is represented in Fig. 3c as a CDF of the ratio of the size of the downloaded content in one sample over the global average of such size. The CDF generated for Pakistan is shown (in green) along with other countries for comparison: Italy (cyan) and U.S.A. (in dark blue); the aggregation level is *country*, thus considering samples for the whole nations regardless of the ISP. The graph shows clearly that the size ratios in Pakistan are close to 0 (i.e. the content size is very small compared with the global average) with relative frequency 1 (always), while for both the other countries the occurrences fall close to 1 (thus same content size as the global average) with relative frequency greater than 0.9 (for U.S.A. 0.91 for a size 1.23 times the average, for Italy 0.95 for a size

1.11 times the average). Comparing with the size ratio threshold (set to 0.3) we notice that the test has correctly separated results in Pakistan from the ones in the other countries. Moreover as the detected condition is above the coherence threshold, the reported results are consistent over each country dataset.

TCP-level tests (Fig.3a, third aggregate, label "TCP reachable") show almost 100% reachability for all the ISPs, thus either no censorship is enacted at this layer, or DNS tampering precedes it. By considering the *default* DNS results for two ISPs "Micronet Broadband (Pvt) Ltd." and "Witribe Pakistan Ltd." no result yields a plausible IP address (i.e. neither a known block page or a failing IP, nor a DNS error), similarly for "Pakistan Telecom Company Ltd." only 11.7% is plausible. These ISPs clearly block the resource with *DNS tampering*. The DNS overall results show equal values for the *default* and the *control* resolvers, thus the inferred technique is DNS *injection*. The ISPs "Transworld Associates" (cyan in Fig. 3b) and "National Wi-Max/IMS" (dark blue) do not perform *DNS tampering* on the resource under analysis; yet for both the *content size ratio* analysis has detected censorship: an *HTTP tampering* technique has been applied. To gather information regarding the *symptom* the user gets in the censored networks, we leverage the detailed DNS analysis, shown in Fig. 3b. It can be noted that, while two ISPs (namely, "Micronet Broadband (Pvt) Ltd." and "Witribe Pakistan Ltd.") both use DNS tampering to provide the user with an explicit *block page*, the ISP "Pakistan Telecom Company Ltd." provides an address that will likely cause an error (either at TCP-level or an HTTP-404), thus confounding the customer without providing explicit notification of censorship.

From the comparison between the summarized view (Fig. 3a) and the DNS analysis details (Fig. 3b) the behavior of one ISP ("Pakistan Telecom Company Ltd.", in magenta) seems inconsistent with the expected *symptom*, as the detected technique ("DNS injection - failing IP") should have elicited an error, and not the high percentages found both in *TCP reachable* and *Content available* bars (3a). By inspecting the collected evidence data it resulted that the IP address returned by the ISP under analysis is `127.0.0.1`, corresponding to `localhost`, i.e. for each machine is the address of the machine itself (network level loopback). While other "specialized" network address ranges [6] are unlikely to be assigned to active hosts in the same LAN of the probe, `localhost` for sure is, and the outcome of a TCP connection to the port 80 and possibly an HTTP request depend on the presence of a service listening on that port, and the response the service will return, if present. The inspection confirms the verdict of the platform, that detected censorship and the actual technique *DNS injection* regardless of the misleading *symptoms* (no errors at any level of the stack - DNS, TCP, HTTP).

3.2   Censorship in Korea

The access to online content in South Korea is regulated by a government body, Korea Communications Standards Commission (KCSC) nominated by the president and in charge of the Ethics of Internet communications. The nation is reported by *ONI* as applying "selective filtering" for *Social* topics and "pervasive filtering" for the *Conflict/Security* category.

Adult Websites. A category of websites that is forbidden per order of the Ethical authority is the one showing adult content (classified among "obscenity and perversion"). The detection algorithm has signaled censorship for URLs such as hardsextube.com, pornhub.com and redtube.com, coherently with the expectations. We will consider the case of hardsextube.com in detail, as the other presents analogous results.

Considering the summarized view for the different tested techniques aggregated by country (Fig. 4a), it becomes evident the peculiar response in Korea with respect to the other tested countries. More specifically, the "content plausible" percentage of tests, result of the analysis based on the size ratio of the downloaded resource, is near 0% while other countries show near 100%, thus limiting to Korea only the issue in accessing the original content. Also no other censorship detection technique has been matched, thus excluding DNS Tampering and TCP-level filtering.

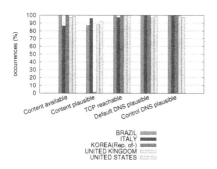

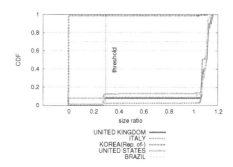

(a) Comparison of censorship evidences results across countries

(b) Empirical CDF of the content size ratio

Fig. 4. Censorship in Korea: porn websites

To inspect in more detail the test that has detected censorship we refer to Fig. 4b, where the Empirical Cumulative Distribution Function is drawn of the ratio of each sample content size over the global average. It can be seen that only results for Korea (in dark blue, close to the top border of the graph) are almost completely (0.98%) below the detection threshold (empirically set to 0.3 as for the preceding analyses). All other countries have the almost totality of samples beyond 1.1, with the exception for U.K., U.S.A., and Brazil, with small fraction (less than 0.16) falling just short of the threshold.

These results have not raised a censorship verdict due to the small relative occurrence (pre-filtering data cleansing ignores cases that represent less than 70% of the results). We have manually checked the content and found that corresponds to mobile versions of the requested website. The detection algorithm based on the size ratio has proved robust to content adaptation [13] in this scenario, but further research should be pursued in order to generalize this result.

To validate the censorship verdict, we have manually inspected the returned resource. We have seen that the returned webpage, result of the *HTTP tampering* technique, consists of a single JavaScript section whose effect when interpreted by the browser is to redirect to the address http://warning.or.kr, the official block page of the Korean authority for Internet censorship.

3.3   Censorship in Italy

Internet censorship in Italy is enforced mainly against websites proposing online gaming, betting and copyright infringement. Another significant motivation for censorship is the block of child pornography, but due to ethical issues in potentially involving volunteers in police investigations the latter has not been tested. Thanks to UBICA we could see that no centralized censoring infrastructure is present, as censoring is detected for different ISPs starting and ending at different times, and censoring techniques are sometimes different (in the vast majority DNS hijacking, and case-specific TCP blocking).

The Italian Agency for State Monopolies (AAMS) [1] provides an official list of domains[2] that have been blocked because of infringement of the Italian laws on online gaming and betting (both require a state license). Another -but non official - source is provided by an independent researcher in his "observatory on censorship" website[3] where a list of censored domains together with the authority that issued the censoring order and the date it was issued are reported.

In the case of blocks of websites proposing online gaming and betting the block is explicit (by means of a blockpage), while for websites related to *file sharing* the block is not motivated, resulting in a network error or a website describing a generic error. The censoring technique used most across all the tested ISPs is DNS hijacking, whose effect is graphically shown in Fig. 5 and in which DNS resolution requested to the probe default resolver is compared between probes from inside Italy (red lines) and USA (blue lines).

A few specific examples are described in the following.

Betting and Gaming. The website http://bet365.com will be used as a representative of the *betting and gaming* website class. The results of censorship analysis algorithms for the resource bet365.com is reported in Fig. 6a. We can see that for the ISP "NGI" the percentage of DNS resolutions performed by the probe default resolver is as little as 4.5%. This is reflected by an analogous percentage of content of plausible size. From the same graph it can be seen that also for "Wind Telecomunicazioni" and "Telecom Italia" providers there

---

[1] Amministrazione Autonoma dei Monopoli di Stato, http://eee.aams.gov.it

[2] http://www.aams.gov.it/sites/aams2008/files/documenti_old/private/downloads/ documentazione/scommesse/Elenco_siti_inibiti/elenco_siti_inibiti.rtf

[3] http://censura.bofh.it/elenchi.html

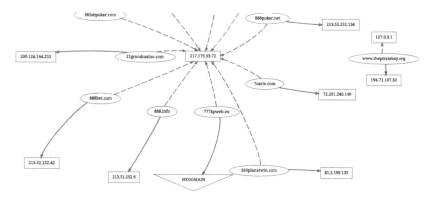

Fig. 5. DNS hijacking in Italy: DNS resolution graph for betting websites. Ellipses contain host names, rectangles contain IP addresses, arrow lines are resolutions requested by probes to their default resolver: for dashed lines probes are inside Italy, while for solid lines the probe is in USA.

are low percentages of plausible DNS resolution (31.2% and 46.1% respectively) and similar percentages of plausible content size (23.8% and 46.1% respectively). Only for the "Center for REsearch And Telecommunication Experimentation" ISP, serviced by the *GARR* [4] , both the DNS resolutions and the downloaded content size are always plausible, showing no censorship on this network for the considered resource.

The verdict for the other ISPs is of *censorship by means of DNS hijacking towards an explicit blockpage*, in fact by comparing the result between the default DNS resolver and the control ones it can be noted that no control DNS is affected.

The reason for the specific kind of DNS hijacking (*blockpage*) is evident when inspecting the results of the DNS analysis, reported as a bar chart in Fig. 6b. Here we can see that for all the three ISPs implementing censorship, the resulting DNS response belongs to the list of known *blockpages*. Thus the adopted censoring technique has the effect of presenting the user with a block webpage explicitly telling him/her of the censorship. From the Fig. 6b it can also be noted that with the exception of "NGI Spa", with 95.4%, no ISP gives percentages close to the totality. The possible causes of this behavior can be: (i) a variability of the censor behavior in the analysis time interval (beginning or ending of censorship); (ii) heterogeneity of the probe environment at a granularity smaller than the *ISP* level. The temporal evolution of the case under description is shown in Fig. 6c. It can be seen that the oscillating results between reachability (upper line) and unreachability is limited to the *default* resolvers (the first two entries in the key, prepended with "DEF:"), while the *control* resolvers always report the domain as uncensored. It can be noted that the default DNS server address - as reported in the DNS reply - corresponds to `localhost`: a local caching application such

---

[4] The "GARR" is the Italian Academic and Research telecommunication network.

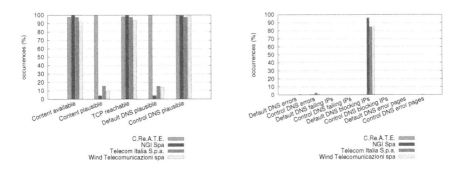

(a) Comparison of censorship techniques   (b) Detail of DNS analysis
per different ISPs

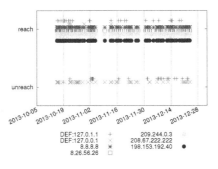

(c) DNS temporal analysis

Fig. 6. Censorship in Italy: gaming and betting websites, the case of bet365.com

as `dnsmasq`[5] is in function on the probe system, preventing the collection of the local default resolver.

Streaming and File Sharing. The second class of websites censored in Italy is constituted by repositories and index directories for file sharing and multimedia streaming. For this class of websites UBICA has reported a much more diverse scenario across the different ISPs; we will describe it in the following taking as an example the index directory http://thepiratebay.sx. The overall behavior of censorship techniques used by different Italian ISPs is summarized in Fig. 7a. Besides the low percentages of *plausible DNS* responses for the default resolver, low percentages are present also for *control* DNS servers. Moreover, differently from the case of betting websites, also the ISP connected through the Academic and Research network GARR presents low percentages (less than 50% for both default and control resolvers, and close to 40% of content availability). Another

---

[5] `dnsmasq` is an open source DNS cache and forwarder, installed by default on several distribution of Linux, including OpenWrt and Ubuntu, main OSes for the UBICA probes. Website: http://www.thekelleys.org.uk/dnsmasq/doc.html

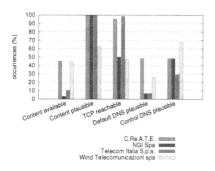
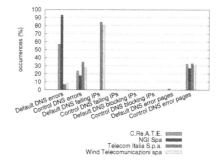

(a) Comparison of results of different techniques

(b) Detail of DNS analysis

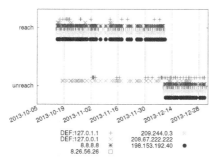

(c) DNS temporal analysis for the "Wind" ISP

Fig. 7. Censorship in Italy: file sharing websites, the case of thepiratebay.sx

notable difference is in the result for TCP reachability: while for the online betting website this measure scored close to 100% reachability for 3 out of 4 ISP (and more than 75% for the remaining one), in the case of the file sharing website 2 ISPs show less than 50% reachability at the TCP level. A more in-depth inspection of the results of DNS tests, reported in Fig. 7b, shows a more diverse condition with respect to the case of betting websites (Fig. 6b).

All the ISPs show different DNS errors, both for default and control DNS servers. One ISP ("Wind Telecomunicazioni") shows a 65.5% responses returning a *failing IP* (127.0.0.1) for the default resolver, and 7.7% of NXDOMAIN or TIMEOUT DNS errors. Different percentages of errors are shown by the other ISPs, each characterized by the presence of multiple symptoms of DNS unreachability in strong discordance with the case of betting websites (each ISP concentrated in one kind of DNS unreachability symptom). The temporal analysis of the DNS measures, represented in the time series of Fig. 7c, helps explaining such combination of results for the "Wind" ISP. In fact, similarly to the case of betting websites (Fig. 6c), there is an oscillation between reachability and unreachability for the default resolvers, spanned over the first half of the timeline, again explainable with the lack of control over the default DNS set for the probe. In this case, however, all the resolvers, no matter if default or control, report unreachability. The unreachability of thepiratebay.sx starting from December 10th 2013 is verified by the probes in *all* the countries, signaling that a server-side event has occurred. From manual check of external information (the news section of the same website, freshly moved to another Top Level Domain: http://thepiratebay.se/blog/234) we can validate the finding of the UBICA platform: the old hostname has been dismissed on December 10th.

4   Conclusions

In this paper we have presented results obtained by means of UBICA (User-based Internet Censorship Analysis), a crowdsourced platform for Internet censorship monitoring. We have ran UBICA for several months on selected targets and we have found evidences of several censorship techniques, such as DNS tampering and content filtering. In this paper we have shown practical results from the following countries: Italy, Pakistan, and South Korea. In these countries we obtained help from local users (and we really thank them) and we validated our analysis using a ground truth built by manual inspection of evidences. We have shown how the UBICA architecture and its main features are able to run an integrated and multi-step analysis to provide a simple but effective dashboard thanks to which censorship events are easily spotted and described also in their temporal evolution. Being based on crowdsourced data and on repeated measurements, the completeness and accuracy of the monitoring depend on user participation: to foster community participation we have provided a lightweight UBICA client for linux platforms and the online access to client reports, both available at http://ubica.comics.unina.it.

References

1. Herdict Project. http://www.herdict.org
2. Anderson, C.: Dimming the internet: Detecting throttling as a mechanism of censorship in iran. arXiv preprint arXiv:1306.4361
3. Chaabane, A., Chen, T., Cunche, M., Decristofaro, E., Friedman, A., Kaafar, M.A., et al.: Censorship in the wild: Analyzing internet filtering in syria. In: ACM SIGCOMM IMC (2014)
4. Chun, B., Culler, D., Roscoe, T., Bavier, A., Peterson, L., Wawrzoniak, M., Bowman, M.: Planetlab: an overlay testbed for broad-coverage services. ACM SIGCOMM Computer Communication Review **33**(3), 3–12 (2003)
5. Clayton, R.C., Murdoch, S.J., Watson, R.N.M.: Ignoring the great firewall of China. In: Danezis, G., Golle, P. (eds.) PET 2006. LNCS, vol. 4258, pp. 20–35. Springer, Heidelberg (2006)
6. Cotton, M., Vegoda, L., Bonica, R., Haberman, B.: Special-Purpose IP Address Registries. RFC 6890 (Best Current Practice), April 2013

7. Dainotti, A., Squarcella, C., Aben, E., Claffy, K.C., Chiesa, M., Russo, M., Pescapé, A.: Analysis of country-wide internet outages caused by censorship. In: SIGCOMM, pp. 1–18. ACM (2011)

8. Dornseif, M.: Government mandated blocking of foreign web content (2003). http://arxiv.org/abs/cs/0404005

9. Eckersley, P.: How unique is your web browser? In: Atallah, M.J., Hopper, N.J. (eds.) PETS 2010. LNCS, vol. 6205, pp. 1–18. Springer, Heidelberg (2010)

10. Filastò, A., Appelbaum, J.: Ooni: Open observatory of network interference. In: USENIX FOCI 2012 (2012)

11. Jones, B., Lee, T.W., Feamster, N., Gill, P.: Automated detection and fingerprinting of censorship block pages. In: ACM SIGCOMM IMC (2014)

12. Khattak, S., Javed, M., Khayam, S.A., Uzmi, Z.A., Paxson, V.: A look at the consequences of internet censorship through an ISP lens. In: ACM SIGCOMM IMC (2014)

13. Md Fudzee, M.F., Abawajy, J.: A classification for content adaptation system. In: iiWAS, pp. 426–429. ACM (2008)

14. Nabi, Z.: The anatomy of web censorship in pakistan. In: USENIX FOCI 2013 (2013)

15. Park, J.C., Crandall, J.R.: Empirical study of a national-scale distributed intrusion detection system: Backbone-level filtering of HTML responses in China. In: ICDCS, pp. 315–326. IEEE (2010)

16. Sfakianakis, A., Athanasopoulos, E., Ioannidis, S.: Censmon: A web censorship monitor. In: USENIX FOCI 2011 (2011)

17. Sundaresan, S., De Donato, W., Feamster, N., Teixeira, R., Crawford, S., Pescapè, A.: Measuring home broadband performance. CACM **55**(11), 100–109 (2012)

18. Verkamp, J.P., Gupta, M.: Inferring Mechanics of Web Censorship Around the World. In: FOCI. USENIX (2012)

19. Xu, X., Mao, Z.M., Halderman, J.A.: Internet censorship in china: where does the filtering occur? In: Spring, N., Riley, G.F. (eds.) PAM 2011. LNCS, vol. 6579, pp. 133–142. Springer, Heidelberg (2011)

How Dangerous Is Internet Scanning?
A Measurement Study of the Aftermath of an Internet-Wide Scan

Elias Raftopoulos[1]([⊠]), Eduard Glatz[1], Xenofontas Dimitropoulos[1,2],
and Alberto Dainotti[3]

[1] ETH Zurich, Zürich, Switzerland
rilias@tik.ee.ethz.ch
[2] FORTH-ICS, Crete, Greece
[3] CAIDA, UC San Diego, San Diego, USA

Abstract. Internet scanning is a de facto background traffic noise that is not clear if it poses a dangerous threat, i.e., what happens to scanned hosts? what is the success rate of scanning? and whether the problem is worth investing significant effort and money on mitigating it, e.g., by filtering unwanted traffic? In this work we take a first look into Internet scanning from the point of view of scan repliers using a unique combination of data sets which allows us to estimate how many hosts replied to scanners and whether they were subsequently attacked in an actual network. To contain our analysis, we focus on a specific interesting scanning event that was orchestrated by the Sality botnet during February 2011 which scanned the entire IPv4 address space. By analyzing unsampled NetFlow records, we show that 2 % of the scanned hosts actually replied to the scanners. Moreover, by correlating scan replies with IDS alerts from the same network, we show that significant exploitation activity followed towards the repliers, which eventually led to an estimated 8 % of compromised repliers. These observations suggest that Internet scanning is dangerous: in our university network, at least 142 scanned hosts were eventually compromised. World-wide, the number of hosts that were compromised in response to the studied event is likely much larger.

Keywords: Botnet characterization · Network scanning · IDS · Netflow

1 Introduction

Botnets of up to millions of compromised computers are presently the most widely-used cyberweapon for executing criminal activities, such as fraud, sensitive data leakage, distributed denial-of-service attacks, and spam. Botnets engage into large-scale scanning to enumerate vulnerable hosts for targeted criminal activities or simply propagation [6,26]. A recent study showed that scanning accounts for 34-67% of all connection attempts in an academic ISP [15]. Besides, recent advances in scanning software make it possible to scan the entire IPv4 address space in

© IFIP International Federation for Information Processing 2015
M. Steiner et al. (Eds.): TMA 2015, LNCS 9053, pp. 158–172, 2015.
DOI: 10.1007/978-3-319-17172-2_11

less than 45 minutes [10], simplifying further the execution of aggressive scanning attacks. In spite of the prevalence of scanning, it is difficult to assess how dangerous it is, i.e., is it simply an innocent background traffic noise or a dangerous threat that is worth investing effort and money for blocking it?

In this work we take a novel look into Internet scanning from the point of view of scan repliers. We combine unsampled Netflow records and IDS alerts collected from a university network to assess the aftermath of a specific scanning event. In particular, we focus on the "sipscan", an Internet-wide scanning event orchestrated from the Sality botnet over 12 days in February 2011 that was analyzed by Dainotti et al. [9]. This event had several interesting characteristics: 1) it used a well-orchestrated stealth scanning strategy; 2) it originated from 3 million IP addresses; 3) it is believed that it scanned the entire Internet address space; and 4) it targeted Session Initiation Protocol (SIP) [25] servers.

We show that this scanning event escalated into persistent exploitation attempts towards the hosts that replied to the sipscan. We use our data to assess the effectiveness of scanning in terms of scan repliers and hosts that were eventually compromised. We find that 2% of the scanned IP addresses replied and at least 8% of the repliers were eventually compromised. Besides, our analysis shows that scanners originated primarily from Eastern countries, while the subsequent exploitation attempts originated from Western countries. This suggests that information about scan repliers was communicated to the subsequent attackers (likely through underground channels). Moreover, we observe 352,350 new scanner IP addresses and show that the sipscan was largely undetected by the IDS used in the observed network, which only raised alerts for 4% of the scan probes.

In summary, our work makes the following contributions:

- We conduct a first measurement study about Internet scanning focusing on scan repliers and the aftermath of scanning.
- We show that significant exploitation activity followed a specific scanning event and estimate the success rate.
- We provide new insights about Internet scanning and the sipscan: 1) we observe a segregation of roles between scanners and exploiters; and 2) that the sipscan originated from 352,350 new IP addresses.

The rest of the paper is structured as follows. We first discuss related research in Section 2. In Section 3 we describe the used data-sets. Then, Section 4 presents how unsampled NetFlow records were used to detect the sipscan and measure scan repliers. Then, in Section 5 we characterize the exploitation activity that followed based on our IDS data. Finally, Section 6 discusses the impact of false-positive IDS alerts on our analysis and Section 7 concludes our paper.

2   Related Work

A long line of measurement studies has analyzed botnets over the last years, following their evolution from centralized IRC-based [7,8] to fully decentralized C&C architectures [17]. The goal of these efforts has been to characterize botnet activities [24], analyze C&C communication methods [8], and estimate the respective botnet size and geographical properties [27]. Their observations have been used to fine tune network defences [14] and tailor novel detection mechanisms [16].

One of the most integral aspects of botnet activity is scanning. Since scanning is widespread [15] and regularly captured by monitoring infrastructures [5,7], it is imperative for security analysts to have a measure regarding its severity and impact on the victim population. However, few studies have focused on the probing characteristics of botnets. In [28] Paxson *et al.* analyzed traffic captured at honeynets in order to study the statistical properties of 22 large-scale scanning events. In a followup study, Li *et al.* [20] extracted botnet scan traffic from honeynet data and used it to infer general properties of botnets, such as population characteristics, blacklisting effectiveness, dynamics of new bot arrivals and scanning strategies. Finally, Yegneswaran *et al.* [7] analyzed the source code of a widely-used botnet malware, revealing the scanning capabilities of basic IRC bots.

Most related to our work, Dainotti *et al* [9] discovered an interesting stealthy scan of the entire IPv4 address space that was carried out by the Sality botnet and analyzed the different phases of the event. However, this study was based solely on packet traces collected at the UCSD network telescope and does not provide insights regarding the effectiveness of scanning and its followup activity. In our work, we detect the sipscan in a large ISP with live hosts, identify the set of hosts that replied to scanners, and analyze the targeted exploitation activity that followed. This way, we provide new insights about the escalation of this event and the effectiveness of scanning in terms of turnover.

3   Monitoring Infrastructure and Data Collection

In this section, we describe the monitored network and the data we use in this study. We collected our measurements from the network of the main campus of the Swiss Federal Institute of Technology at Zurich (ETH Zurich). The ETH Zurich network is large and diverse. During our data collection period, which spanned 5 months (between the 1st January and the 31th of May 2011), we observed in total 79,821 internal hosts. On these hosts, the IT policy grants full freedom to users regarding the software and services they can use.

We select two data sources that provide complementary views into the studied event. First, we collect unsampled NetFlow data from the only upstream provider of ETH Zurich. Netflow produces summary records for *all* flows crossing the monitoring point. However, Netflow lacks context, since it does not provide information regarding the type of activity that triggered a flow. To fill this gap, we use

IDS data collected from a Snort sensor, which captures and analyzes all traffic crossing our infrastructure's border router. Snort uses signature-based payload matching to perform protocol analysis, revealing more information about the type of activity that triggered an observed packet sequence. The two passive monitoring data sets complement each other, since they capture flow summaries for all traffic and finer (payload/header) details for packets that trigger IDS signatures. A detailed description of our data collection methodology can be found in our accompanying technical report [11].

4 Sipscan Detection

To extract sipscan traffic from NetFlow data, we rely on heuristics introduced by Dainotti *et al.* [9], which are based on the analysis of the payload of sipscan packets. However, because flow data do not include packet payload contents, we adapted the extraction rules. We focus on the UDP part of sipscan traffic, which is sufficient to detect sipscan activity and identify sipscan sources. Specifically, we identify a sipscan flow as a single-packet one-way flow towards port 5060/udp having a size in the range of 382 to 451 bytes.

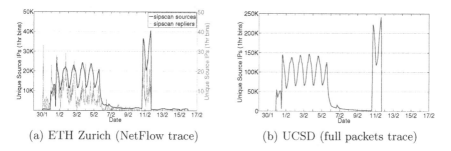

(a) ETH Zurich (NetFlow trace)   (b) UCSD (full packets trace)

Fig. 1. Number of IP addresses per hour sourcing or replying to scan flows in ETH Zurich and in the UCSD network telescope

In Figure 1a, we highlight how the host population sourcing attacks towards the SIP service port evolved over 16.7 days (from 31/01/2011 to 16/02/2011). In Figure 1b, we illustrate how the same event was captured by the UCSD network telescope. Note that Dainotti *et al.* [9] used full packet traces collected at the network telescope in order to estimate the scanning population. The similarity in these two patterns, indicates that our heuristic adapted to Netflow records, is able to capture the same phenomenon as seen on our network. We observe two major sipscan outbreaks in terms of participating attackers along with a minor fraction of hosts engaged continuously in SIP scanning. The first outbreak starts at 2011.01.31 21:30 UTC and lasts until approximately 2011.02.06 22:40, while the second outbreak starts at 2011.02.11 14:10 and lasts until 2011.02.12

15:00 UTC. In total, 952,652 scanners participated in the scan. A significant number (352,350) of hosts targeting our infrastructure were not observed in the population of Sality scanners detected by the UCSD network telescope, which were 2,954,108 [9]. This finding indicates that the size (expressed in terms of source IP addresses) of the botnet was at least 11.9% larger than the lower bound estimated in the previous work. At the victim side, 77,158 hosts within ETH Zurich were scanned at least once during the 16.7 days period, meaning that the coverage of the scan in our infrastructure was 96.6%. The scan was largely stealthy, in terms of generated alerts from the IDS, since only 4% of the respective probing flows triggered a scan-related IDS signature.

In contrast to [9], our data set allows us to identify those target hosts that reply to the sender of a sipscan flow. For this purpose, we search for two-way flows matching a relaxed filter (i.e., requiring port 5060/UDP only). Additionally, we look at the number of attacker-victim host pairs where a sipscan flow is answered with an ICMP flow. For this answer type, we see a weak correlation of ICMP flow counts with the two sipscan outbreaks. On the other hand, when looking at host pairs where we have biflows, we observe a strong correlation of biflow counts with the sipscan outbreaks indicating that sipscan attacks significantly result in bidirectional communication between attacker and victim. In Figure 1a we present the number of unique internal IP source addresses responding to the sipscan. In total, we identify 1,748 sipscan repliers, whereas during the scan we find 3.8 new unique internal IPs responding to the scan every hour. For 80.2% of the repliers we detected a TCP reply originating from the respective host, whereas for 8.3% of the repliers, the sipscan was answered with an ICMP flow. 0.2% of the replies involved both a TCP and an ICMP flow, while the remaining 11.5% used neither TCP or ICMP.

5   Aftermath of the Sipscan

5.1   Inbound Exploitation Attempts

In this section, we study the impact of the sipscan on the target host population within ETH Zurich. We first investigate if scanning was a precursor of subsequent exploitation attempts targeting hosts that replied to the scanners. Recall that our IDS data cover 5 months, including one month before the beginning of the sipscan (31/01/2011) and approximately 3.5 months after its end (16/02/2011).

In Figure 2a, we show how the daily number of exploitation alerts per target host triggered by inbound traffic changed after the sipscan. We consider alerts of the VRT rule sets *exploit.rules*, *exploit-kit.rules*, and *indicator-shellcode.rules* and of the ET rule set *emerging-exploit.rules*. These rule sets [11] are tailored to detect exploit activity, including buffer overflow attacks, remote command execution, brute force authorization and privilege escalation attempts. In Figure 2a, we also show the daily number of exploitation alerts per target host for the *baseline*, i.e., the ETH Zurich hosts that did not reply to the scanners according to our data. The *baseline* accounts for 78,073 hosts, whereas the number of sipscan

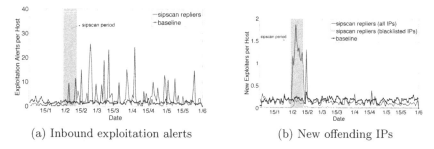

(a) Inbound exploitation alerts   (b) New offending IPs

Fig. 2. Daily number of inbound exploitation alerts and new offending IPs per target host over a period of 5 months. The shaded region marks the duration of the sipscan.

repliers is 1,748. In the pre-sipscan period sipscan repliers were involved on average in 122 exploitation alerts per day. During the sipscan period we see that this number increases to 842 alerts per day, whereas after the sipscan it remains high at 931 alerts per day. In sharp contrast, the inbound exploitation activity associated with the *baseline* remains low after the sipscan. On average, each host is a target to 1.2 alerts per day, which is a baseline noise caused by automated threats attempting to propagate and false alerts. The respective noise level for the sipscan repliers in the pre-sipscan period is 0.4 alerts per day. After the sipscan, this number increases to 3.7 alerts per day. The high number of exploitation alerts towards sipscan repliers persists even 4 months after the end of the sipscan, although it is more intense during the first two months (from 31/1 to 28/2), when 68% of the total exploitation alerts are triggered. Out of the 1,748 sipscan repliers, we observe that 852 were involved in inbound exploitation alerts.

Next, we study whether the observed increase in exploitation activity comes from new offenders. Figure 2b illustrates the daily number of new offending IP addresses per target host for sipscan repliers and for the baseline. We report IP addresses that appear in exploitation alerts, however we consider an address new only when it has not previously appeared in the entire alert trace. A baseline host records a new external attacker approximately every four days consistently throughout the 5-month period. However, this number increases sharply for sipscan repliers during the sipscan, when each victim is attacked on average by 1.4 new IP addresses per day. Moreover, we investigate whether these IP addresses are known blacklisted hosts using four public blacklists [1–4]. Figure 2b shows that only 7% of the new offenders were already blacklisted, while this number drops to almost 0 before and after the sipscan period.

In addition, we explore how persistent the attacking hosts are in terms of generated exploitation alerts, and examine whether the attackers targeting the sipscan repliers are more persistent compared to the ones targeting the baseline. In Figure 3a, we compare the average number of exploitation alerts per target for sipscan repliers and baseline attackers, respectively. We see that the former group tends to be more persistent triggering in the median case 4 exploitation alerts per target, whereas the same number for the latter group is 2 alerts. The

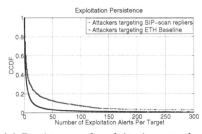
(a) Persistence of exploitation attackers

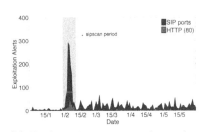
(b) Exploitation attempt alert volume

Fig. 3. Persistence of exploitation attackers and alert volume for exploitation attempts targeting SIP related ports

Table 1. Top 10 countries used by the sipscanners compared to the respective countries for exploitation attack originators. Geo location data for sipscan sources and exploitation attack originators was obtained using the MaxMind GeoIP Lite Database[21].

	sipscanners CAIDA		*sipscanners ETH*		*Exploiters ETH*	
Rank	%	Country	%	Country	%	Country
1	12.55	Turkey	10.06	Indonesia	27.11	United States
2	12.54	India	9.72	Turkey	12.70	Canada
3	8.64	Brazil	7.32	China	9.90	China
4	7.23	Egypt	6.86	Brazil	7.01	Switzerland
5	5.77	Indonesia	6.52	Egypt	4.98	Germany
6	5.59	Romania	5.94	India	4.78	Taiwan
7	5.58	Russian Federation	4.80	Thailand	4.31	Japan
8	5.36	Vietnam	4.06	Philippines	3.31	India
9	5.10	Thailand	3.71	Russian Federation	2.95	Russian Federation
10	3.01	Ukraine	3.20	Romania	2.88	Brazil

increased persistence towards sipscan repliers is more prominent in the tails of the distributions. We see that the top 10% most active attackers towards sipscan repliers launch up to 73 alerts on average per target, whereas the respective number for the baseline is only 21 alerts.

We also investigate the similarity between the IP addresses of scanners (extracted from NetFlow) and of exploiters (extracted from Snort alerts towards sipscan repliers). Surprisingly, we observe that out of 6,676 exploiter and 1.3 million scanner IP addresses, only 17 are in common. This suggests that there is a clear separation between scanners and bots wielded to exploit target hosts. In Table 1, we compare the geographical distribution of the scanners detected in our infrastructure and in the UCSD network telescope [9] with the exploiters targeting the ETH Zurich sipscan repliers. The geographical distribution of scanners seen in the UCSD network telescope and in ETH Zurich is very similar with the exception of China. In our data set China is a significant source of SIP scanning accounting for 7.32% of the total scanners population. On the UCSD data set China is ranked 27th. More importantly, the geographical distribution of exploiters is particularly interesting, since it is dominated by Western countries and United States in particular, which is the most strongly represented country with 27.11% of the exploiters. In contrast, the geographical distribution of scanners is dominated by Eastern countries. US is not sourcing sipscanning, which is remarkable since the analysis of the botnet has shown a strong presence in the United States [13]. This observation shows that information about scan repliers was communicated from scanning to attacking bots through unknown channels.

Finally, we examine the exploitation activity on port numbers related to SIP. Figure 3b shows the number of exploitation alerts targeting sipscan repliers on ports 5060, 5061, 5070 and 80. Ports 5060, 5061 and 5070 are used by SIP for control and data traffic. Moreover, the sipscan binary attempts to open a connection and gain administration privileges on port 80, where an HTTP server may provide remote administration to SIP servers [12]. Figure 3b shows a sharp increase of exploitation activity targeting SIP ports during and after the sipscan. Before, the sipscan we observe on a daily basis less than 12 exploitation alerts targeting SIP ports and 3 alerts targeting port 80. During the sipscan period, these numbers jump to 135 and 27, respectively, exhibiting approximately a ten-fold increase. Moreover, during the sipscan period 22% of all inbound exploitation alerts are on SIP ports. In the post-scan period we observe that these values drop, but still remain significant compared to the pre-sipscan period. Specifically, the daily number of exploitation alerts targeting SIP ports and port 80 are 5 and 21, respectively.

To summarize the key findings of this section, we first observe a steep increase in exploitation alerts against sipscan repliers right after the sipscan, which is associated only with sipscan repliers and not with other hosts in the monitored infrastructure. Second, we observe that the attackers associated with the increase appear for the first time during the sipscan and were not active before. Third, we observe a sharp increase in exploitation alerts towards SIP ports and show that these exploitation attempts happen in close temporal proximity to the sipscan. We believe these findings constitute sufficient evidence that the sipscan was the precursor of a subsequent large-scale exploitation activity targeting sipscan repliers.

5.2   Sality Alert Classification and Outbound Exploitation Activity

In Sections 4 and 5.1, we analyzed the inbound scanning and exploitation activity towards the monitored network. In this section, we shift our attention to IDS alerts raised by outbound traffic originated by sipscan repliers, and analyze the new behavioral patterns that emerge. A comprehensive overview of the activity exhibited by the Sality bot based on the forensics investigation of compromised hosts can be found in our technical report [11].

In Table 2, we list the Snort identifiers (SIDs) and their official short description for relevant signatures that are triggered in our data. To compile the list, we manually analyzed the outbound alerts generated by sipscan repliers. We found the new types of alerts that emerged in the post-scan period and inspected their signatures in order to identify specific behaviors. We group signatures into four categories shown in Table 2.

Table 2. Snort signatures related to Sality bot lifecycle

SID	Signature Description
	[C&C Communication] Communication with botnet controller.
2404138:2404156	ET DROP Known Bot C&C Server Traffic TCP/UDP
2000348	ET ATTACK_RESPONSE IRC - Channel JOIN on non-std port
2000334	ET P2P BitTorrent peer sync
2009971	ET P2P eMule KAD Network Hello Request
2008581	ET P2p BitTorrent DHT ping Outbound
2010142	ET P2P Vuze BT UDP Connection Outbound
2008584	ET P2P BitTorrent DHT announce_peers request
2181	P2P BitTorrent transfer
	[Exfiltration] Possible leakage of sensitive user data.
5	SENSITIVE-DATA Email Addresses Outbound
2006380	ET Policy Outgoing Basic Auth Base64 HTTP Password detected unencrypted
2010784	ET CHAT Facebook Chat POST Outbound
2000347	ET ATTACK_RESPONSE IRC - Private message on non-std port
1463	CHAT IRC message Outbound
	[Propagation] Attempted infection of vulnerable hosts.
2007695,2008070	ET User-Agent Malware overflow attempt
4060	POLICY RDP attempted administrator connection request
2006546	ET SCAN LibSSH Based SSH Connection - BruteForce Attack
2002383	ET SCAN Potential FTP Brute-Force attempt
3817	TFTP GET transfer mode overflow attempt
2010643	ET SCAN Multiple FTP Administrator Login Attempts- Brute Force Attempt
2001972	ET SCAN Behavioral Unusually fast Terminal Server Traffic, Potential Scan or Infection
2001569	ET SCAN Behavioral Unusual Port 445 traffic
	[Egg Download] Possible download of malicious executable.
2009897	ET MALWARE Possible Windows Executable sent when remote host claims to send a Text File
19270	POLICY attempted download of a PDF with embedded Javascript
15306	WEB-CLIENT Portable Executable binary file transfer
2003546	ET USER Agents Suspicious User agent Downloader
2007577	ET TROJAN General Downloader Checkin URL
2012648	ET Policy Dropbox Client Downloading Executable
2009301	ET Policy Megaupload file download service access

Signatures in the group *C&C Communication* detect the activity triggered by a bot when calling its controller for instructions. In the case of the HTTP version of the Sality bot, the signatures in the SID range *(2404138:2404156)* are triggered when a set of known blacklisted C&C servers are contacted, whereas the signature *(2000348)* detects the setup of an IRC channel, which is used by the bot and the controller to communicate. The remaining alerts are related to the P2P version of the bot and are triggered when the bot is either attempting to join the P2P network, instantiating a new P2P connection, or fetching the latest peers list.

Signatures in the group *Exfiltration* are tailored to detect the exfiltration of confidential data. The SIDs *(5,2006380)* are triggered when passwords or email addresses are sent from the intranet unencrypted. The signature *(2010784)* is triggered when the bot is attempting to leak sensitive information using Facebook's POST mechanism. This alert should be expected to generate a significant amount of false positives, since it is also triggered when a user sends a legitimate Facebook message. However, a sudden sharp increase in the amount of Facebook POST operations could signify a malicious activity. The signatures with SIDs *(2000347,1463)* are triggered when information is exfiltrated using an IRC channel.

Signatures in the group *Propagation* are generated when the bot is attempting to infect exposed vulnerable hosts. The main targeted vulnerabilities are the MS-LSASS buffer overflow and the MS-WebDav vulnerability related to services used for accessing remote network shares. The set of signatures shown in Table 2 are fine-tuned to detect brute force privilege escalation attacks (*4060,2006546, 2002383,2010643*), buffer overflow exploitation attempts (*2007695,2008070, 3817*), and targeted scanning on these services (*2001972 ,2001569*).

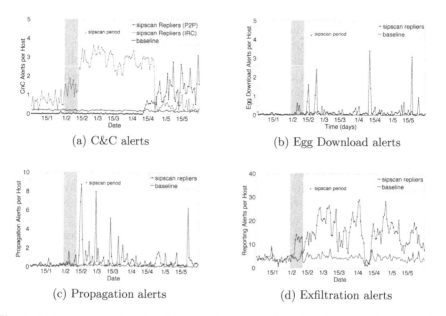

(a) C&C alerts

(b) Egg Download alerts

(c) Propagation alerts

(d) Exfiltration alerts

Fig. 4. Daily number of different types of alerts per host for sipscan repliers and for baseline hosts over a period of 5 months

Finally, signatures in the group *Egg Download* correspond to attempts made by the bot to fetch a malicious binary from a remote domain. The downloaded executable can be either an update of Sality's own code or can correspond to a new malware pushed to the infected population. Signatures with SIDs (*15306,2003546,2007577*) detect the activity of Sality's downloader module when attempting to check a suspicious URL or when a binary download is initiated. Sality tries to obfuscate the downloaded binary by hiding it in seemingly legitimate files, such as Text and PDF documents. This activity is detected by signatures with SIDs (*2009897,19270*). The obfuscation is used to evade detection by cloud providers, such as Dropbox and Megaupload, which are exploited in order to host the malicious content. Signatures with SIDs (*2012648,2009301*) detect the download of executables from these sites.

Figure 4a shows the average number of C&C alerts triggered by sipscan repliers and baseline hosts. For sipscan repliers, we differentiate between IRC and P2P C&C alerts, whereas for the baseline we include both types of alerts. After the sipscan, we see a sharp increase in the IRC C&C alerts, which indicates that hosts are attempting to contact known malicious IRC servers operating as controllers. This behavior continues for approximately two months, during which we see daily on average 2.4 C&C alerts per sipscan replier. However, on April 11 (day 111) there is a clear shift in the pattern of triggered signatures: the volume of IRC alerts suddenly drops, while the volume of P2P alerts rises. This signifies a likely upgrade in the mode of C&C communication of the Sality botnet.

Figure 4b illustrates the daily number of *Egg Download* alerts per sipscan replier and baseline host. After the sipscan, we observe 4 malware downloading spikes, during which the daily alert count ranges from 1.6 to 3.4 per sipscan replier. The spike that occurs on April 11 (day 111), seems to be associated with the shift in the communication method used to contact the controller shown in Figure 4a. We believe that during that event the Sality botnet pushed a major update to the infected population, upgrading itself from the centralized HTTP to the fully decentralized P2P version.

In Figure 4c, we show the daily number of *Propagation* alerts per local host for sipscan repliers and baseline hosts. We see that after the sipscan the number of outbound exploitation attempts originating from the sipscan repliers increases drastically, exhibiting an average daily value of 1.2 alerts per host compared to only 0.21 alerts per baseline host. The most dominant alerts of this group are the privilege escalation attempts with SIDs *(4060,2006546,2002383,2010643)* accounting for 72% of the observed activity.

Finally, Figure 4d illustrates the daily number of information leakage alerts per local host for sipscan repliers and baseline hosts. Again we see a sharp increase in the number of exfiltration alerts for sipscan repliers in the post-sipscan period, where the daily average increases from 4.7 to 18.2 alerts per host. The triggered alerts are dominated by the signature *ET CHAT Facebook Chat POST Outbound*, which accounts for 83% of all alerts. However, this signature is also triggered by legitimate user activity and may introduce a significant number of false positives. This is reflected in the high baseline in the pre-sipscan period, which accounts on average for 4.7 alerts per host. Although the baseline for this alert group is high, we can still see a clear increase in the post-sipscan period when its alert volume quadruples. Summarizing the key finding, we discovered major changes in the alert patterns of sipscan repliers that correlate with the behavior of the Sality bot.

5.3   Sality-Bot Infections

In this section, we build a heuristic to identify this behavioral shift and extract likely Sality infections. We use our heuristic to conservatively estimate a lower bound on the success rate of the sipscan in terms of infected hosts. Note, that we do not have the goal to build a general purpose detector, but rather a systematic way to identify infected sipscan repliers in the monitored network.

Our heuristic is summarized in Algorithm 1. We focus on sipscan repliers that were subsequently attacked. Then we find repliers that exhibit a persistent increase in outbound exploitation activity for the four signature classes listed in Table 2, while their respective activity in the pre-sipscan period is low. In particular, for the four classes in Table 2, we first compute the number of alerts per day each internal host generates. Our heuristic then finds and keeps hosts that trigger in the pre-sipscan period fewer alerts per day than the corresponding baseline of that day plus a tolerance of 1.5× the inter-quartile range of the baseline. If a host has more alerts per day even for a single day, then it is discarded from further consideration because it is either already infected or it generates a large number of false positives. Second, our heuristic makes the same comparison in the post-sipscan period. If the daily alert count is consistently above the tolerance threshold, then it constitutes an indication of compromise activity. To assess whether this increase persists, we count the number of daily bins where it is above the threshold and tolerate only 5% of the post-sipscan bins where this condition is not met. We consider only the bins in which a host has generated at least one alert of any type.

Input:
B_T^S : mean count of S type alerts generated by Baseline hosts on day T
I_T^S : IQR of S type alerts generated by Baseline hosts on day T
R_T^S : mean count of S type alerts generated by sipscan repliers on day T
S={CnC Communication, Reporting, Propagation, Egg Download}
Result: Returns *true* if the examined host is infected, *false* otherwise.
foreach *alert type S* **do**
    $BelowThreshCount = 0$;
    for $T_i = 1{:}T_{max}$ **do**
        if *isHostActiveAt(*T_i*)* eq false **then**   *next;*;
        $SignificanceThresh = B_{T_i}^S + 1.5 * I_{T_i}^S$;
        if $T_i \le T_{scan}$ **then**
            if $R_{T_i}^S > SignificanceThresh$ **then**
                 return *false*;
            end
        else
            if $R_{T_i}^S \le SignificanceThresh$ **then**
                $BelowThreshCount += 1$;
            end
        end
        if $BelowThreshCount/(T_{max} - T_{scan}) > 0.05$ **then**
             return *false*;
        end
    end
end
return *true*;

Algorithm 1. Pseudo-code for identifying Sality-bot infections

---

Our heuristic takes a conservative approach by introducing several conditions to make a Sality infection assessment. It is possible, however, that a Sality bot exhibits some of the post-sipscan behaviors presented in Section 5.2, but not all. For example, some examined hosts show persistent signs of C&C communication and attempts to propagate, but do not attempt to leak data. Others attempt to exfiltrate data, but do not frequently visit malicious domains to fetch malware. By tailoring our heuristic to only make an assessment if all alert types in the post-sipscan period exhibit a persistent increase, we attempt to minimize possible false positives even if we introduce a number of false negatives. This way, we believe we can estimate a lower bound of the Sality infections that occurred in our infrastructure.

Our heuristic identified a total of 142 Sality infections in our IDS data set. In the first stage of reconnaissance, 77,158 exposed ETH Zurich IPs were scanned. Out of these only 1,748 (2%) hosts replied to the scanners. Almost half of the sipscan repliers, specifically 48%, were subsequently the targets of inbound exploitation attacks. Based on our heuristic we identified that 142 hosts showed persistent signs of infection during the post-sipscan period. Therefore, the sipscan turnover, i.e. the percentage of hosts that were infected out of the sipscan repliers, was 8%.

6   Discussion about IDS False Positives

The quality of IDS alerts we study in Section 5 heavily relies on the accuracy of the inferences made by the Snort sensor deployed in our infrastructure. Snort has been criticized for generating an excessive number of false positives, often exceeding 99% [18,19]. Such high false positive rates can introduce significant bias in our measurements, resulting in skewed results. However, in this work we have focused on signatures which, based on our previous work [22,23], were shown to be reliable, generating only a small number of false positives. Specifically, in [22] we performed a thorough evaluation of the alerts being triggered by Snort in our infrastructure and identified signatures that generate a large number of false positives. These alerts have been excluded from the current work. Moreover, in [23] we introduced a complexity criterion to evaluate the effectiveness of a Snort signature in terms of correctly identifying malicious activity. The alerts analyzed in Section 5 are triggered by highly complex signatures, which our analysis in [23] has shown to be more reliable, generating a low number of false positives.

7   Conclusions

In this work, we analyzed the aftermath of an Internet-wide scanning event [9] in a university network focusing on scan repliers. Using a unique combination of unsampled Netflow records and IDS alerts we found that the sipscan was followed by significant exploitation activity that led to at least 142 infected hosts in the studied network and likely many more worldwide. The effectiveness of scanning in terms of targeted hosts that replied and repliers that were eventually compromised was 2% and at least 8%, respectively. We also observed a segregation of roles between scanners and exploiters, which originated from different geographical locations. We therefore conclude that Internet scanning is dangerous as it leads to many compromised hosts. Understanding how these observations differ across networks and scanning events is an interesting subject for future research.

References

1. Anonymous postmasters early warning system. http://www.apews.org
2. Dshield: Internet storm center (2014). http://www.dshield.org/
3. Shadowserver foundation (2014). https://www.shadowserver.org/
4. Threatexpert - automated threat analysis (2014). http://www.threatexpert.com/
5. Bacher, P., Holz, T., Kotter, M., Wicherski, G.: Know your enemy: Tracking botnets (2008). http://www.honeynet.org/papers/bots
6. Bailey, M., Cooke, E., Jahanian, F., Xu, Y., Karir, M.: A survey of botnet technology and defenses. In: CATCH 2009, Washington, District of Columbia, USA (2009)
7. Barford, P., Yegneswaran, V.: An inside look at botnets. In: Malware Detection, Advances in Information Security, vol. 27 (2007)
8. Cooke, E., Jahanian, F., Mcpherson, D.: The zombie roundup: Understanding, detecting, and disrupting botnets, pp. 39–44 (2005)
9. Dainotti, A., King, A., Claffy, K., Papale, F., Pescap, A.: Analysis of a "/0" stealth scan from a botnet. In: ACM IMC 2012 (2012)
10. Durumeric,Z., Wustrow, E., Halderman, J.A.: ZMap: fast internet-wide scanning and its securityapplications. In: USENIX 2013 (2013)
11. Dimitropoulos, X., Raftopoulos, E., Glatz, E., Dainotti, A.: The days after a "/0" scan from the sality botnet (2014), Technical Report 358. http://www.csg.ethz.ch/people/rilias/publications/Sality_RaDi14.pdf
12. Falliere, N.: A distributed cracker for voip (2011)
13. Falliere, N.: Sality: Story of a peer-to-peer viral network (2011)
14. Freiling, F.C., Holz, T., Wicherski, G.: Botnet Tracking: Exploring a Root-Cause Methodology to Prevent Distributed Denial-of-Service Attacks (2005)
15. Glatz, E., Dimitropoulos, X.: Classifying internet one-way traffic. In: Proc. of the 2012 ACM Conf. on Internet Measurement. ACM, NY (2012)
16. Gu, G., Junjie, Z., Lee, W.: BotSniffer: detecting botnet command and control channels in network traffic. In: NSDI (2008)
17. Holz, T., Steiner, M., Dahl, F., Biersack, E., Freiling, F.: Measurements and mitigation of peer-to-peer-based botnets: a casestudy on storm worm. In: LEET 2008 (2008)
18. Julisch, K., Dacier, M.: Mining intrusion detection alarms for actionable knowledge. In: The 8th ACM Conference on Knowledge Discovery and Data Mining
19. Kruegel, C., Robertson, W.: Alert verification - determining the success of intrusion attempts. In: DIMVA (2004)
20. Li, Z., Goyal, A., Chen, Y., Paxson, V.: Towards situational awareness of large-scale botnet probing events. Transactions on Information Forensics and Security
21. MaxMind Lite. http://dev.maxmind.com/geoip/legacy/geolite/
22. Raftopoulos, E., Dimitropoulos, X.: Detecting, validating and characterizing computer infections in the wild. In: Proceedings of IMC (2011)
23. Raftopoulos, E., Dimitropoulos, X.: A quality metric for ids signatures: In the wild the size matters. EURASIP Journal on Information Security
24. Rajab, M.A., Zarfoss, J., Monrose, F., Terzis, A.: A multifaceted approach to understanding the botnet phenomenon. In: Proc. of the ACM IMC 2006 Conference (2006)
25. Rosenberg, J., Schulzrinne, H., Camarillo, G., Johnston, A., Peterson, J., Sparks, R., Handley, M., Schooler, E.: Sip: Session initiation protocol (2002)

26. Shin, S., Lin, R., Gu, G.: Cross-analysis of botnet victims: new insights and impli-
    cations. In: Sommer, R., Balzarotti, D., Maier, G. (eds.) RAID 2011. LNCS, vol.
    6961, pp. 242–261. Springer, Heidelberg (2011)
27. Stone-gross, B., Cova, M., Cavallaro, L., Gilbert, B., Szydlowski, M., Kemmerer,
    R., Kruegel, C., Vigna, G.: Your botnet is my botnet: Analysis of a botnet takeover
28. Yegneswaran, V., Barford, P., Paxson, V.: Using honeynets for internet situational
    awareness. In: HotNets IV (2005)

Investigating the Nature of Routing Anomalies: Closing in on Subprefix Hijacking Attacks

Johann Schlamp[1]([✉]), Ralph Holz[2], Oliver Gasser[1], Andreas Korsten[1],
Quentin Jacquemart[3], Georg Carle[1], and Ernst W. Biersack[3]

[1] Technische Universität München, München, Germany
{schlamp,korsten,carle,gasser}@net.in.tum.de
[2] NICTA, Sydney, Australia
Ralph.Holz@nicta.com.au
[3] Eurecom Sophia Antipolis, Biot, France
{jacquemart,biersack}@eurecom.fr

Abstract. The detection of BGP hijacking attacks has been at the focus of research for more than a decade. However, state-of-the-art techniques fall short of detecting subprefix hijacking, where smaller parts of a victim's networks are targeted by an attacker. The analysis of corresponding routing anomalies, so-called subMOAS events, is tedious since these anomalies are numerous and mostly have legitimate reasons.

In this paper, we propose, implement and test a new approach to investigate subMOAS events. Our method combines input from several data sources that can reliably disprove malicious intent. First, we make use of the database of a Internet Routing Registry (IRR) to derive business relations between the parties involved in a subMOAS event. Second, we use a topology-based reasoning algorithm to rule out subMOAS events caused by legitimate network setups. Finally, we use Internet-wide network scans to identify SSL-enabled hosts in a large number of subnets. Where we observe that public/private key pairs do not change during an event, we can eliminate the possibility of an attack. We can show that subprefix announcements with multiple origins are harmless for the largest part. This significantly reduces the search space in which we need to look for hijacking attacks.

1 Introduction

Autonomous Systems (ASes) use the Border Gateway Protocol (BGP) to propagate information about paths to certain destinations. Despite being vital to traffic forwarding on the Internet, BGP does not feature any security mechanisms like origin or neighbor authentication. Reports such as [1,2,8,11] have shown that attacks do occur and are real threats. Systems like S-BGP [5] and RPKI [4] have been developed to add integrity protection and origin authentication to BGP. However, due to the considerable resources needed to deploy them, they are not widely used. Consequently, a number of mechanisms to (at least) detect attacks on BGP have been developed [7,9,12,14,15]. Although they are

© IFIP International Federation for Information Processing 2015
M. Steiner et al. (Eds.): TMA 2015, LNCS 9053, pp. 173–187, 2015.
DOI: 10.1007/978-3-319-17172-2_12

able to detect certain attacks like the hijacking of entire IP prefixes, they suffer from relatively high rates of false-positive alarms.

In this paper, we investigate a particularly interesting phenomenon in BGP that is elusive to investigations yet can be an indication of a serious threat: subprefix hijacking where rogue ASes announce routes to prefixes that are *fully contained* inside prefixes originated by other, legitimate ASes. We call these subMOAS events. Such an attack leads to a 'black hole' for a victim's network since BGP generally prefers routes to more specific prefixes. However, business relationships between ASes and their customers naturally lead to a very large number of subMOASes as well. It is an unsolved challenge to tell the many benign events apart from the (rarer) malicious ones: on average, we observe nearly 75 subMOASes *per hour* with peaks of several hundred events.

Our contribution in this work is a filter system to identify legitimate sub-MOAS events such that a much more reasonable number of 'still suspicious' cases remains. These can either be manually inspected or serve as the input for future detection systems. Our approach is to combine data sources that are external to BGP to draw conclusions about the legitimacy of subMOAS events. First, we use information from the RIPE database to infer business and management relationships between the IRR objects stored in the database. Such information can only be altered by entities with valid access credentials. Our assumption is that an attacker does not have these credentials. Second, we use a topology algorithm to reason whether an attacker targets subprefixes of his own upstream provider. This is highly unlikely as the victim would simply be able to filter out the malicious BGP updates. Third, we use data from Internet-wide scans of the SSL/TLS landscape to determine hosts whose public/private key combinations are unique and remain stable over a longer period of time. These hosts serve as beacons. If their public/private key pair remains the same during a subMOAS event, we can rule out malicious interference. The assumption here is that a BGP hijacker cannot compromise hosts in hijacked prefixes and steal their keys. In our evaluation, we will see that our methods are very effective on the input data. Since their coverage can still be increased, this is an encouraging result.

The remainder of this paper is organised as follows. Section 2 presents related work. We describe our methodology in Section 3 and present our results and the lessons learned in Section 4.

2   Related Work

There is a huge body of relevant and related literature. In the following, we can only focus on a few selected contributions. Evidence that BGP hijacking attacks occur has been provided in several publications, *e.g.*, by Ramachandran and Feamster [10] (short-lived tampering with BGP for spam purposes) and Schlamp *et al.* [11] (a longer-lived occurrence). Possibly the first attempt to detect hijacks was made by Lad *et al.* [7]: a control-plane technique focusing exclusively on reporting multiple-origin AS (MOAS) prefixes. The authors of [9] provided heuristics to assess that the announced MOAS paths comply with standard economy-based routing policy. Wählisch studied the correlation between routing policies and RPKI-invalid announcements in [13]. The authors of [15] use a hop-count metric to evaluate the number of IP hops between a monitor and a target network—changes in this number indicate a topology change. Argus [12] uses multiple monitors for ping measurements to distinguish between two zones affected and unaffected by the respective BGP updates. Importantly, these techniques focus primarily on MOAS. In contrast, we focus on subMOAS events. Here, active probing to detect an affected and an unaffected part of the Internet topology is not possible, since all of the Internet topology is affected by a corresponding BGP update (due to BGP's preference of routes to more specific prefixes). The above methods would thus not work. The authors of [3] discuss detection techniques for subMOASes. Their approach requires that upstream providers allow IP spoofing, which is not always the case. The mechanism in [14] can detect network cut-offs from inside a victim's network, but works on a local level only.

3   Methodology

Our methodology consists of four steps. First, we determine actual subMOAS events from BGP routing tables and update messages. Subsequent steps focus on eliminating subMOAS events with legitimate causes. To this end, we establish a filter chain. First, we use the RIPE IRR database to infer the ownership for certain so-called IRR resources. If we find that an alleged attacker actually is the legitimate owner of a resource or has been delegated authority over it, we consider such a subMOAS event as legitimate. Our filter is currently limited to the RIPE space, but can be extended to other IRR databases. The next filter is a topology-based reasoning algorithm: the idea is that an attacker is unlikely to hijack his own upstream provider as this provider could simply counter the attack by filtering out malicious BGP udpates. The last filter uses data from active SSL/TLS scans. For a given prefix in a subMOAS event, we verify if Web hosts in this prefix presented the same public key before and during a subMOAS occurence. If so, we may assume that the prefix is not hijacked as the attacker would have to be in possession of the private key, too, to fake a successful connection. This leaves us with a much smaller remainder of subMOAS events.

3.1   Identification of subMOASes

In a subMOAS-based attack, an attacker uses his AS to attract a victim's traffic by advertising a subprefix of a victim's (less specific) prefix. This effectively blackholes a part of the victim's network. To discover subMOAS events, we analyze RouteViews Oregon's routing table. We store prefix announcements in a binary prefix tree, where nodes hold information about the origin of an announcement. We only consider *effective* subMOAS: we discard cases where affected prefixes are fully announced by multiple origins, *i.e.*, regular MOAS cases. Instead, we look for more specific prefixes that are originated by a different AS than the

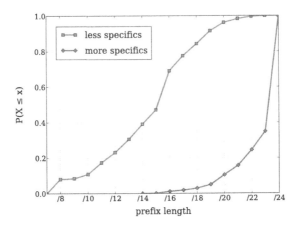

Fig. 1. Distribution of prefix lengths for subMOAS announcements (CDF)

enclosing prefix. We thereby compare the most specific parts of a prefix, *i.e.*, those parts that are decisive with respect to longest prefix matching, with its directly enclosing prefix to obtain all IP ranges that are affected by a subMOAS announcement. For instance, if the prefixes `10.0.0.0/22` and `10.0.0.0/24` are originated by the same origin AS, we would still recognize a subMOAS event for the `/22` prefix if `10.0.0.0/23` is originated by a different AS.

As of June 1, 2014, RouteViews Oregon's routing table holds 511,118 announced prefixes ($\approx$62.7% of the IPv4 space). A total of 76,121 prefixes are subMOAS announcements (covering $\approx$3.44% of the IPv4 space). These figures emphasize that subMOAS are a very common and naturally occuring phenomenon, with attacks hard to detect in the large number of benign events. On average, more specific subMOAS prefixes are longer than corresponding less specifics by a factor of 2^8 (see Figure 1). Hence, it will be essential to identify a great number of SSL/TLS-enabled hosts in advance in order to allow for the comparison of public keys before and during *any* new event.

3.2   Utilizing IRR Databases

All five Internet Routing Registries (IRR) maintain databases that contain information pertaining to the management of Internet resource holders. A recent study [6] matched prefixes and ASes observed in BGP and IRR by looking for appropriate database objects. We provide a generalized set of inference rules for benign subMOAS events, which take into account multiple origins observed in BGP as well as complex relationships between the affected prefixes and a suspicious origin AS.

Our filter is designed for the RIPE database as RIPE provides daily snapshots with a precise data model and a certain amount of consistency enforced. Still, IRR databases are updated by individual resource holders and can thus be outdated or even hold conflicting information. Our filter accounts for this. Note that filters for other IRR databases are easy to design; this is ongoing work.

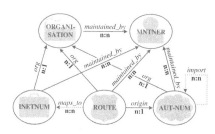

Fig. 2. Entities and relations in the RIPE database relevant for our filter

Table 1. Information stored in our graph database, June 2014

Instance	Nodes	Relations
MNTNER	**48,465**	
←*maintained_by*− [*]		5,307,883
ORGANISATION	**81,260**	
←*org*− [*]		199,644
AUT-NUM	**27,616**	
←*import*− AUT-NUM		221,690
←*origin*− ROUTE		245,831
INETNUM	**3,871,827**	
ROUTE	**236,604**	

Data Model. Since February 2012, we download and evaluate daily snapshots of the RIPE database. Figure 2 shows entities and relations in the RIPE database that are of significance for our work. We use a graph database to store the extracted data using the same schema as in the figure. We also track all changes over time. The RIPE database models access rights with MNTNER objects. Only maintainers with valid credentials can modify or delete objects. For any object, this is expressed by adding a *maintained_by* reference pointing to the respective MNTNER object. ORGANISATION objects are optional and mainly used to provide administrative contact details. The RIPE snapshots remove details for privacy reasons but preserve the references to the objects themselves. INETNUM objects represent allocated or assigned IPv4 prefixes managed by RIPE. ROUTE objects are created by resource holders and are used to document or confirm intended prefix announcements by specific ASes. To create a ROUTE object, a resource holder needs to provide valid maintainer credentials for both the INETNUM and the AUT-NUM object. The corresponding *maps_to* relation is computed by our parsing algorithm. AUT-NUM objects represent AS numbers and may be referenced as the *origin* of ROUTE objects. Our parsing algorithm also deduces *import* relations from free-text description fields, which are often used to model routing policies in the so-called Routing Policy Specification Language (RPSL). When resources are deleted from the RIPE database, RPSL definitions may still reference (now) non-existing ASes. We account for this by tracking such orphaned *import* relations.

As of June, 2014, our database holds more than 4 million nodes and 5 million relations extracted from the RIPE database. Figure 1 provides details for selected objects that are relevant for our approach. We can see that less than 50,000 MNTNER objects share more than 5 million incoming *maintained_by* references. Although optional, roughly 80,000 ORGANISATION objects are referenced by almost 200,000 other objects. Less than 30,000 AUT-NUM objects *import* routing policies from more than 220,000 other AUT-NUM objects. Nearly 250,000 ROUTE objects bind prefix announcements to less than 30,000 AUT-NUM objects. We will see that these figures allow our filter to be very effective.

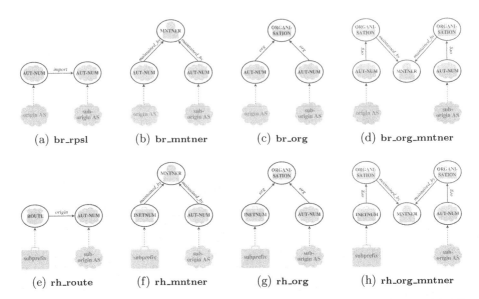

Fig. 3. IRR inference rules used for the legitimization of subMOAS events (a)–(d) Legitimate business relationships   (e)–(h) Legitimate resource holders

Infering Resource Ownership. Recall that our fundamental assumption is that an attacker does not have the credentials to change the RIPE database in order to cover his attack. Accordingly, we look for legitimate relationships between the parties involved in a subMOAS event to disprove an attack. Given a routing change that results in a subMOAS, we map the affected AS numbers and prefixes to AUT-NUM and INETNUM objects in our graph database. We then traverse the graph along a path of legitimizing relations. We look for paths between a) the two affected AS or b) the more specific prefix and its origin AS. If we succeed with a), we can infer a valid business relation between the victim and the suspected attacker. If we succeed with b), the suspected attacker holds ownership rights for the more specific prefix and is thus authorized to originate it from his AS.

Legitimizing paths are formed by one or more of the following relations: *import, origin, maintained_by* and *org*. Figure 3 shows the complete set of our inference rules. Entities without surrounding circles represent subMOAS information derived from BGP data, encircled items represent nodes in our database. We first look for an *import* relation from the alleged victim to the attacker (Figure 3 (a)). This would imply that the suspected victim deliberately updated the RIPE database to document his willingness to accept the suspected attacker's route updates. This indicates a business relationship rather than an attack, and we consider it proof for a legitimate subMOAS event. Similar arguments apply for the victim's AUT-NUM object being maintained by the attacker's MNTNER object (Figure 3 (b)) since no victim would grant his attacker such privileges. Relations to a common ORGANISATION object (Figure 3 (c)) and even a path from different affected organisations to a common MNTNER (Figure 3 (d)) can also be considered strong evidence for an underlying business relationship.

If we are not able to find a path with the above rules, we look for evidence that a suspected attacker is in fact the legitimate holder of a subprefix resource in question. We first check if we can map the subprefix to a ROUTE object. If so, we search for an *origin* relation to the suspected attacker's AUT-NUM object (Figure 3 (e)). To create such a ROUTE object, valid maintainer credentials are needed for the AUT-NUM object, but also for the implicitly given INETNUM object represented by the subprefix. If the alleged attacker is able to provide both, we consider him the owner of the subprefix and the subMOAS case to be legitimate. Note that we also check for ROUTE objects that bind less specific prefixes to the suborigin AS. This implies that the attacking AS is the owner of the corresponding larger IP range, of which only a part is advertised in BGP. As network operators are free to announce their networks in any given size, such cases are legitimate, too.

The remaining rules in Figure 3 (f)–(h) are similar to those in (b)–(d): we aim to identify a legitimizing path based on shared MNTNER or ORGANISATION objects—in these cases between the subprefix mapped to an INETNUM object and the AUT-NUM object of the originating AS. Once again, we do not look for exact matches to the INETNUM object but also allow for larger IP ranges since a resource holder is not required to advertise his assigned prefixes as a whole.

Our figures from Table 1 show that these rules have the potential to be highly effective, since we observe a high degree of interconnections: On average, MNTNER objects are referenced by 110 other objects, and ORGANISATION objects have at least eight incoming relations. In addition, we have nearly ten times more ROUTE objects and *import* relations than AUT-NUM objects. It is therefore promising to look for objects with common references to these objects. Note that our approach does not require the RIPE database to be complete, and not even to be conflict-free. Our inference rules are solely based on legitimate objects. In case of absent or conflicting database objects, we are unable to establish a legitimizing path—we cannot wrongly legitimate a subMOAS event this way.

3.3   Topology Reasoning

The next filter in our chain is topology-based. For each subMOAS occurrence, we extract all AS paths that lead to the affected subprefixes and build a directed graph. In essence, this graph represents all possible paths to the subprefixes' origins, regardless of the selected route. We use the graph to check if at least one of the observed AS paths to the more specific origin AS contains the origin AS of the less specific one. If this is the case, we consider the subMOAS event to be legitimate: if it were illegitimate, the owner of the less specific prefix would not forward malicious BGP updates upstream. The legitimate scenario occurs, for example, when a smaller Internet service provider obtains Internet connectivity and a block of IP addresses from a larger carrier; other reasons might be multihoming setups or the use of static routes invisible to BGP.

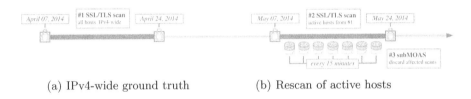

(a) IPv4-wide ground truth   (b) Rescan of active hosts

Fig. 4. Timeline for obtaining our ground truth

3.4 Cryptographic Assurance with SSL/TLS

Our final filter uses data sets obtained from our regular Internet-wide scans of the SSL/TLS protocols on port 443 (HTTPS). The idea is to identify legitimate subMOAS events by checking the public/private key pair used in SSL/TLS handshakes. We assume that an attacker cannot obtain cryptographic keys from a victim. Thus, if a host uses the same key pair before and during a subMOAS event, we may infer the legitimacy of an event. For this to work, we first need to establish a ground truth: a collection of mappings of IP addresses to public keys. Due to the fluctuating nature of the Internet in terms of IP address assignments, routing paths and change-overs of SSL/TLS keys, we carry out two subsequent scans to establish a ground truth.

First, we initiate a SSL/TLS scan of the entire routable IP space. To reduce the intrusiveness and to avoid our probes being dropped by destinations, the scans are carried out much more slowly than it would be technically possible. We also inform a number of CERTs, research institutes and blacklist providers before a scan, and maintain our own blacklist of networks based on feedback from operators.

Figure 4 shows the timeline for obtaining our ground truth. Our first scan lasted from 7-24 April 2014. It yielded 27.2 million IP addresses where we could retrieve certificate chains in the SSL/TLS handshake. For our ground truth, we focus on particularly stable hosts with unchanging IP addresses and stable, unique public keys. We thus scanned the 27.2 million hosts a second time one month later (7-24 May 2014) and filtered out all IP addresses for unresponsive hosts or for which the public key had changed. We arrived at 5.4 million stable hosts. The final step was to discard hosts that had already been affected by subMOAS events. This is necessary since a subMOAS event at the time of the scan would mean we would have connected to a host possibly under the control of an attacker. By checking against *all* BGP messages received in intervals of 15 minutes, roughly 20,000 hosts were discarded in this step. Note that discarded hosts may be eventually reincluded into the ground truth by rescanning on a periodic basis, thus mitigating the effects of short-lived subMOAS events. The resulting set of 5,356,634 hosts can be considered stable: for each host, both its IP address and corresponding public key had remained unchanged, and no subMOAS event occured during our connection to the host.

Note that our ground truth naturally becomes less effective over time due to long-term changes of hosts. The implication for our methodology, however, is once again unproblematic, since we gradually miss out on legitimizing subMOAS events, but we cannot accidentally overcount. In addition, we update our ground truth on a monthly basis to overcome a decrease in our coverage.

With this ground truth available, we can now reliably detect whether hosts affected by an emerging subMOAS event still present the same public key as before the event. To this end, we are in need of a real-time framework to timely initiate the re-scanning of affected hosts.

3.5   Real-Time Framework

subMOAS events may be of long duration (in the range of several months), but we also observed events that lasted much shorter (*e.g.,* for several hours or minutes only). To account for this variability in duration, we set up a real-time framework to continously analyze subMOAS events. Note that it is imperative that our SSL/TLS scans are carried out *before and within* the life time of an event, *i.e.,* we need to perform our scans quickly after a subMOAS arises.

Our real-time framework comprises several steps that are executed every two hours. First, we obtain the latest BGP data: a two-hour old RIB dump and all BGP update messages until present time. We extract all subMOAS events that started within this time frame and have not been withdrawn yet. Next, we apply our IRR filters and identify legitimate events. We also apply our topology reasoning algorithm and use our ground truth scan to look up stable SSL/TLS hosts contained in the more specific prefixes to initiate SSL/TLS scans.

At the same time, we obtain all scan results from the previous run and compare cryptographic host keys to those obtained in our ground truth scan. Note that, in general, one must not assume that a scan always reaches the more specific prefix. At the moment we observe a subMOAS event, routing may have already changed along the path of our upstreams, hence our BGP view might be out-dated. Due to such propagation delays inherent to BGP, this issue cannot be resolved by a tight coupling of our SSL/TLS scanner to the subMOAS detection alone. Instead, we sanitize our scan results with the help of a subsequent validation process. After we have collected a new set of cryptographic keys, we further evaluate the following two hours of BGP data, and discard scan results for which the subMOAS event changed or vanished within this time frame. Note that man-in-the-middle attacks where an attacker is able to forward our scans to the legitimate destination are beyond the scope of our work. Besides, our approach does not allow us to analyze events that last shorter than two hours. However, this is no inherent limitation and can be mitigated by selecting a shorter analysis period (*i.e.,* investing more resources).

4   Evaluation

We begin our evaluation with an analysis of the frequency of subMOAS events during the time frame of our experiment. We then show how much each filter in our chain can contribute to identify legitimate events. Based on our results, we discuss lessons learned at the end of this section.

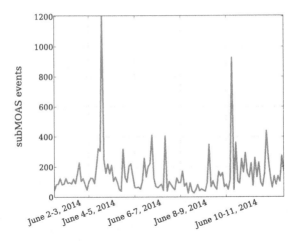

Fig. 5. subMOAS events observed over the duration of our experiment

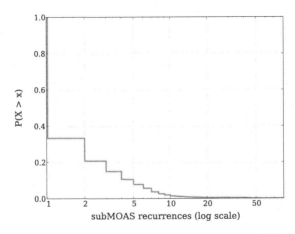

Fig. 6. Distribution of subMOAS recurrences, CCDF

4.1 subMOAS Analysis

Figure 5 shows the frequency of subMOAS events we observed in the period of 2-12 June 2014. On average, we encountered 148.2 events over two hours (the minimum number is 27; the maximum number is 1,206). Figure 6 gives details on subMOAS events that occurred more than once, *i.e.*, concerned the same prefixes and ASes. On average, subMOASes recurred 2.2 times, with a maximum of 84 occurrences.

During the duration of our experiments, we observed a total of 8,071 unique subMOAS events. We were able to legitimize 46.5% of these events by subsequent application of our filter chain. Table 2(a) presents an overview of individual filter results. IRR-based analysis could rule out 10.8% legitimate events; topology reasoning could contribute about 31.7%, and SSL/TLS about 22.9%.

Table 2. Overview of our results

	total	in %
All subMOAS events	**8,071**	**100%**
IRR analysis	870	10.78%
topology reasoning	2,560	31.72%
SSL/TLS scans	1,851	22.93%
Legitimate events (cum.)	**3,755**	**46.53%**

(a) Combined filter results

	total	in %
Individual SSL/TLS scans*	**37,043**	**100%**
with different SSL/TLS key	773	2.09%
no response (port closed)	3,302	8.91%
with same SSL/TLS key	32,968	89.0%
Covered subMOAS events	**2,116**	**100%**
Legitimate events	**1,851**	**87.48%**

(c) SSL/TLS scan results.
*986 scans were removed due to routing changes

	total	in %
Covered subMOAS events	**1,048**	**100%**
br_rpsl	362	34.54%
br_mntner	519	49.52%
br_org	51	4.87%
br_org_mntner	145	13.84%
rh_route	692	66.03%
rh_mntner	599	57.16%
rh_org	159	15.17%
rh_org_mntner	160	15.27%
Legitimate events (cum.)	**870**	**83.02%**

(b) IRR analysis results

With our combined filter chain, we are able to legitimize nearly half of all subMOAS events present in today's routing tables. We emphasize that this is not an upper limit that would be inherent to our methodology: it is simply because, at this point, we only use sources that cover about 60% (4,795) of all events. Rather, the results for the individual filters suggest that adding further data source like other IRRs (ARIN, APNIC, etc.) or other cryptographic protocols (SSH, IMAPS, etc.) have the potential to shrink the result space much further.

IRR Analysis. Table 2(b) shows how effective our IRR-based filters are at eliminating legitimate subMOAS events for prefixes registered by RIPE. Rules that aim at capturing business relationships can eliminate about 65% of these events. Rules that establish legitimate resource holding can eliminate about 72%. In combination, we find that **83.0%** of events that are based in the RIPE service region are legitimate. Our previous analysis with Table 1 indicated that IRR inference rules based on MNTNER and ROUTE objects could perform best; the results presented above confirm this finding.

SSL/TLS Scans. Table 2(c) shows the total numbers of observed keys. In terms of legitimized subMOAS events, we are able to rule out **87.5%** of events with at least one SSL/TLS-enabled host in the respective subprefixes. Figure 7 shows the distribution of SSL/TLS hosts per subMOAS prefix. 75% of the prefixes host at least one SSL/TLS-enabled machine, 25% even contain more than 10 hosts.

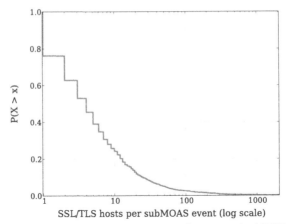

Fig. 7. Distribution of SSL/TLS hosts per subMOAS subprefix (CCDF). Only subprefixes with at least one SSL/TLS host have been considered.

Note that for more than 75% of all subMOAS events, we have more than one host available to use for cryptographic confirmation. We even have more than ten hosts available in about 25% of all events. The average number of SSL/TLS hosts per subMOAS subprefix is 17; the minimum and maximum numbers are 1 and 2,070, respectively. These figures allow our SSL/TLS filter to be highly robust against short outages of single hosts, since it is enough for us to confirm that *at least one* cryptographic key remains unchanged per subMOAS event.

Figure 8 shows that the populations of unchanging and changing keys remain relatively stable for the lifetime of our ground truth. While a certain decline is evident, it remains in the range of 5% or less. Finally, Figure 9 shows the percentages of hosts that became unresponsive during our live scans, which increases very slowly, too. These findings suggest that the interval for obtaining new ground truth hosts can be set to one month or even longer. Note that outliers with a larger fraction of changed certificates or unresponsive hosts are the result of a lower initial number of available ground truth hosts.

4.2   Lessons Learned

The results from our filters are quite encouraging. Given that we achieve high elimination rates for the IP space we can currently cover (already 60%), we offer the following conclusions.

First, data obtained from IRR databases is highly useful to identify legitimate subMOAS events, even if some data may be incomplete or outdated. Our results encourage us to extend our IRR analysis to the remaining databases in other service regions—we expect a significant increase of our coverage. Furthermore, we would encourage IRR operators to publish database snapshots on a daily basis to aid in this effort at demystifying routing anomalies.

Second, active scans are equally powerful. The coverage of our methodology corresponds exactly to the number of Web hosts that use unique keys, a set of

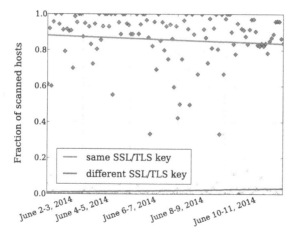

Fig. 8. Percentage of same and different SSL/TLS keys during our experiment

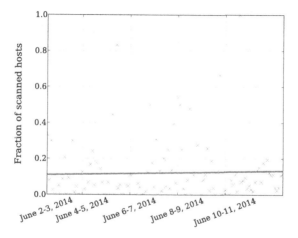

Fig. 9. Number of unresponsive SSL/TLS hosts over the duration of our experiment

hosts that remained pleasingly stable throughout our experiments. The coverage can be even increased in the future by focusing on additional cryptographic protocols, e.g. like IMAPS and SSH. We intend to perform regular ground truth scans and to deploy our filter techniques continously.

Our work aims at the detection and analysis of subMOAS events. It is thus not applicable to other types of routing anomalies that do not exhibit subMOAS conflicts, e.g. interception attacks. However, our ultimate goal is to be able to reduce the huge search space for subprefix hijacking attacks to a manageable size for manual inspection, and to allow automated reasoning about subMOAS routing anomalies. Our analysis chain lends itself well to integration of future detection systems: a) to narrow down the number of suspicious routing anomalies and b) to cross-check the resulting alarms.

5 Conclusions and Outlook

We introduced a methodology that allows us to reliably identify subMOAS events with legitimate causes. Our method combines data from several sources and proves promising: although coverage for the entire Internet can be improved, our individual filter techniques are highly effective. Our findings show that both IRR databases and active scans are useful tools to reason about routing anomalies in-depth. Moreover, we outlined straightforward steps to increase coverage, which puts manual inspection of the remaining subMOAS events within reach. Finally, we intend to grow our framework into a service that makes its data publicly available on a continuous and permanent basis. This framework promises to be greatly beneficial for future systems to detect subprefix hijacking. We invite the research community to participate in this effort. We would be delighted to have our results used as input for further detection systems or by seeing further filters developed by fellow researchers.

Acknowledgments. This work has been supported by the German Federal Ministry of Education and Research (BMBF) under support code 01BY1203C, project *Peeroskop*, and by the European Commission under the FP7 project *EINS*, grant number 288021.

References

1. Ballani, H., Francis, P., Zhang, X.: A study of prefix hijacking and interception in the Internet. In: Proc. ACM SIGCOMM 2007, pp. 265–276 (2007)
2. Hepner, C., Zmijewski, E.: Defending against BGP man-in-the-middle attacks. Talk at BlackHat 2009 (2009)
3. Hu, X., Mao, Z.M.: Accurate real-time identification of IP prefix hijacking. In: Proc. IEEE Symposium on Security and Privacy, pp. 3–17 (2007)
4. Huston, G., Bush, R.: Securing BGP and SIDR. IETF Journal **7**(1) (2011)
5. Kent, S., Lynn, C., Seo, K.: Secure Border Gateway Protocol (SBGP). IEEE Journal on Selected Areas in Communications **18**(4), April 2000
6. Khan, A., Kim, H.-C., Kwon, T., Choi, Y.: A comparative study on ip prefixes and their origin ases in bgp and the irr. SIGCOMM Comput. Commun. Rev. **43**(3), 16–24 (2013)
7. Lad, M., Massey, D., Pei, D., Wu, Y., Zhang, B., Zhang, L.: PHAS: a prefix hijack alert system. In: Proc. 15th USENIX Security Symposium, vol. 15 (2006)
8. Pilosov, A., Kapela, T.: Stealing the Internet: An Internet-scale man in the middle attack. In: Talk at DEFCON 16 (2008)
9. Qiu, J., Gao, L.: Detecting bogus BGP route information: going beyond prefix hijacking. In: Proc. 3rd Int. Conf. on Security and Privacy in Communication Networks (SecureComm) (2007)
10. Ramachandran, A., Feamster, N.: Understanding the network-level behavior of spammers. In: Proc. ACM SIGCOMM 2006 (2006)
11. Schlamp, J., Carle, G., Biersack, E.W.: A forensic case study on as hijacking: the attacker's perspective. ACM SIGCOMM CCR **43**(2), 5–12 (2013)

12. Shi, X., Xiang, Y., Wang, Z., Yin, X., Wu, J.: Detecting prefix hijackings in the Internet with argus. In: Proc. ACM SIGCOMM IMC (2012)
13. Wählisch, M., Maennel, O., Schmidt, T.C.: Towards Detecting BGP Route Hijacking Using the RPKI. ACM SIGCOMM CCR **42**(4), 103–104 (2012)
14. Zhang, Z., Zhang, Y., Hu, Y.C., Mao, Z.M., Bush, R.: iSPY: Detecting IP prefix hijacking on my own. IEEE/ACM Trans. on Networking **18**(6), 1815–1828 (2010)
15. Zheng, C., Ji, L., Pei, D., Wang, J., Francis, P.: A light-weight distributed scheme for detecting IP prefix hijacks in real-time. In: Proc. ACM SIGCOMM 2007 (2007)

The Abandoned Side of the Internet: Hijacking Internet Resources When Domain Names Expire

Johann Schlamp[1]([✉]), Josef Gustafsson[1], Matthias Wählisch[2],
Thomas C. Schmidt[3], and Georg Carle[1]

[1] Technische Universität München, München, Germany
{schlamp,gustafss,carle}@net.in.tum.de
[2] Freie Universität Berlin, Berlin, Germany
m.waehlisch@fu-berlin.de
[3] HAW Hamburg, Hamburg, Germany
schmidt@informatik.haw-hamburg.de

Abstract. The vulnerability of the Internet has been demonstrated by prominent IP prefix hijacking events. Major outages such as the China Telecom incident in 2010 stimulate speculations about malicious intentions behind such anomalies. Surprisingly, almost all discussions in the current literature assume that hijacking incidents are enabled by the lack of security mechanisms in the inter-domain routing protocol BGP.

In this paper, we discuss an attacker model that accounts for the hijacking of network ownership information stored in Regional Internet Registry (RIR) databases. We show that such threats emerge from abandoned Internet resources (e.g., IP address blocks, AS numbers). When DNS names expire, attackers gain the opportunity to take resource ownership by re-registering domain names that are referenced by corresponding RIR database objects. We argue that this kind of attack is more attractive than conventional hijacking, since the attacker can act in full anonymity on behalf of a victim. Despite corresponding incidents have been observed in the past, current detection techniques are not qualified to deal with these attacks. We show that they are feasible with very little effort, and analyze the risk potential of abandoned Internet resources for the European service region: our findings reveal that currently 73 /24 IP prefixes and 7 ASes are vulnerable to be stealthily abused. We discuss countermeasures and outline research directions towards preventive solutions.

1 Introduction

Internet resources today are assigned by five Regional Internet Registrars (RIRs). These non-profit organisations are responsible for resources such as blocks of IP addresses or numbers for autonomous systems (ASes). Information about the status of such resources is maintained in publicly accessible RIR databases, which are frequently used by upstream providers to verify ownership for customer networks. In general, networks are vulnerable to be hijacked by attackers due to

© IFIP International Federation for Information Processing 2015
M. Steiner et al. (Eds.): TMA 2015, LNCS 9053, pp. 188–201, 2015.
DOI: 10.1007/978-3-319-17172-2_13

the inherent lack of security mechanisms in the inter-domain routing protocol BGP. Real attacks have been observed in the past that led to the development of a variety of detection techniques and eventually of security extensions to BGP [8,11]. Common to these attacks is a malicious claim of IP resources at the routing layer. However, claims of network ownership can be also made at RIR level, a fact that has received little attention so far.

In a history of more than three decades, a vast number of Internet resources have been handed out to numerous users under varying assignment policies. Some ASes or prefixes have never been actively used in the inter-domain routing, others changed or lost their original purpose when companies merged or vanished. It is not surprising that some Internet resources became abandoned, i.e. resource holders ceased to use and maintain their resources.

In this paper, we focus on threats that emerge from abandoned Internet resources. Currently, there is no mechanism that provides resource ownership validation of registered stakeholders. Instead, the control over email addresses that are stored with RIR database objects is often considered a proof of ownership for the corresponding resources. Our contribution is a generalized attacker model that takes into account these shortcomings. We thoroughly evaluate the risk potential introduced by this attack by drawing on several data sources, and show that the threat is real. Since this kind of attack enables an attacker to fully hide his identity, it makes hijacking more attractive, and significantly harder to disclose. Consequently, we show that state-of-the-art detection techniques based on network measurements are ill-suited to deal with such attacks. Even so, these attacks have been evidenced in practice, and should thus be taken into account by future research.

We continue the discussion by establishing our attacker model in Section 2. In Section 3, we estimate the risk potential of abandoned resources, and show that there is a real threat. As a result, we outline an approach to mitigate this threat, and discuss limitations of related work in Section 4. In particular, we outline the need for a system that provides resource ownership validation. We conclude our discussion in Section 5.

2   Attacker Model

Conventional attacks on BGP are based on its lack of origin validation, which allows an attacker to originate arbitrary prefixes or specific subnets from his own AS. We propose a new attacker model that accounts for attackers to take ownership of abandoned resources. In such a scenario, an attacker is able to act on behalf of his victim, in particular to arrange upstream connectivity. Misled upstream providers unknowingly connect one or several ASes including prefixes of the victims as instructed by an attacker who successfully hides his true identity. Following this model, the anonymous attacker can participate in the cooperative Internet exchange at arbitrary places without any formal incorrectness. In the following, we generalize a real incident to derive preconditions that enable this kind of attack.

2.1 Background: The LinkTel Incident

In previous work [17], a corresponding attack has been observed in practice, which is known as the *LinkTel incident*. The authors studied this attack and showed that a victim's prefixes originated from his own AS, while the victim itself abandoned his business. The authors reconstructed the attacker's course of action to claim ownership of the abandoned resources. The LinkTel incident thereby revealed a major flaw in the Internet eco-system: validation of resource ownership is most often based on manual inspection of RIR databases. In this context, it was shown that the attacker was able to gain control over the victim's DNS domain, and thus over corresponding email addresses. The involved upstream provider presumably validated that the attacker's email address was referenced by the hijacked resources' RIR database objects. Given this proof of ownership, the upstream provider was convinced by the attacker's claim to be the legitimate holder of the resources. Surprisingly, the attacker captured the victim's DNS domain by simply re-registering it after expiration.

For several months, the attacker's abuse of the hijacked resources remained unnoticed. By combining several data sources, the authors showed that the hijacked networks were utilized to send spam, to host web sites that advertised disputable products, and to engage in IRC communication. After the victim recovered his business, he learned that his networks were listed on spamming blacklists. However, the attacker's upstream provider refused to take action at first, since the victim was unable to refute the attacker's ownership claims.

2.2 Preconditions for an Attack

Based on the insights gained from the LinkTel incident, we show that the attacker's approach can be generalized. To enable hijacking of Internet resources, the following preconditions have to be met: (a) Internet resources are evidentially abandoned and (b) the original resource holder can be impersonated.

If an organisation goes out of business in an unsorted manner, these conditions are eventually met. As a first consequence, the organisation ceases to use and maintain its resources. If this situation lasts over a longer period of time, the organisation's domain name(s) expire. Since day-to-day business lies idle, re-registration and thus impersonation becomes practicable for an attacker. At that moment, upstream connectivity can be arranged on behalf of the victim, since face-to-face communication is not required in general. Routers can be sent via postal service, or even be rented on a virtualized basis. Details on BGP and network configuration are usually exchanged via email, IRC, or cellular phone, and payment can be arranged anonymously by bank deposits or other suitable payment instruments. Without revealing any evidence about his real identity, the attacker is able to stealthily hijack and deploy the abandoned resources.

2.3 Implications

The implications of this attacker model are manifold. First, an attacker may act on behalf of a victim, thereby effectively hiding his own identity and impeding disclosure. This makes hijacking more attractive as it enables riskless network abuse. It hinders criminal prosecution, and could be used to deliberately create tensions between organisations or even countries. Due to the lack of a system for resource ownership validation, these attacks only depend on idle organisations or missing care by legal successors of terminated businesses. Even after the discovery of such an attack, it is difficult for the victim to mitigate since reclaiming ownership is the word of one person against another at first. The LinkTel incident [17] proves that this is not only a realistic scenario: such attacks are actually carried out in practice.

The benefit of attacks based on abandoned resources can even be higher than in the case of conventional attacks. Hijacking productive networks rarely lasts for more than a few hours, since the victim can receive great support in mitigating the attack. Moreover, for most cases, the benefit is reduced to blackholing a victim's network – with the Youtube-Pakistan incident being a prominent example. In addition, monitoring systems for network operators exist that raise alarms for unexpected announcements of their prefixes. However, due to the very nature of abandoned resources, virtually no one is going to take notice of an attack. Our attacker model thus accounts for stealthily operating attackers who aim at persistently maintaining malicious services.

3   Abandoned Internet Resources

We identify readily hijackable Internet resources by searching RIR databases for unmaintained resource objects. Subsequently, we distinguish between resources that are still in use, with potential for network disruption, and resources that are fully abandoned and ready to be abused stealthily. Such resources are especially attractive for attackers for two reasons. First, the resource is assigned to an organisation for operational use and thus represents a valid resource in the Internet routing system. Second, an attacker can easily claim ownership by taking control of the contact address referenced by corresponding RIR database objects, ie by re-registering a domain name.

Consequently, we look for RIR database objects that reference email addresses with *expired DNS names*. Since the inference of invalid domain names can also be the result of poorly maintained resource objects or typing errors, it is important to take into account recent database activities for individual resource owners, and to correlate this information with BGP activity.

The following analysis is based on archived RIPE database snapshots over 2.5 years (23 February, 2012 till 9 July, 2014). Our results are representative for the European service region only, but similar analyses can be done with little effort for other service regions, too.

3.1   Resource Candidates from RIR Database

RIPE, like all other RIRs, provides publicly available database snapshots on a daily basis. Most of the personally related information is removed due to privacy

Table 1. Data objects stored in the RIPE database, and references to DNS names. 9 July, 2014.

Object type	Frequency	DNS references	
inetnum	3,876,883	1,350,537	(34.84 %)
domain	658,689	97,557	(14.81 %)
route	237,370	50,300	(21.19 %)
inet6num	231,355	8,717	(3.77 %)
organisation	82,512	0	(0.00 %)
mntner	48,802	0	(0.00 %)
aut-num	27,683	6,838	(24.70 %)
role	20,684	14,430	(69.76 %)
as-set	13,655	2,500	(18.31 %)
route6	9,660	723	(7.48 %)
irt	321	162	(50.47 %)
Total	**5,239,201**	**1,531,764**	**(29.24 %)**

concerns. Some attributes, however, remain unanonymized, which we utilize to extract DNS names.

Available Data Objects. The RIPE database holds more than 5.2 million objects. These objects can be updated from the Web or via email. Most of these objects optionally hold an email address in the `notify` field, to which corresponding update notifications are sent. Despite anonymization, we found that these `notify` fields are preserved in the publicly available database snapshots, which is also the case for `abuse-mailbox` attributes. To extract DNS names, we parse these email addresses where applicable.

Table 1 shows the distribution of stored objects by type along with the number of DNS names we were able to extract. Although we found more than 1.5 million references to DNS names, the total number of *distinct* names is only 21,061. This implies that, on average, more than 72 objects reference the same DNS name. The overall fraction of objects that reference a domain name is 29.24 %, which is surprisingly high since the database snapshots are considered to be anonymized.

Hijackable Internet resources are given by `inetnum` and `aut-num` objects, which represent blocks of IP addresses and unique numbers for autonomous systems respectively. Exemplary database objects are provided in Figure 1, further details on the RIPE database model and update procedures are available at [16].

It is worth noting that the attacker neither needs authenticated access to the database nor does the attacker need to change the database objects. The attacker only needs to derive a valid contact point. We assume that the (publicly available) notification address usually belongs to the same DNS domain as the technical contact point. Detailed analysis is subject to future work; in our study, we disregard groups of objects that reference more than a single DNS domain as a precaution.

```
inetnum:      194.28.196.0 - 194.28.199.255
netname:      UA-VELES
descr:        LLC "Unlimited Telecom"
descr:        Kyiv
notify:       internet@veles-isp.com.ua
mnt-by:       VELES-MNT

aut-num:      AS51016
as-name:      VALES
descr:        LLC "Unlimited Telecom"
notify:       internet@veles-isp.com.ua
mnt-by:       VELES-MNT
```

Fig. 1. Examples of RIPE database objects (`inetnum` and `aut-num` objects)

Grouping Objects by Maintainer. The RIPE database is mostly maintained by resource holders themselves. Its security model is based on references to `mntner` (maintainer) objects, which grant update and delete privileges to the person holding a `mntner` object's password. This security model allows us to infer objects under control of the same authority by grouping objects with references to a common `mntner` object. We use these *maintainer groups* to estimate the impact of an attack for individual authorities: On average, we observed nearly 110 such references per `mntner` object, with a maximum of up to 436,558 references[1]. The distribution of the number of objects per maintainer group is presented in Figure 2.

For each of the maintainer groups, we obtain the set of all DNS names referenced by a group's objects. To unambiguously identify maintainer groups with expired domains, we merge disjoint groups that reference the same DNS domain, and discard groups with references to more than one DNS name. From an initial amount of 48,802 maintainer groups, we discard (a) 937 groups of zero size, i.e. unreferenced `mntner` objects, (b) 31,586 groups without domain name references, and (c) 4,990 groups with multiple references. The remaining 11,289 groups can be merged to 8,441 groups by identical DNS names. We further discard groups that do not include any hijackable resources, i.e. `inetnum` and `aut-num` objects, which finally leads us to 7,907 object groups.

Note that the number of these groups is a lower bound: an attacker could identify even more with access to unanonymized RIPE data. As discussed above, each of these groups is maintained by a single entity. If a group's DNS name expires, we consider the entity's resources to be a valuable target for an attacker.

3.2 Refinement by Activity Measures

To confirm that a set of resources is abandoned, our approach is based on complementary data sources. We start with domain names that expire, which is a

---

[1] The meta information refers to *Interbusiness Network Administration Staff* of Telecom Italia.

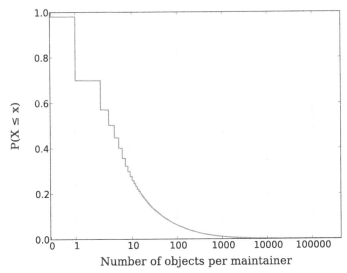

Fig. 2. RIPE database objects grouped by references to a common maintainer object (CCDF)

strong yet inconclusive indication for a fading resource holder. We gain further evidence by considering only resources that are neither changed in the RIPE database nor announced in BGP. Including both administrative (DNS, RIPE) and an operational (BGP) measures gives a comprehensive picture on the utilization of the resources.

Lifetime of Domain Names. We used the *whois system* to query expiry dates for all extracted DNS names (cf., Sect. 3.1). Figure 3 shows the distribution of these dates. At the time of writing, 214 domain names have been expired. Another 121 names expire within the week, given that the owners miss to renew their contracts. The most frequent top level domains are .com (27.9 %), .ru (21.5 %), and .net (13.0 %), while the most frequent *expired* TLDs are .ru (20.1 %), .it (16.4 %), and .com (9.81 %). The longest valid domains are registered until 2108 and mostly represent governmental institutions. The longest expired domain has been unregistered for nearly 14 years. With respect to the maintainer groups derived above, a total of 65 groups that reference expired DNS names remain. These groups hold 773 /24 networks and 54 ASes, and are subject to closer investigation.

RIPE Database Updates. For each of the 7,907 maintainer groups – divided into 7,842 valid groups and 65 with expired DNS names – we extracted the minimum time since the last change for any of its database objects. Note that we filtered out automated bulk updates that affected *all* objects of a certain

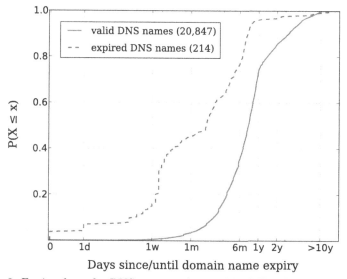

Fig. 3. Expiry dates for DNS names referenced by RIPE database objects

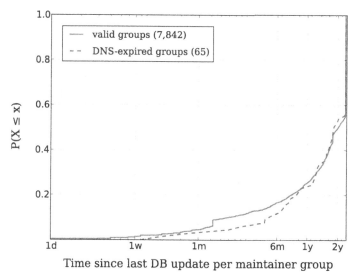

Fig. 4. RIPE database updates by maintainer group (CDF)

type[2]. Figure 4 shows the distribution of database updates for groups with valid and for groups with expired domain names. While about 10 % of the valid groups show changes within two months, DNS-expired groups differ strikingly: the 10 %-quantile is at nearly 5 months. Hence, given these long times without updates, we consider resource groups that exhibit an object update within 6 months to

---

[2] For instance, RIPE added a new `status` attribute to all `aut-num` objects on 27 May, 2014.

be still maintained and not abandoned. Note that we do not assume inactivity in absence of such changes.

BGP Activity. To confirm inactivity, we correlate the RIPE database updates with activities in the global routing system. For that, we analyze all available BGP update messages from the RouteViews Oregon's feed for the same time frame. This data set comprises 83,255 files with 18.4 billion announcements and 1.04 billion withdraw messages for resources assigned by RIPE. Given this data, we are able to extract two indicators: (1) the time since an *IP prefix* was last visible from the RouteViews monitor, and (2) the time since the last deployment of a RIPE-registered *AS number* by looking at AS path attributes. Figure 5 shows the distribution of last activity in BGP for any Internet resource in our maintainer groups. Nearly 90 % of resources in valid groups are visible in BGP at the moment. Surprisingly, most of the remaining groups did not show any activity at all during the last 2.5 years. About 75 % of the DNS-expired resources are present in today's routing table – and are thus still actively used. The remaining resources did show some activity in the past (10 %) or were never observed in BGP during our analysis period (15 %).

These findings confirm our assumption that inactivity in the RIPE database does not necessarily imply operational shutdown. While up to 85 % of the expired resources were seen in BGP within the last 2.5 years, Figure 4 indicates that not more than 55 % of the expired resources received an update in the RIPE database. We further learn that some expired resources did show BGP activity in the past, and do not show any activity today. Note that we disregard resources with recent BGP activity. These resources could potentially be hijacked already; however, attacks that started before our analysis are beyond the scope of our approach.

3.3   Hijackable Resources

So far, we learned that 65 maintainer groups with a total of 773 /24 networks and 54 ASes reference expired DNS names. Our activity measures further indicate that valid groups yield higher activity than expired groups. By combining these measures, we are able to infer resources that are inactive from both an administrative and an operational point of view. Figure 6 shows the time since the latest change by any of these measures, i.e., the minimum value of both measures.

This combined activity measure clearly splits the 65 expired maintainer groups into two disjoint sets: 52 cases were active within the last 3 months, while 13 cases did not show any activity for more than 6 months. We consider these remaining 13 cases to be effectively abandoned. These resource groups represent a total number of 15 `inetnum` objects (with an equivalent of 73 /24 networks) and 7 `aut-num` (i.e., AS number) objects.

Now that we have identified vulnerable resources, we feel obliged to protect these resources. Since any attacker could repeat our analysis, we are going to

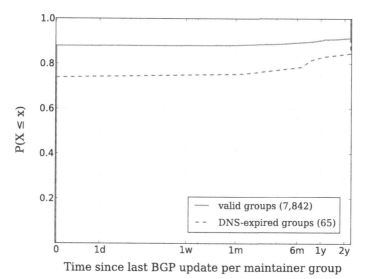

Fig. 5. BGP update messages observed by maintainer group (CDF)

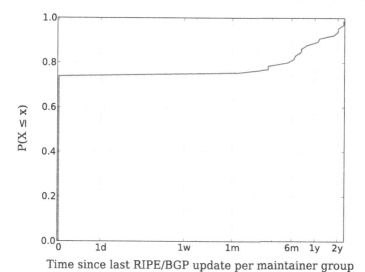

Fig. 6. Combined RIPE/BGP activity by maintainer group (CDF)

contact endangered resource holders before publishing our findings. Although communication via e-mail is futile due to expired domains, we can fall back on telephone numbers provided in the RIPE database to reach out for the operators.

4   Research Agenda

For the problem of abandoned Internet resources, one might argue that the threat is not caused by a technical but a social problem because operators agree to their peering relations based on a weak authentication scheme. This scheme can be replaced by stronger verification – the required data already exists. RIRs have contracts with the owners of delegated resources and thus are aware of more reliable contact points (e.g., telephone numbers). However, the current situation shows that we need mechanisms, tools, and procedures which are not tedious for operators but allow for easy resource verification. Our approach to identify abandoned resources can be easily extended to continuously monitor resources of all RIRs. This would allow us to warn network operators about potential risks. Finding scalable approaches to implement early warning and prevention in real-time, though, is an open research issue.

4.1 Limitations of Related Work

Current research is particularly focused on the detection of BGP hijacking attacks. Proposed mitigation techniques look on the control plane, the data plane, or both. *Control plane* monitoring is used to identify anomalies in BGP routing tables to infer attacks [1,6,9,14,21]. Such approaches are prone to false positives due to legitimate causes for anomalies. Techniques based on *data plane* measurements account for changes of the router topology [22,23], or of hosts in supposedly hijacked networks [4,5,18]. These approaches rely on measurements carried out before and during an attack. Beyond that, studies on the malicious intent behind hijacking attacks exist [15,17,19,20].

All detection approaches require the observation of suspicious routing changes. Attacks based on our attacker model take place outside the routing system, and thus do not lead to noticeable routing changes – apart from a supposedly legitimized organisation starting to reuse its Internet resources. Hence, current detection systems are incapable to deal with this kind of attack.

The DNS has been widely studied in the context of malicious network activities, mainly concerning spammers or fraud websites. Proactive blacklisting of domain names [3] does not help in our scenario as the threat is effective on the routing layer. Identifying orphaned DNS servers [7] is also out of scope of this paper as the attacker does not leverage the DNS server but the expiring domain.

4.2 Resource Ownership Validation

Despite its effectiveness, we consider our approach to detect and monitor abandoned resources as outlined above an intermediate solution only. In fact, we argue that there is a need for resource ownership validation.

There is ongoing effort to increase the deployment of a *Resource Public Key Infrastructure (RPKI)* [11]. In its present state, the RPKI allows for validation of route origins by using cryptographically secured bindings between AS numbers and IP prefixes. This mechanism prevents common hijacking attacks. In terms of hijacking abandoned resources, however, this system is ineffective in its current form since the abandoned origin AS is taken over as well, and origin validation performed by BGP routers [13] will indicate a valid BGP update.

Even though the RPKI itself can be misused [2], at the moment it represents the only mechanism for proofing securely ownership of Internet resources. We merely lack a clear procedure in the context of abandoned Internet resources. One approach could be the following operational rule: a peering request is only established when resource objects of the requesting peer exist in the RPKI. Recent time stamps for these objects indicate that the requesting peer has control over the resources as only authorized users can create such objects. Such a scheme seems feasible from the operational perspective and might even increase the incentives to deploy RPKI.

RPKI is part of *BGPsec*, an even larger effort to secure BGP. This extension to the protocol remedies the risk of hijacking abandoned resources due to its path validation capabilities: in our model, an attacker cannot provide valid crypto-graphic keys to sign update messages as specified by BGPsec [10]. However, the development of BGPsec is at an early stage, and the benefit compared to pure origin validation is questionable in particular in sparse deployment scenarios [12].

Future research should be carried out on enabling Internet service providers to validate resource ownership of customers. We see the potential of such a system not only in preventing attackers from hijacking abandoned Internet resources. It would also establish trust in customer-provider and peer-to-peer relationships, as well as in resource transfers issued by RIRs or LIRs.

5   Conclusion

Motivated by a real-world case study, we introduced a generalized attacker model that is aimed on the hijacking of abandoned Internet resources. We showed that such an attack is feasible with little effort, and effectively hides the attacker's identity by acting on behalf of a victim. By studying orthogonal data sources over a period of more than 30 months, we could give evidence of a high risk potential of such attacks. Only in the European RIR database, we found 214 expired domain names that control a total of 773 /24 networks and 54 ASes, all of which can be easily hijacked. About 90 % of these resources are still in use, which enables an attacker to disrupt operational networks. The remaining 10 % of the resources are fully abandoned, and ready to be stealthily abused.

Our findings led us to the conclusion that state-of-the-art systems are limited to deal with this kind of attack. More importantly, we argued that there is a need for *resource origin validation*. Such a framework would not only prevent attacks, but could also strengthen today's Internet eco-system by establishing trust in resource ownership.

Ethical Considerations. In this paper, we sketched a new attack vector. Up until now, it is unclear how common such attacks are; our findings thus might trigger new malicious activities. However, we also showed that this attack is already known to attackers, and we sketched countermeasures to mitigate this concern. In addition, we contact the holders of vulnerable resources before publication of our findings.

Acknowledgments. This work has been supported by the German Federal Ministry of Education and Research (BMBF) under support code 01BY1203C, project *Peeroskop*, and by the European Commission under the FP7 project *EINS*, grant number 288021.

References

1. Ballani, H., Francis, P., Zhang, X.: A study of prefix hijacking and interception in the internet. In: Proc. ACM SIGCOMM 2007, pp. 265–276 (2007)
2. Cooper, D., Heilman, E., Brogle, K., Reyzin, L., Goldberg, S.: On the risk of misbehaving RPKI authorities. In: Proc. of HotNets-XII. ACM, New York (2013)
3. Felegyhazi, M., Kreibich, C., Paxson, V.: On the potential of proactive domain blacklisting. In: Proc. of the 3rd USENIX LEET Conference. USENIX Association, Berkeley (2010)
4. Hong, S.-C., Ju, H.-T., Hong, J.W.: IP prefix hijacking detection using idle scan. In: Hong, C.S., Tonouchi, T., Ma, Y., Chao, C.-S. (eds.) APNOMS 2009. LNCS, vol. 5787, pp. 395–404. Springer, Heidelberg (2009)
5. Hu, X., Mao, Z.M.: Accurate real-time identification of IP prefix hijacking. In: Proc. IEEE Symposium on Security and Privacy, pp. 3–17 (2007)
6. Jacquemart, Q., Urvoy-Keller, G., Biersack, E.: A longitudinal study of BGP MOAS prefixes. In: Dainotti, A., Mahanti, A., Uhlig, S. (eds.) TMA 2014. LNCS, vol. 8406, pp. 127–138. Springer, Heidelberg (2014)
7. Kalafut, A.J., Gupta, M., Cole, C.A., Chen, L., Myers, N.E.: An empirical study of orphan DNS servers in the internet. In: Proc. of the 10th ACM SIGCOMM IMC, pp. 308–314. ACM, New York (2010)
8. Kent, S., Lynn, C., Seo, K.: Secure Border Gateway Protocol (SBGP). IEEE Journal on Selected Areas in Communications 18(4), April 2000
9. Lad, M., Massey, D., Pei, D., Wu, Y., Zhang, B., Zhang, L.: PHAS: A prefix hijack alert system. In: Proc. 15th USENIX Security Symposium, vol. 15 (2006)
10. Lepinski, M.: BGPSEC Protocol Specification. Internet-Draft - work in progress 00, IETF, March 2011
11. Lepinski, M., Kent, S.: An Infrastructure to Support Secure Internet Routing. RFC 6480, IETF, February 2012
12. Lychev, R., Goldberg, S., Schapira, M.: Bgp security in partial deployment: Is the juice worth the squeeze?. In: Proc. of ACM SIGCOMM, pp. 171–182. ACM, New York (2013)
13. Mohapatra, P., Scudder, J., Ward, D., Bush, R., Austein, R.: BGP Prefix Origin Validation. RFC 6811, IETF, January 2013
14. Qiu, J., Gao, L.: Detecting bogus BGP route information: going beyond prefix hijacking. In: Proc. 3rd Int. Conf. on Security and Privacy in Communication Networks (SecureComm) (2007)
15. Ramachandran, A., Feamster, N.: Understanding the network-level behavior of spammers. In: Proc. ACM SIGCOMM 2006 (2006)
16. RIPE NCC. RIPE Database Update Reference Manual. http://www.ripe.net/data-tools/support/documentation/RIPEDatabaseUpdateManual20140425_edit.pdf
17. Schlamp, J., Carle, G., Biersack, E.W.: A forensic case study on as hijacking: the attacker's perspective. ACM SIGCOMM CCR **43**(2), 5–12 (2013)

18. Shi, X., Xiang, Y., Wang, Z., Yin, X., Wu, J.: Detecting prefix hijackings in the Internet with argus. In: Proc. ACM SIGCOMM Internet Measurement Conference (IMC) (2012)
19. Vervier, P.-A., Thonnard, O.: SpamTracer: How stealthy are spammers? In: 5th Int. Workshop on Traffic Monitoring and Analysis (TMA 2013) (2013)
20. Vervier, P.-A., Jacquemart, Q., Schlamp, J., Thonnard, O., Carle, G., Urvoy-Keller, G., Biersack, E.W., Dacier, M.: Malicious BGP hijacks: appearances can be deceiving. In: IEEE ICC Communications and Information Systems Security Symposium (ICC CISS 2014) (2014)
21. Wählisch, M., Maennel, O., Schmidt, T.C.: Towards Detecting BGP Route Hijacking Using the RPKI. ACM SIGCOMM CCR **42**(4), 103–104 (2012)
22. Zhang, Z., Zhang, Y., Hu, Y.C., Mao, Z.M., Bush, R.: iSPY: Detecting IP prefix hijacking on my own. IEEE/ACM Trans. on Networking **18**(6), 1815–1828 (2010)
23. Zheng, C., Ji, L., Pei, D., Wang, J., Francis, P.: A light-weight distributed scheme for detecting IP prefix hijacks in real-time. In: Proc. ACM SIGCOMM 2007, pp. 277–288 (2007)

New Protocols

DoS Amplification Attacks – Protocol-Agnostic Detection of Service Abuse in Amplifier Networks

Timm Böttger[1]([⊠]), Lothar Braun[1], Oliver Gasser[1], Felix von Eye[2], Helmut Reiser[2], and Georg Carle[1]

[1] Technische Universität München, Munich, Germany
{boettget,braun,gasser,carle}@net.in.tum.de
[2] Leibniz Supercomputing Centre, Munich, Germany
{voneye,reiser}@lrz.de

Abstract. For many years Distributed Denial-of-Service attacks have been known to be a threat to Internet services. Recently a configuration flaw in NTP daemons led to attacks with traffic rates of several hundred Gbit/s. For those attacks a third party, the *amplifier*, is used to significantly increase the volume of traffic reflected to the victim. Recent research revealed more UDP-based protocols that are vulnerable to amplification attacks. Detecting such attacks from an abused amplifier network's point of view has only rarely been investigated.

In this work we identify novel properties which characterize amplification attacks and allow to identify the illegitimate use of arbitrary services.

Their suitability for amplification attack detection is evaluated in large high-speed research networks. We prove that our approach is fully capable of detecting attacks that were already seen in the wild as well as capable of detecting attacks we conducted ourselves exploiting newly discovered vulnerabilities.

1 Introduction

Denial-of-Service attacks aim at making services unavailable to their intended users. Attackers can use different methods to consume bandwidth or deplete other resources of the victim. One method to exhaust bandwidth is called Distributed Reflection Denial-of-Service (DRDoS) attack: an attacker sends forged requests to several servers with the victim's spoofed source address. In response the servers will send replies to the victim. If these replies are significantly larger than the requests the attack is called an *amplification attack*.

Recent research has shown that at least 14 UDP-based protocols are vulnerable to such attacks [10]. Reports show that current amplification attacks can result in more than 100 Gbit/s of bandwidth consumption [11]. The spam blocklist provider Spamhaus was attacked by a DNS amplification attack in March 2013 with an unprecedented traffic rate of up to 300 Gbit/s [8].

© IFIP International Federation for Information Processing 2015
M. Steiner et al. (Eds.): TMA 2015, LNCS 9053, pp. 205–218, 2015.
DOI: 10.1007/978-3-319-17172-2_14

Researchers proposed many different mechanisms to identify and protect victims of DRDoS attacks. Furthermore commercial products for this purpose exist. One provider of such products is CloudFlare [1], who successfully mitigated the above mentioned attack against Spamhaus. In contrast the development of approaches to detect actual service abuse received less attention. Operators of amplifier networks (i.e. networks in which services are abused as amplifiers) are in a good position to take effective countermeasures if they are aware of that their services are used in an attack. However, to enable service operators to employ countermeasures, they first must know that their services are abused as amplifiers. Unfortunately detecting amplification attacks on the border of an amplifier network is more challenging, because illegitimate incoming requests might look the same as legitimate requests.

In this paper we present a novel method to detect service abuse of arbitrary UDP-based protocols in amplifier networks. Our method leverages knowledge on amplification attacks to distinguish legitimate client requests from spoofed attack requests. We evaluate our method with measurements in a large-scale university network. Furthermore, we inject our own attacks into the network for protocols that are known to be exploitable, but for which we did not observe any real world attacks yet.

The remainder of the paper is structured as follows: In Sect. 2 we discuss related work on amplification attacks and DRDoS detection. The following Sects. 3 and 4 present our detection mechanism: we start with already known yet still important prerequisites in Sect. 3 and continue with describing our new approach in Sect. 4. We evaluate the approach in Sect. 5, followed by a discussion on the approach's limitations in Sect. 6. Finally, we conclude the paper in Sect. 7.

2   Related Work

Denial-of-Service attacks have been an active research topic for many years. Specht and Lee provide a taxonomy of attacks, tools and countermeasures and give a good overview of different DoS attack types [12]. Among other attacks, the authors discuss amplification as one way to generate large amounts of attack traffic. Certain protocols, e.g. DNS or SNMP, have long been known to be vulnerable to amplification attacks: Several studies analyze amplification attacks based on the DNS protocol and researchers proposed different methods to identify attack victims [4], [9], [14]. The majority of these studies aims at finding attacks on the border of the victim's network or at detecting attacks which target specific application layer protocols.

Other protocols have recently been identified to be vulnerable to amplification attacks. Rossow revisits a number of UDP-based applications and identifies 14 of them to be vulnerable [10]. He describes how these protocols can be used to conduct attacks and analyzes their possible impact. Even though the list of vulnerable protocols is impressive and contains protocols that have not been known to be vulnerable, it is also known that further protocols such as SIP are vulnerable as well [2]. Based on such findings, one can presume that other protocols could be vulnerable to amplification attacks as well. Therefore we see the need for an amplification attack detection mechanism that works independently from specific protocols. The detection method presented in this paper is protocol-agnostic and thus differs from previous approaches focusing mostly on individual protocols.

Rossow presents a first detection approach for amplifier networks that is based on NetFlow data [10]. He compares the amount of request and response data sent between a client and a server and reports an attack if a certain threshold is exceeded. The approach is restricted to network protocols that are known to be vulnerable and operate on a fixed UDP port. At the same time he also acknowledges that protocols which exhibit a download-like behavior, e.g. the also vulnerable BitTorrent protocol, will lead to false positives.

Rossow also discusses other approaches for detecting amplification attacks and compares them to his own proposal. Since our work relies on the same considerations as his work, all his considerations apply to our approach as well. We therefore refer the reader to the paper by Rossow [10] for further discussion and comparison with other related work.

3   Important Prerequisites

Some important prerequisites needed for our detection approach to work were already formalized and described by Rossow in [10]:

To identify attacks the communication between a server and a client has to be modeled. In certain protocols, e.g. DNS, the client uses a new port for each request message. The communication between a single client and server can therefore result in multiple UDP flows. To aggregate such a set of flows Rossow proposes to use a so-called *pairflow* for each server/client pair:

$$pairflow :=< C_{IP}, S_{IP}, S_{port}, B_{2s}, B_{2c}, t > \qquad (1)$$

In a pairflow C_{IP} matches the client IP, S_{IP} and S_{port} are the server's IP and port. Furthermore the payload bytes sent to the server (B_{2s}) and to the client (B_{2c}) are assessed. The duration t of the pairflow is recorded for calculating average rates. To identify the server in a communication flow a fixed set of 14 well-known UDP server ports is used.

In addition Rossow defines the so-called *bandwith amplification factor* (BAF) to characterize the amount of traffic exchanged between client and server. The BAF is calculated per pairflow as:

$$BAF = \frac{len(UDP\ payload)\ amplifier\ to\ victim}{len(UDP\ payload)\ attacker\ to\ amplifier} \qquad (2)$$

Communication between a server and a client with at least a 10 kBit/s data exchange rate, a BAF larger than five and a server that sends more than 10 MB of payload is classified to be an amplification attack.

4   Detection Approach

Our detection approach exploits characteristics of attack traffic to distinguish it from legitimate traffic. For modeling the communication relationship between server and client we rely on the foundations laid by Rossow as explained in the previous section. We also stick to his thresholds, i.e. classifying a pairflow as an attack if it exhibits a BAF of five and more than 10MB of traffic are sent towards the victim. These thresholds are reasonable as amplification attacks are characterized by an amplifier which sends a lot more traffic than it receives. Hence we expect pairflows corresponding to an amplification attack to exhibit a (relatively) large BAF. The threshold of 10MB is probably large enough to not be easily reached with simple requests but at the same time should be small enough such that amplification attacks certainly reach it.

In contrast to Rossow we want to provide a protocol-agnostic approach that does not depend on a fixed set of well-known UDP server ports. To build a pairflow, however, we need to identify the client and server roles of the communication. As these roles can not be reliably determined we assume that the servers are within our network. This simplification is reasonable because we want to detect amplifiers within the monitored network. However, this might lead to internal clients being treated as servers, potentially resulting in false positives.

As opposed to Rossow we are not working with NetFlow data, thus we chose to apply ten minutes active/inactive timeouts to each pairflow.

4.1   Characteristic Properties of an Amplification Attack

Even though the bandwidth and BAF criteria are surely fulfilled by every amplification attack relying only on these two criteria is, as we will show later in Sect. 5, not sufficient because they are also fulfilled by legitimate service usage (e.g. Peer-to-Peer or VPN traffic). Hence more criteria are needed to prevent false positive alarms from being generated.

To derive further criteria it is beneficial to discuss certain aspects of an amplification attack in more detail: To conduct an amplification attack the attacker sends requests to an amplifier service, which she expects to be answered with responses larger than the requests. These responses are in turn sent to the victim. In order to accomplish this task, the attacker must use the IP address of the victim as source address for her requests.[1] If the attacker is not located on the same broadcast domain as the amplifier or the victim, which is the common case we focus on, then the attacker will not see any response packets from the amplifying service.

---

[1] It seems reasonable to assume that nowadays filter mechanisms to mitigate IP spoofing are widely deployed. Unfortunately the Spoofer Project reports that roughly 40% of all AS' worldwide allow (at least partially) for using spoofed sender IP addresses [13]. Furthermore to effectively prevent IP spoofing all AS' must filter their traffic, because the attacker needs to find only one AS allowing spoofed IP addresses. Hence we must IP spoofing expect to happen.

Therefore an attacker can neither establish shared state with the amplifying service through the request packets, nor can she be sure that her requests produce the desired response. As a consequence she cannot send arbitrary requests to the amplifying service, but only those that do not require shared state. She furthermore is interested in sending requests where she is reasonably sure to produce a large response. As the possible requests an adversary would use are limited, we expect highly similar messages from the attacker during a single attack. In turn the responses generated by the amplifier are also expected to share similarities.

If an attacker is successful with provoking the amplifier to generate messages, then the victim will receive many unsolicited messages, i.e. messages that it did not request and hence not expects. A reasonable network stack should react to such unsolicited messages by sending ICMP port unreachable messages. Therefore in the early stages of an attack, when the resources are not yet depleted, such ICMP messages sent by the victim might be observed.

4.2   Improved Amplification Attack Detection Criteria

Based on the previous considerations we propose to use the following additional criteria for amplification attack detection:

Request and Response Packet Size Similarity: The attacker wants to obtain a large amplification factor while at the same time she is, as argued above, restricted in the requests she can send. Thus she is likely to only use a very small set of different requests, for which she verified in advance that they will generate large responses. A simple attacker might even stick to using only the one request which yields the highest amplification factor. In conclusion the attacker will only use a few different short requests, so we expect the sizes of the request messages to be very similar.

The amplifying service on the other hand cannot rely on shared state with the attacker, therefore, if not returning random information, the responses to the same request are expected to be similar. Likewise, as the attacker only uses a few different request messages, the amplifying service can only generate a few different responses. Thus we also expect the sizes of the response messages to be similar between all responses belonging to a single attack. To measure this similarity we assess the packet's payload sizes in both directions of the communication.

Request and Response Payload Similarity: We already justified that an attacker will only rely on a very restricted set of requests. For a single attack we therefore expect the payloads of the requests sent by the attacker to be very similar. The responses from the amplifier are expected to exhibit the same characteristic as these responses are generated by only a small set of different requests.

In order to assess the similarity of the messages, we apply the deflate compression as provided by the zlib library [16] to the payloads and use the ratio of compressed and uncompressed size for a similarity estimation. The deflate algorithm uses both Huffmann coding and LZ77 compression to create the compressed data. To save resources on the monitoring system we sample 100 packets per direction of a pairflow after this pairflow reached the BAF threshold and then apply the compression to this sample only. Using the payloads we calculate a *similarity factor* (SF) per traffic direction as

$$SF = 1 - \frac{len(deflate(concatenated\ UDP\ payload))}{len(concatenated\ UDP\ payload)}. \tag{3}$$

A similarity factor close to one indicates good compressible and hence similar payloads, a similarity factor close to zero indicates rarely compressible and hence unsimilar payloads. This calculation is performed separately for each direction.

Unsolicited Messages: The messages from the amplifying service that the victim receives are unsolicited messages. A network stack should react on these messages with ICMP port unreachable messages if no service is running on the port that receives the UDP frame. As a further attack indicator we count the number of ICMP port unreachable messages for any possible victim.

IP Spoofing: We use the IP header field of incoming requests to determine the path length between the sender of the request and the amplifier service. Initial TTL field values are set by the operating system and differ between the OS[2]. Each IP router on the way decrements the TTL by one. We record the TTL of the incoming requests and calculate the IP path length by comparing the value to the nearest known initial value for different operating systems. If we receive an ICMP reply from the victim, we also extract the path length in the same way. We can use the difference between those values to check whether the path length of the request from the attacker and the path length of the victim differ. If we do not receive any ICMP messages, we try to obtain the path length ourselves by performing trace routes to the victim.

Other Criteria: Surely there will be further criteria that can be used to distinguish legitimate and attack traffic. One possible criterion might be the client's inter-arrival times. For an attack we would expect very small, almost similar inter-arrival times, whereas for an interactive session we would expect higher inter-arrival times with a higher variance. However, so far we restrict our attention to the four criteria mentioned above and leave further criteria for future research.

---

[2] Linux and many BSD variants use an initial TTL of 64, Windows networking stacks have an initial value of 128 and some Unix variants start with a TTL of 255.

5   Evaluation

We implemented our method as a module of an Intrusion Detection System (IDS) and evaluated it on real traffic traces. Sect. 5.1 describes our measurement setup in a large university network. As only a small subset of all vulnerable protocols is currently used in real-world attacks, we additionally conducted attacks ourselves to also evaluate our approach on the other protocols, which we describe in Sect. 5.2. Our measurements in a high-speed research network are explained in Sects. 5.3, 5.4 and 5.5. We begin by briefly presenting the individual measurement runs, continue with using a subset of one run for deriving detection thresholds and finish by applying these thresholds to all three measurement runs.

5.1   Measurement Setup

We conducted the traffic measurements in the Munich Scientific Network (MWN) which is operated by the Leibniz Supercomputing Centre (LRZ). This network infrastructure connects the different sites of the Munich universities, many student residence halls, the Bavarian Academy of Science and Humanities, the Bavarian State Library, Max Planck and Fraunhofer Society institutes and various museums. In the course of one month the LRZ handles more than 1200 TByte of inbound and 730 TByte of outbound traffic. On average the measured link transmitted 2.6 GBit/s of incoming and approximately 1.5 GBit/s of outgoing traffic.

The traffic measurements were conducted on a dated commodity server running a Linux 3.2 kernel. It employs a 3.2 GHz Intel Core i7 CPU with four cores with hyperthreading and 12 GB RAM. The machine is connected to a monitoring session at the LRZ's border gateway router via an Intel 10 GE network card that is based on the 82598EB chipset. The card is driven by PF_RING and *Direct NIC Access* (DNA) [6], which is a zero-copy solution that allows the network card to directly copy packets into the userspace application without any CPU overhead. The capturing was configured to pass only UDP and ICMP traffic to the user space application, because we expect IP address spoofing to happen only on UDP.

5.2   Generated Attack Traffic

During our initial investigation, we realized that the only real-world attacks in the network were abusing DNS and NTP services. However, recent prior research showed that additional protocols are vulnerable [10]. In order to evaluate whether our approach is suitable to detect those cases, we created our own attacks on known vulnerable protocols. We searched for freely available attack tools for amplification attacks and found several that supported attacks on SNMP, DNS and NTP. None of the other vulnerable protocols were supported by these tools, so we added support for these protocols. The functional extensions are implemented to exploit the vulnerabilities as outlined in [2] and [10] .

Some of the vulnerable protocols could easily be exploited: NTP, DNS, SNMPv2, Chargen and SIP have implementations that are simple to exploit if the service is provided to the open Internet. For some protocols we had to alter the standard configurations, as per default the services are configured securely.

Other services posed more difficulties: The legacy Quote-of-the-Day (QOTD) service's exploitability strongly depends on the actual implementation and the size of the returned quotes. Implementations following the recommendations of the RFC [7] only send quotes with 512 or less characters. Therefore they can only produce low bandwidth attacks. Nevertheless exploiting the protocol is possible.

For aMule, Quake3 and Steam we are able to confirm their vulnerability. However, all of them include hard-coded rate-limits which effectively prohibit the generation of significant attack traffic. Thus we could not include them in our evaluation. Similarly many BitTorrent clients employ rate-limiting for their vulnerable DHT protocol. However, when intially writing this paper we discovered that the Mainline DHT plugin of Vuze [15] was vulnerable. More recent versions seem not to be vulnerable to our attacks any longer.

We created attacks using services we deployed in the monitored amplifier network. Both attacker and victim networks were placed outside the monitored networks. This setup allowed us to inject the attack traffic and simultaneously monitor it as part of our live traffic measurements. Our attacks lead to amplification factors (BAFs) ranging from roughly five (BitTorrent) and ten (SIP) up to 2,500 (NTP). Using the NTP protocol we generated 500MB per attack, using BitTorrent we generated roughly 100MB and using SIP only 30MB.

5.3   The Measurement Runs

For the final evaluation of our detection approach we conducted three measurement runs. The first one took place from June 7 until June 13, 2014 and lasted for 144 hours. The second run lasted for 96 hours from September 26 until September 30, 2014. The last run was performed from September 30 until October 1, 2014 and captured another 24 hours. For each run we logged all the pairflows exceeding the BAF-thresholds mentioned in the beginning of Sect. 4. The information in Table 1 thus refers to all logged pairflows only. We only conducted own attacks during measurement run #1.

Table 1. Measurement Runs

	Run #1	Run #2	Run #3
Duration (in h)	144	96	24
Total Bytes Sent	7,340.66 GB	3,425.62 GB	734.67 GB
Total Packets Sent	6,589,456,476	3,208,724,852	674,865,692
Total Pairflows Reported	77,693	45,747	10,974
Unique Server-Port-Client Triples	22,428	14,567	4,058
Unique Server-Port Pairs	3,324	1,682	504
Unique Servers	530	309	204

5.4   Deriving Detection Thresholds

If we want to use the criteria explained above to detect amplification attacks, we must first define detection thresholds. For that we extracted a sample set of pairflows, which we manually classified as attacks or legitimate traffic. This training set was chosen as a subset of the first measurement by only considering an 8 hour timeframe. It was chosen in such a way that it includes most of the attacks we conducted ourselves. The training set covered roughly 5% of the traffic captured during the first measurement run. Table 2 contains further details about the size of the training set.

Table 2. Training Set

	Training Set	Run #1	Share
Duration (in h)	8	144	5.55%
Total Bytes Sent	380.19 GB	7,340.66 GB	5.18%
Total Packets Sent	365,076,992	6,589,456,476	5.54%
Total Pairflows Reported	4,883	77,693	6.28%
Unique Server-Port-Client Triples	1,573	22,428	7.01%
Unique Server-Port Pairs	348	3,324	10.47%
Unique Servers	146	530	27.54%

In the following we will separately deal with our attacks using the Quote-of-the-Day (QOTD) protocol. They are unique in the sense that for the same request the server can reply with an arbitrary quote. This will significantly interfere with our detection criteria as we assumed that for a reasonable service the replies to the same request will be the similar. But as QOTD is the only[3] service exhibiting this behavior network operators will be able to compensate for attacks using this one special service. Nevertheless dealing with QOTD services even today is relevant as identifying a thousand exploitable QOTD services in the Internet took Rossow less than four minutes on average [10]. It is true that also for other attacks the attacker can try to evade the detection by using different requests. However, to achieve a significant impact she will still have to stick to a set of requests yielding a high amplification factor. Thus by just sampling more packets per pairflow the similarity can still be detected and this problem can be remediated. But so far we did not observe any attacks with varying request patterns.

We begin with how the similarity factors differ between attack and legitimate traffic. Please not that in the following each pairflow is only displayed once. Hence multiple attacks from the same attacker towards the same victim using the same protocol only result in one data point plotted. According to Fig. 1 the similarity factors already seem to provide a measure to distinguish the two classes of traffic:

---

[3] Every other service exhibiting this behavior can be seen as QOTD service with a very broad set of quotes.

As we claimed above for attacks we observe high similarity factors whereas for legitimate traffic the similarity factors are significantly lower. As expected the QOTD-attacks exhibit a significantly lower similarity factor as the other attacks. Based on our training set we choose to require similarity factors of 0.75 or more in each direction to classify a pairflow as an attack. This choice ensures that all attacks are captured while at the same time the vast majority of legitimate pairflows is not captured. The SF-values less than zero are artifacts caused by our packet capture method. They stem from pairflows from which due to active timeouts only a few packets were sampled. This lead to an increased size after compression.

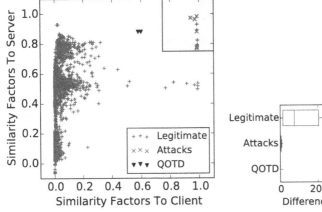

Fig. 1. Similarity Factors   **Fig. 2.** Packet Sizes To Client

As second criterion we want to evaluate the difference in the sizes of the packets. We calculated the difference between the average packet size and the minimal resp. maximal packet size and took the smaller of the two differences. As Fig. 2 and 3 indicate these differences are also different for attack and non-attack traffic. In accordance with these figures the remainder of this paper requires a difference of 25 or less bytes of the packet sizes in either direction to client or direction to the server for an amplification attack to happen.

We also tried exploiting the ICMP unreachable replies. As shown in Fig. 4 it is true that for attack traffic we observe more ICMP unreachable replies as for legitimate traffic. But even in our small subset of mostly controlled attacks the number of ICMP unreachable replies varies largely. As we cannot assure that for every attack ICMP unreachable replies are present, we will not further use this criterion for our attack detection. However as their presence still is a strong indicator for an undesired behavior resp. an attack, the generated alarms should be enriched with the number of observed ICMP unreachable replies.

The same is true for the path length detection. We could only obtain path length information for a minority (roughly 20%) of all pairflows. Thus we cannot

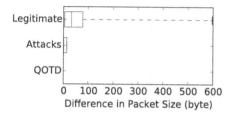 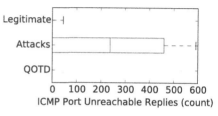

Fig. 3. Packet Sizes To Server   **Fig. 4.** ICMP Port Unreachable Replies

rely on mismatches in path length for the actual attack detection, but for a pairflow classified as attack the path length information can be used to harden the detection result.

As the MWN connects different types of users like universities, student halls or research institutions, the traffic we observe is a representative cross-section of different network types. We therefore believe that for other networks similar thresholds as the ones we derived here can be used.

5.5 Live Measurement Evaluation

To evaluate the decisiveness of our new criteria and thresholds we applied them to all pairflows exceeding the BAF-thresholds. After applying them we manually verified all pairflows that were marked as an attack. For the pairflows classified as legitimate traffic we only verified that we did not miss an attack using one of the well-known vulnerable protocols.

We grouped alerts by the triple of server, port and client, hence a long-lasting attack resulting in several pairflows is counted only once. Table 3 summarizes the detection results and proves that our approach is capable of very precisely distinguishing legitimate from attack traffic. It detected all attacks that took place and at the same time produced only very few false positive alarms.

Table 3. Detection Summary

	Run #1	Run #2	Run #3
BAF identified services	3,324	1,682	504
BAF identified alarms	22,428	14,567	4,058
True positive alarms	277	30	18
False positives alarms	3	9	0
True negative alarms	22,149	14,534	4,041
False negatives alarms	0	0	0

For the true positives we encountered some attacks (roughly five per run) using the SIP-protocol, which were similar to our own attacks. Thus we classify them as amplification attacks, while we cannot distinguish them from enumeration attacks for sure. In any case, administrators should be informed about them.

All the false positive alarms were mainly raised due to highly similar payload content. For all of them we determined the used application layer protocol with nDPI [5] resulting in six alarms for BitTorrent, one for Skype and two for unknown protocols. In all cases we could manually verify the similarity of the payloads due to the presence of repeating byte patterns. For Skype and BitTorrent we cannot explain what caused the similarity. For the unknown protocol a lot of null-bytes were observed which were probably used for payload padding.

This evaluation further proves that our additional criteria are necessary. When omitting them and only relying on the BAF-criteria from the beginning of Sect. 4, all pairflows that our approach classified as true negative alarms would be classified as amplification attacks. Thus applying only the BAF-criteria to all server ports without additional checks leads to a large amount of false positive alarms.

6   Detection Evasion and Limitations

In the following we will discuss evasion strategies and limitations of our approach.

Evading Detection: Our detection approach imposes assumptions on the attacker's behavior which can be used by an attacker to evade the detection. First of all we require a certain BAF and amount of traffic to be sent. An attacker can clearly evade our detection by generating less traffic. However, by doing so, she reduces the impact of the attack, which is desirable from our point of view. When reducing the amount of traffic sent below our detection rate, the impact of this attack is very low and hence neglectable. To overcome this an adversary could employ several amplifiers and forging requests such that each amplifier does not send more than 10 MB of traffic in ten minutes. However, to achieve a significant impact many amplifiers must be used as for this scenario each single amplifier may not exceed an average outgoing traffic rate of 136 kBit/s.

Instead of reducing the amount of attack traffic, an attacker can try to adapt his request packet lengths and payload entropy. She has two ways to achieve this goal: Firstly, she can send garbage messages to the amplifying service that are not legitimate messages. Since we have a generic protocol-independent approach, we cannot detect this. However, the attacker will reduce his amplification factor if she sends such messages. Secondly, she can try to employ different types of messages in his attack, which still result in large response messages. In general, however, this decreases the amplification factor as typically only a few requests yield high amplification ratios. This can be further dealt with by sampling more packets per pairflow to get a better estimate of the message similarity. Figure 1 indicates that there is a large gap between attacks and legitimate traffic when evaluating the similarity factors. Hence lowering the detection threshold should allow for detecting even attacks with a varying request message scheme while at the same time only very few additional false positive alarms are raised. Evading the detection of our approach would therefore reduce the impact that an attacker can have with his amplification attack.

Limitations of the Approach: We rely on estimating the entropy of the communication. If an attacker succeeds in generating encrypted amplification traffic, this criterion will fail as encrypted traffic looks rather random. However, we argue that generating encrypted amplification traffic is not easily achievable. Setting up encryption requires holding state which in case of an amplification attack as explained above is not possible.

The approach is designed for networks that can be monitored at a single point, in the simplest case for networks having only one uplink. If a network is connected through multiple uplinks our approach can still be applied if the traffic running through the uplinks is consolidated in a suitable way at single monitoring points. This might be achieved by consolidating all traffic at one monitoring point or at multiple monitoring points by applying a suitable splitting scheme. Nevertheless monitoring a network with multiple uplinks is a more general problem set which is out of the scope for this paper.

7 Conclusion

Distributed Reflection Denial-of-Service attacks are responsible for significant disruptions in the Internet. Recent research mainly has focused on detection of DRDoS-attacks on the edge of the victim's network. The potential countermeasures against such attacks that service operators in amplifier networks can employ remained unused, as detection of such attacks was hardly possible. In this paper we presented a novel approach to successfully solve this shortcoming.

As detection base we reused ideas from an already existing detection approach. Our key contributions are two novel detection criteria which allow for distinguishing between legitimate and attack traffic for any arbitrary application protocol. We showed that our protocol-agnostic approach enhances the detection process by not only defending against attacks on static port numbers, but also to thwart novel DRDoS attacks. Our practical evaluation in a large scientific network revealed that with our approach we were able to detect real attacks as well as artificial attacks that used new vulnerabilities.

In comparison to other mitigation strategies, like e.g. BCP 38 [3], our approach is applicable in the amplifier network, where the BCP 38 approach focuses on filtering in the attacker's network. Patching or disabling affected services also is a possible solution, however simply patching or disabling might not always be possible. With our approach network operators can at least detect ongoing amplification attacks. Additionaly our method only requires modest hardware; we used a dated commodity server.

In the future the detection scheme can be improved by changing it to a feedback-driven approach using machine-learning capabilities. We are confident that the criteria we developed in this paper will be suitable features for such an approach. Additionally measures to detect IP spoofing will surely help to strengthen the detection results.

Acknowledgments. This work has been supported by the German Federal Ministry of Education and Research (BMBF) under support code 01BY1203C, project *Peeroskop*, and 16BP12304, EUREKA project *SASER*, and by the European Commission under the FP7 project *EINS*, grant number 288021.

References

1. CloudFlare. https://www.cloudflare.com/ (last accessed: December 2014)
2. Özavci, F.: VOIP Wars: Return of the SIP, DEFCON 21, August 2013. http://www.defcon.org/images/defcon-21/dc-21-presentations/Ozavci/DEFCON-21-Ozavci-VoIP-Wars-Return-of-the-SIP-Updated.pdf (last accessed: December 2014)
3. Ferguson, P., Senie, D.: Network Ingress Filtering: Defeating Denial of Service Attacks which employ IP Source Address Spoofing. RFC 2827 (Best Current Practice), May 2000. http://www.ietf.org/rfc/rfc2827.txt, updated by RFC 3704
4. Kambourakis, G., Moschos, T., Geneiatakis, D., Gritzalis, S.: Detecting DNS amplification attacks. In: Lopez, J., Hämmerli, B.M. (eds.) CRITIS 2007. LNCS, vol. 5141, pp. 185–196. Springer, Heidelberg (2008)
5. nDPI-Homepage. http://www.ntop.org/products/ndpi/ (last accessed: December 2014)
6. Direct NIC Access - Gigabit and 10 Gigabit Ethernet Line-Rate Packet Capture and Injection. http://www.ntop.org/products/pf_ring/dna/ (last accessed: December 2014)
7. Postel, J.: Quote of the Day Protocol. RFC 865 (INTERNET STANDARD), May 1983. http://www.ietf.org/rfc/rfc865.txt
8. Prince, M.: The DDoS That Almost Broke the Internet, March 2013. http://blog.cloudflare.com/the-ddos-that-almost-broke-the-internet (last accessed: December 2014)
9. Rastegari, S., Saripan, M.I., Rasid, M.F.A.: Detection of Denial of Service Attacks against Domain Name System Using Neural Networks. International Journal of Computer Science Issues (IJCSI) 7(4) (2009)
10. Rossow, C.: Amplification hell: Revisiting network protocols for DDoS abuse. In: Proceedings of the 2014 Network and Distributed System Security (NDSS) Symposium, San Diego, CA, February 2014
11. Soluk, K.: NTP ATTACKS: Welcome to The Hockey Stick Era, February 2014. http://www.arbornetworks.com/asert/2014/02/ntp-attacks-welcome-to-the-hockey-stick-era/ (last accessed: December 2014)
12. Specht, S., Lee, R.: Distributed denial of service: Taxonomies of attacks, tool and countermeasures. In: Proceedings of the ISCA 17th International Conference on Parallel and Distributed Computing Systems, San Francisco, CA, September 2002
13. Spoofer Project: State of IP Spoofing. http://spoofer.cmand.org/summary.php (last accessed: December 2014)
14. Sun, C., Liu, B., Shi, L.: Efficient and low-cost hardware defense against DNS amplification attacks. In: IEEE Global Telecommunications Conference (GLOBE-COM 2008). IEEE (2008)
15. Vuze homepage. http://www.vuze.com/ (last accessed: December 2014)
16. zlib Homepage. http://www.zlib.net/ (last accessed: December 2014)

Measuring DANE TLSA Deployment

Liang Zhu[1]([✉]), Duane Wessels[2], Allison Mankin[2], and John Heidemann[1]

[1] University of Southern California, Angeles, US
liangzhu@usc.edu
[2] Verisign Labs, San Francisco, US
{dwessels,amankin}@verisign.com

Abstract. The DANE (DNS-based Authentication of Named Entities) framework uses DNSSEC to provide a source of trust, and with TLSA it can serve as a root of trust for TLS certificates. This serves to complement traditional certificate authentication methods, which is important given the risks inherent in trusting hundreds of organizations—risks already demonstrated with multiple compromises. The TLSA protocol was published in 2012, and this paper presents the first systematic study of its deployment. We studied TLSA usage, developing a tool that actively probes all signed zones in .com and .net for TLSA records. We find the TLSA use is early: in our latest measurement, of the 485k signed zones, we find only 997 TLSA names. We characterize how it is being used so far, and find that around 7–13 % of TLSA records are invalid. We find 33 % of TLSA responses are larger than 1500 Bytes and will very likely be fragmented.

1 Introduction

The Domain Name System (DNS) is central to Internet use. Originally used mainly to map between names and IP addresses or services, DNS has grown to support many other applications. To protect DNS information from modification or forgery, DNS Security Extensions (DNSSEC) provides integrity of DNS data via a cryptographic chain of trust following the DNS hierarchy. Traditional public-key infrastructure (PKI) places trust in multiple Certification Authorities (CAs, or PKI-CAs). Rather than the PKI's many roots and shallow tree, DNSSEC provides a single root and deeper hierarchy, decreasing the size of the root of trust and thus its vulnerability to compromise.

DANE (DNS-based Authentication of Named Entities) takes advantage of the DNSSEC-provided root of trust to authenticate TLS (Transport Layer Security) certificates. It places *TLSA records* in the DNS hierarchy and uses DNSSEC to validate their integrity. DANE TLSA therefore complements PKI Certificate Authorities, allowing TLS-users to better control certificates validation and protect against classes of CA compromise (as has occurred before [5,6]).

The DANE standard was published in 2012 [14], relatively recently. Although standardized, little is known about how actively DANE is being used. After two years, how many domains are using DANE? How widely used is TLSA? In this paper, we start to answer these questions.

© IFIP International Federation for Information Processing 2015
M. Steiner et al. (Eds.): TMA 2015, LNCS 9053, pp. 219–232, 2015.
DOI: 10.1007/978-3-319-17172-2_15

This paper presents the first systematic study of DANE TLSA deployment. Its first contribution is to describe an efficient methodology to actively probe DANE TLSA deployment status for three protocols on six ports. We apply this method to get a *complete* view of DANE usage at the two largest generic top-level domains (gTLDs): .com and .net for more than four months. (Passive monitoring would provide an incomplete view.) Our second contribution is to track DANE TLSA growth. We see that deployment remains very early, with only 997 TLSA names of the 485k DNSSEC zones, but *use is steadily increasing* (§4.1). Our third contribution is to evaluate DANE usage in two ways. We check for *correct* use of TLSA, and we consistently find 7%-13% of TLSA records are invalid: no IP address, no certificate, or a mismatch between the TLSA record and the certificate (§4.3). This high rate of misconfiguration suggests that DANE remains experimental, not mandatory. DANE has several operational modes, so we also characterize which are most popular, finding that DANE is most often used (76% of the time) to establish trust independent of the public CA hierarchy (§4.4). Our final contribution is to evaluate how DANE interacts with UDP. We find that find 33% of TLSA responses exceed the Ethernet MTU and will be fragmented at the IP layer, raising potential performance issues (§4.5).

2   Background and Related Work

We next briefly review DNS, DNSSEC, and DANE TLSA, and prior work observing DNS.

2.1   DNS

DNS is a protocol that maps *domain names* to *Resource Records* (RRs) using globally distributed servers to provide a consistent global namespace distributed across millions of servers [20,21]. There are many types of RRs, from A and AAAA for IPv4 and IPv6 addresses, or MX for the mail server for a given domain. RRs are stored in *zones*, with each zone managing part of the namespace (*.example.com). An *authoritative* name server provides the answer for a zone.

2.2   DNSSEC

DNS originally assumed a cooperative internet, so its basic design did not protect against malicious attempts to alter or pollute the namespace. DNSSEC was developed to protect the integrity of DNS responses by cryptographically signing the zone, allowing anyone to verify that RRs are what the zone owner intended [2–4]. For most users, DNSSEC trust is anchored in the single, signed root zone. The chain of trust extends to lower levels of the namespace via signed delegations in the form of Delegation Signer (DS) records. The operator of a signed zone is responsible for publishing its DS records in its parent zone.

2.3 DANE TLSA

DANE (DNS-based Authentication of Named Entities) is the idea that DNSSEC allows the DNS hierarchy to provide a root of trust for different types of information. DANE can compliment the traditional public-key infrastructure (PKI) Certification Authorities (CAs, or PKI-CAs) by giving operators of TLS-based services more control over how they indicate the authenticity of their TLS certificates. The CA model has come under scrutiny recently due to CA compromises and a lack of transparency and choice in the set of trusted CAs.

The DANE framework can provide trust for many different applications. DANE TLSA [14] is the first of these, providing methods to verify X.509 server certificates used in Transport Layer Security [9]. This paper addresses the deployment of DANE TLSA; studies of TLSA design and TLS performance with DANE are not our focus.

In DANE TLSA, domain name owners publish "certificate association data" in the DNS as TLSA RRs. TLSA RRs specify how applications can verify an X.509 certificate. Options range from providing the X.509 certificate itself, identifying a particular already-known intermediate CA, any already-known intermediate CA, or specify a new CA to serve as trust anchor. It can further specify whether the entire certificate, or only the public key, must be matched, and whether matching is based on hashes or an exact match of the given data. Figure 1 highlights the different ways that TLSA complements and constrains traditional CA methods.

TLSA associates records with particular network services to support different certificates for different services on the same host. TLSA names are prefixed with a port number and protocol name. For example, the TLSA record for the HTTPS service at www.example.com is stored under the name _443._tcp.www.example. com.

2.4 Related Work

We are not the first to scan the DNS. Several groups have walked the DNS reverse hierarchy, and ISC makes this data available publicly [16]. Others have used active DNS queries to study potential DNSSEC DDoS attacks [33], and uncover operational practices of EDNS-Client-Subnet (ECS) adopters [32]. SecSpider has tracked DNSSEC deployment and health since 2005 [26]. NIST monitors DNSSEC deployment of a set of government, industry and university domains [23]. Our probing is similar to these measurements, but targeted tracking growth of DANE TLSA. The Internet Society also provides pointers to DNSSEC deployment reports [8]. We provide data about DANE TLSA that could fit in such a report.

To support testing, several organizations have created correct or intentionally misconfigured DANE sites [7,24,37]. Other groups have created websites or tools that allow one to validate DANE TLSA (and DNSSEC) by request [10,19,22], both with IPv4 and IPv6 [1,31], and published DANE TLSA enabled mail servers [19]. Our measurements complement test cases and on-demand tests by evaluating deployment correctness as seen in the field, at least for two large TLDs.

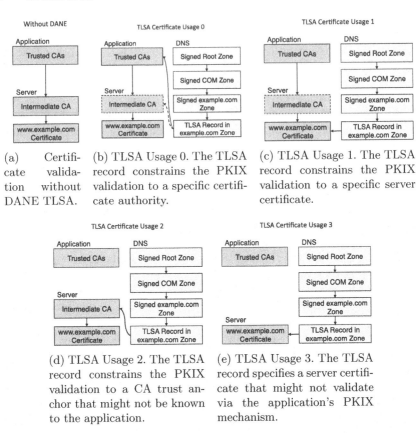

(a) Certificate validation without DANE TLSA.

(b) TLSA Usage 0. The TLSA record constrains the PKIX validation to a specific certificate authority.

(c) TLSA Usage 1. The TLSA record constrains the PKIX validation to a specific server certificate.

(d) TLSA Usage 2. The TLSA record constrains the PKIX validation to a CA trust anchor that might not be known to the application.

(e) TLSA Usage 3. The TLSA record specifies a server certificate that might not validate via the application's PKIX mechanism.

Fig. 1. The different ways that DANE TLSA complements and constrains certificate validation in applications

3 Monitoring DANE TLSA Deployment

To understand current DANE TLSA deployment we are interested in long-term observations of its use and growth. We have developed *PryDane*, a new tool that takes a set of zone names as input, then evaluates all those that use DNSSEC to see which also use TLSA. For zones with TLSA records, it also validates whether records match the the servers' certificates.

3.1 How to Track TLSA-Enabled Names

Our goal is to track increased deployment of DANE TLSA over time. Since the DNS is large, TLSA records are currently rare, and we need to probe regularly, our first challenge is to *efficiently* search DNS for TLSA use. Two possible methods present themselves: passive collection from live traffic, and TLD zone files. Each has advantages and disadvantages.

```
for all $DOMAIN in DS records of COM and NET zones do
  check _443._tcp.$DOMAIN
  check _443._tcp.www.$DOMAIN
  for SMTP $PORT 25, 465, 587 do
    if MX record points to $MX then
      check _$PORT._tcp.$MX
    else
      check _$PORT._tcp.$DOMAIN
  for $NAME _xmpp-client._tcp.$DOMAIN, _xmpp-server._tcp.$DOMAIN do
    if $NAME SRV record points to $PORT and $TARGET then
      check _$PORT._tcp.$TARGET
    else
      for XMPP $PORT 5222, 5269 do
        check _$PORT._tcp.jabber.$DOMAIN
        check _$PORT._tcp.xmpp.$DOMAIN
```

Fig. 2. Pseudo code of our probing system

Passive collection of DNS (for example, [11]) can provide usage and popularity with basic DNS data. It also can collect data across the entire DNS namespace. However, passive collection is likely incomplete, missing zones that never happen to be used during observation, and collection can be complex and sometimes unreliable.

Zone files are available for all gTLDs through ICANN's Centralized Zone Data Service [15]. We find that zone files are generally more reliable and easier to process, and they guarantee complete coverage within the TLD. They do not, however, indicate which names are actually being queried, and do not cover the entire DNS namespace since most ccTLDs do not make their zone files available. Nonetheless, for this study, we have chosen to use TLD zone files as our data source. So far we have only used the .com and .net zone files. See Section 5 for details about the zone files we used. Including more gTLDs is future work.

To get a set of meaningful targets to probe, we select *all* DNSSEC signed names by extracting those delegations that have accompanying DS records. We ignore non-DNSSEC names because TLSA records are only trustworthy when their integrity is ensured, and use of TLSA without DNSSEC is an error.

We probe several services that are TLSA early-adopters: HTTPS, SMTP (mail [29]), and XMPP (Jabber [18,28]). Other services that may use TLS are VPNs and secure SIP, but we omit these because we know of no deployments that support DANE TLSA. Table 1 lists when protocol support for TLSA began, and our gradual addition of protocol coverage. We look for DANE TLSA use with service discovery methods specific to each protocol as shown in Figure 2. Generally these probe only with the target domain, but some MX records point to e-mail servers in domains outside our targets (.com and .net).

Table 1. Protocol and implementation support for TLSA, and when our coverage begins for each

protocol	port	TLSA Support date	probing start
HTTPS [9]	443	2013-03-04 [10]	2014-07-14
SMTP [13]	587	2014-01-15 [29]	2014-07-14
	25		2014-10-02
	465		2014-10-02
XMPP [27]	5222	experimental	2014-10-14
	5269	[18, 28]	2014-10-14

Table 2. Number of TLSA names on Dec. 3, 2014. We discovered a few TLSA names outside the zone of .com and .net, since some mail servers are not in those two TLDs.

scanned size	130.30M	(100%)	
non-DNSSEC	129.82M	(99.63%)	
DNSSEC	485k	(0.37%)	
non-TLSA zones	~485k		
TLSA zones	443		[100%]
com and net	365		[82.4%]
other zones	78		[17.6%]
TLSA names	997		{100%}
HTTPS (443)	393		{39.5%}
SMTP (25)	314		{31.5%}
(465)	87		{8.7%}
(587)	105		{10.5%}
XMPP (5222)	49		{4.9%}
(5269)	49		{4.9%}

4 Observations and Findings

Our measurements provide several key findings: estimates of DANE TLSA deployment, growth, and correctness.

4.1 The Number of TLSA Enabled Names

As of Dec. 3, 2014, PryDane monitors 485k DNSSEC secured .com and .net zones. Among those, 997 TLSA names are found (Table 2).

Our measurement shows the deployment of DANE TLSA is steady increasing overall (Figure 3), although the fluctuation of the curve also exists, which we think is caused by the experimental deployment and occasional DNS failure. Adding protocols results in jumps in the number of total names that we find on 2014-10-02 and 2014-10-14. We also find that port-443 TLSA names increase faster than port-587 names which does not increase much (almost flat curve). If we project the current linear trend, the population will double in 6 months.

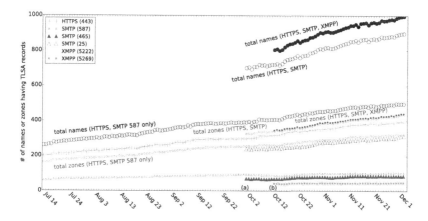

Fig. 3. Number of TLSA names and zones over 142 days. New probes are added during our measurement: (a) add probing SMTP port 25 and 465; (b) add probing XMPP port 5222 and 5269.

Table 3. Sample zone numbers and penetration of DNSSEC and DANE TLSA at the end of our current observation

zone	date	total	DNSSEC	TLSA	P_{dnssec}	P_{tlsa}
com	2014-12-03	115.2M	405k	183	.0035	.0005
net	2014-12-03	15.1M	79k	182	.0053	.0023

Growth so far is largely linear but our collection methodology will allow longer observation to determine if usage increases and follows an S (sigmoid) curve.

Currently there are only few applications, such an add-on [10] available for common browsers and Postfix mail server [29], supporting DANE TLSA. Deployment of DANE TLSA should pick up quickly as the application support is implemented.

4.2 Compare DANE TLSA and DNSSEC Deployment

To understand the deployment of DANE TLSA, we compare the growth of DNSSEC and DANE TLSA over time. We find DANE TLSA is growing well given it's relative immaturity.

To compare them we consider the penetration of each technology into its base of possible users. We define the penetration of DANE TLSA (P_{tlsa}) as the fraction of the number of TLSA zones over all DNSSEC zones (N_{tlsa}/N_{dnssec}). Since N_{tlsa} is limited by N_{dnssec} (DANE TLSA replies on DNSSEC for authentication), we normalize by the number of DNSSEC zones. We consider a zone to be *TLSA active* if that zone contains at least one TLSA record. Similarly, the penetration of DNSSEC (P_{dnssec}) is the fraction of zones using DNSSEC over all active zones (N_{dnssec}/N_{all}).

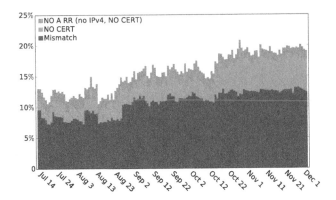

Fig. 4. TLSA validation (ports 443 and 587 only) without cert usage 0 over 142 days. There are consistently 7%-13% TLSA enabled names do not match servers' certificates (lower red bars).

We obtain DNSSEC data from TLDs operators. Combining those with our measurement results, we track P_{tlsa} and P_{dnssec} during our time of observation. The absolute values of penetration are small for both TLDs (less than 0.6%) Table 3, indicating DNSSEC deployment is still modest, 9 years after standardization. Compared to current DNSSEC deployment, DANE TLSA seems promising given its novelty (only 2 years after standardization). We observe $P_{dnssec} > P_{tlsa}$ because of greater DNSSEC maturity. Ideally we would compare the first year of DNSSEC deployment with current DANE TLSA deployment. However, the correct data of early DNSSEC deployment is not available because many zones had DNSSEC signed names before the signing of .com and .net zones.

4.3 TLSA Record Validation

Having found TLSA records, we also check them for correct usage. We find 7–13% TLSA records are consistently showing invalid over two months (Figure 4). We identify several problems: no IP address, no certificate, or a mismatch between the TLSA record and the certificate at the IP address. We categorize our TLSA validation results in the following.

No IPv4: There are some domain names having an associate TLSA record, but without an A record (no IPv4 address). In this case, it's impossible to get a certificate through IPv4, thus no validation could be done. Over 142 days of our observation, 24 unique domain names in total fall into this case. Among those, 5 domain names consistently report no IPv4 addresses every day. To further study the consistent no-IPv4 names, we queried AAAA record (IPv6) for those names. We found 3 of them pointing to the same CNAME record having a IPv6 address, one of them has an IPv6 address, and the rest don't have IPv6 address.

No certificate: For some TLSA records, we were unable to retrieve the server's certificate. In these cases our call to the `OpenSSL` command timed out. We believe this problem is cased by the remote server, since the probing machine is well connected to internet and has no problems fetching certificates in all the other cases.

Mismatching: Sometimes the TLSA record and certificate exist, but they don't match based on the given options in the TLSA record. We think this is mostly caused by expiration of either certificate or TLSA record, and one of them is not updated correspondingly. This accounts for most of the invalid cases. The lacking of feedback from users also makes web operators pay little attention to those deployed TLSA records, since TLSA is not widely used at this time.

We plan to add more functionality to our TLSA validation process. We validate the certificate through IPv4 addresses after getting a TLSA record. We would like to also check certificates through IPv6, however our probing systems currently sit on a network without global IPv6 reachability. We leave validating IPv6 certificate as a future work. For simplicity, we currently assume DNS integrity without validating DNSSEC chain, and only checks whether the certificate matches the corresponding TLSA records or whether a trust anchor is found, based on the different options. To support DNSSEC validation in our measurement, we plan to use cache to avoid constantly fetching common DNSSEC keys, potentially improving performance. TLSA records in an unsigned domain is also an error because their integrity cannot be protected by DNSSEC. Measuring this kind of error would require probing *all* domains, an expensive task inconsistent with our goal of minimizing network traffic. Exploration of this class of error is possible future work.

There are several websites built to allow one to validate DANE TLSA and DNSSEC by request [10,22,31]. Our measurements complement these on-demand tests and show a broader view of DANE TLSA healthiness.

4.4   Observed TLSA Parameters

TLSA can specify several different trust relationships, such as requiring a specific CA or certificate. More explanation about TLSA option is presented in subsection 2.3. We next study which are currently in use.

We study the latest one-day sample (Figure 5). We observe that the major group of combination is domain-issued certificate (76%, certificate usage: 3) matching full certificate (71%, selector: 0) with SHA-256 (84%, matching type: 1), and this does not change much over the time of our observation. The dominant use of domain-issued certificate indicates that most DANE TLSA cases are actually independent from CA without serving its trust source. SHA-256 is currently strong enough and it's not necessary to use stronger algorithm bringing more bits in DNS response, causing the problem of larger DNS packets subsection 4.5. There is a small number (1.5%) of TLSA records using exact matching (matching type: 0) which may bring the problems of large response packets subsection 4.5. We recommend not to use full certificate matching unless TLSA record is used to deliver the server's certificate.

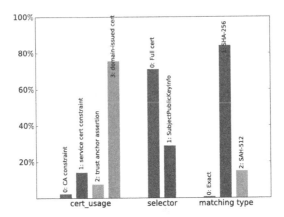

Fig. 5. Distribution of different options in TLSA record. This figure shows one sample of total 1123 TLSA records in 997 TLSA responses captured on Dec. 3, 2014.

4.5 Problematically Large TLSA Packets

When TLSA response blows up to more than 1500 bytes, it suffers IP fragmentation causing various problems: resend-all loss recovery [17], middleboxes block fragments [38], and fragmentation attacks [12]. Large TLSA packets also force DNS to fallback to retry using TCP, and fragments have to be re-assembled, adding the extra resolving latency.

There are several causes leading to large TLSA response. First, a TLSA response can contain multiple TLSA records, either for certificate rollover or for different assertions [14]. In the sample of Dec. 3, 2014, we observe 9.5% out of 997 TLSA responses contain more than one TLSA record. As number of TLSA records increases, the packet size rises correspondingly. Second, the exact matching of certificate in TLSA record without using a hash value adds much more to response packets. We examine the sizes of current SSL certificates by using data collected by Rapid7 Labs [30]. We find median size of X.509 certificate is 774 B, indicating that a TLSA response containing 2 full certificates gets IP fragmented. Third, with DNSSEC enabled and multiple RRs in authority and additional sections, a TLSA response is more likely to be problematically large, which is the common problem of DNS response, not limited to TLSA. To examine the actual TLSA response sizes, we actively query the corresponding authoritative servers for those TLSA names we found. We find that 33% TLSA responses are larger than 1500 bytes, leading to the problems of IP fragmentation (Figure 7). Those large response packets are mostly caused by the several RRs with different names in authority and additional sections.

We suggest that DNS zone operators limit the number of TLSA records for one domain name, use hash matching instead of exact matching, and limit the number of RRs in authority and additional sections to avoid future possible IP fragmentation.

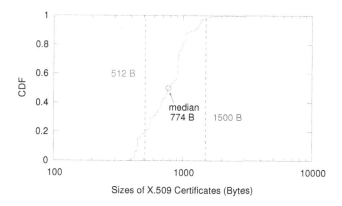

Fig. 6. Cumulative distribution of certificate sizes based on IPv4 SSL certificate data from Rapid7 Labs [30]. Date: 2014-09-29

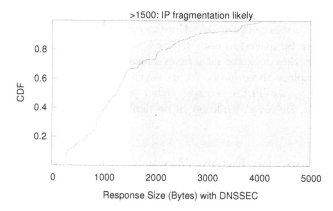

Fig. 7. Cumulative distribution of the response sizes with DNSSEC from authoritative servers of the 997 TLSA names on Dec. 3, 2014

4.6   Different Certificates Through IPv4 and IPv6

The difference between IPv4 and IPv6 certificates is problematic for DANE TLSA with usage "domain-issued certificate", because one domain names normally (more than 90% as we observed) has one associated TLSA record, in which case, one TLSA record cannot match two different certificates.

To detect this circumstance (different IPv4 and IPv6 certificates for the same name), we conduct additional measurement from another vantage point with working IPv6 access. (Our main probing server does not have IPv6 connectivity.) For each TLSA enabled name we detect, we actively fetch certificate through IPv4 and IPv6 if they have one, and we compare the two certificates. As of Oct 1, 2014, we find 238 out of 390 TLSA names have both IPv4 and IPv6 certificates, among which we detect 15 names (under 10 different sub-domain) have different certificates between IPv4 and IPv6. Operators might forget to update one of them when rolling over the certificates, leading to this inconsistency. We suggest domain name owners pay attention attention to this problem if they prepare to deploy DANE TLSA in their domain.

5   Representativeness of Our Results

Although we study two of the largest TLDs (.com and .net), they are only a subset of the Internet. Some other TLDs have as many or more signed delegations, however those ccTLD zone files are not generally available. We believe the data we study is large enough to provide an overview of current deployment of DANE TLSA. We do not know of any bias in the subset that we measure.

Our dataset is large: as of Dec. 3 2014, there are 115.2M and 15.1M active zones in .com and .net respectively [34, 36].

Second, we probed *all* DNSSEC signed sub-zones from these two TLDs, by extracting *all* DS records in the zone files. On Dec. 3 2014, we probed 405k DNSSEC signed .com zones, and 79k signed .com zones [35]. We only probe DNSSEC signed zones because DANE relies on DNSSEC for integrity. While a TLSA record can be placed in non-DNSSEC-signed zones, such records are not effective because they lack the integrity verification provided by DNSSEC.

Third, we explore three major secure services (HTTPS, SMTP and XMPP) that are most likely to use TLSA records. Other services using TLS are VPN and SIP applications. However, we know of no deployments using DANE TLSA for them.

6   Conclusion and Future Work

This paper presents the first measurement of DANE TLSA deployment. The main results are summarized as follows. Current CA-based certificate authentication works well in most cases and people don't feel the need to use a completely new authentication protocol, although DANE provides several benefits, such as reducing attack surface and making Secure/Multipurpose Internet Mail Extensions (S/MIME) global deployment possible [25]. Our measurement shows DANE TLSA use is early. However, the increasing trend of DANE TLSA deployment emerges. Our TLSA validation shows current DANE deployment has security inconsistency. Among TLSA records found, there are consistently around 7%-13% TLSA records mismatching server's certificates over the time of our observation. We observed that the most common (71%-84%) usage of TLSA record is: domain-issued certificate matching full certificates with SHA-256. We find 33% TLSA responses suffering IP fragmentation, resulting in fragmentation attacks and additional latency of query processing.

Our monitoring system PryDane is continuously running to keep track of new deployment of DANE. We are working on releasing the source code. (Pseudocode is shown in Figure 2.) We are exploring different services leading to TLSA records deployed in DNS, other than SMTP and HTTPS. We are also extending PryDane to capture other possible DANE cases, such as OPENPGPKEY [39], and adding

IPv6 certificate validation. Our current measurements cover .com and .net with direct access to the zones; future work may explore other DNSSEC signed zones, or passive DNS analysis of TLSA.

Acknowledgments. Liang Zhu began this work on an internship at Verisign. The work of Liang Zhu and John Heidemann in this paper is partially sponsored by the Department of Homeland Security (DHS) Science and Technology Directorate, HSARPA, Cyber Security Division, via SPAWAR Systems Center Pacific under Contract No. N66001-13-C-3001, and via BAA 11-01-RIKA and Air Force Research Laboratory, Information Directorate under agreement number FA8750-12-2-0344. The U.S. Government is authorized to make reprints for Governmental purposes notwithstanding any copyright. The views contained herein are those of the authors and do not necessarily represent those of DHS or the U.S. Government.

References

1. NLnetLabs. Ldns (ldns-dane). http://www.nlnetlabs.nl/projects/ldns/
2. Arends, R., Austein, R., Larson, M., Massey, D., Rose, S.: Dns security introduction and requirements. RFC **4033**, March 2005
3. Arends, R., Austein, R., Larson, M., Massey, D., Rose, S.: Protocol modifications for the dns security extensions. RFC **4035**, March 2005
4. Arends, R., Austein, R., Larson, M., Massey, D., Rose, S.: Resource records for the dns security extensions. RFC **4034**, March 2005
5. Bhat, S.: Gmail Users in Iran Hit by MITM Attacks, August 2011. http://techie-buzz.com/tech-news/gmail-iran-hit-mitm.html
6. Comodo. Comodo Fraud Incident, March 2011. https://www.comodo.com/Comodo-Fraud-Incident-2011-03-23.html
7. Deploy360 Porgramme. Dane test sites. http://www.internetsociety.org/deploy360/resources/dane-test-sites/
8. Deploy360 Porgramme. Dnssec statistics. http://www.internetsociety.org/deploy360/dnssec/statistics
9. Dierks, T., Rescorla, E.: The transport layer security (tls) protocol version 1.2. RFC **5246**, August 2008
10. DNSSEC/TLSA Validator. https://www.dnssec-validator.cz
11. Edward Bjarte Fjellskal. PassiveDNS tool. https://github.com/gamelinux/passivedns
12. Herzberg, A., Shulmanz, H.: Fragmentation considered poisonous. In: Proc. of IEEE Conference on Communications and Network Security (CNS), October 2013
13. Hoffman, P.: Smtp service extension for secure smtp over transport layer security. RFC **3207**, February 2002
14. Hoffman, P., Schlyter, J.: The dns-based authentication of named entities (dane) transport layer security (tls) protocol: Tlsa. RFC **6698**, August 2012
15. ICANN. The Centralized Zone Data Service. https://czds.icann.org/
16. Internet Systems Consortium. Internet domain survey, January 2008. web page http://www.isc.org/solutions/survey
17. Kent, C.A., Mogul, J.C.: Fragmentation considered harmful. SIGCOMM Comput. Commun. Rev. **25**(1), 75–87 (1995)
18. Learmonth, I., Gunasekaran, S.: Bootstrapping Trust with DANE, April 2014. https://www.hackerleague.org/hackathons/kings-of-code-hack-battle-at-tnw-europe-conference-2014/hacks/bootstrapping-trust-with-dane

19. Mail Server Security Test. https://www.tlsa.info/
20. Mockapetris, P.: Domain names - concepts and facilities. RFC **1034**, November 1987
21. Mockapetris, P.: Domain names–implementation and specification. RFC **1035**, November 1987
22. NIST. Danelaw. https://www.had-pilot.com/dane-tests.html
23. NIST. Estimating ipv6 and dnssec external service deployment status. http://fedv6-deployment.antd.nist.gov
24. NIST. Tlsa test tree. https://www.had-pilot.com/tlsa-test.html
25. Osterweil, E., Kaliski, B., Larson, M., McPherson, D.: Reducing the x. 509 attack surface with dnssecs dane. SATIN: Securing and Trusting Internet Names, March 2012
26. Osterweil, E., Ryan, M., Massey, D., Zhang, L.: Quantifying the operational status of the dnssec deployment. In: Proceedings of the 8th ACM SIGCOMM Conference on Internet Measurement, IMC 2008, pp. 231–242. ACM, New York, NY, USA (2008)
27. Saint-Andre, E.P.: Extensible messaging and presence protocol (xmpp): Core. RFC **3920**, October 2004
28. Pennock, P.: XMPP & DANE with Prosody, May 2014. http://bridge.grumpy-troll.org/2014/05/xmpp-dane-with-prosody
29. Postfix. http://www.postfix.org/TLS_README.html
30. Schloesser, M., Gamble, B., Nickel, J., Guarnieri, C., Moore, H.: Project Sonar: IPv4 SSL Certificates, September 2014. https://scans.io/study/sonar.ssl
31. SIDN labs. Tlsa validator. https://check.sidnlabs.nl/dane
32. Streibelt, F., Böttger, J., Chatzis, N., Smaragdakis, G., Feldmann, A.: Exploring edns-client-subnet adopters in your free time. In Proceedings of the 2013 Conference on Internet Measurement Conference, IMC 2013, pp. 305–312. ACM, New York, NY, USA (2013)
33. van Rijswijk-Deij, R., Sperotto, A., Pras, A.: Dnssec and its potential for ddos attacks: A comprehensive measurement study. In: Proceedings of the 2014 Conference on Internet Measurement Conference, IMC 2014, pp. 449–460. ACM, New York, NY, USA (2014)
34. Verisign. Daily zone counts. http://www.verisigninc.com/en_US/channel-resources/domain-registry-products/zone-file-information/index.xhtml
35. Verisign. Dnssec scoreboard. http://scoreboard.verisignlabs.com
36. Verisign. The Domain Name Industry Brief, December 2014. www.verisigninc.com/assets/domain-name-report-december2014.pdf
37. Verisign Labs. Dane/tlsa demonstration. http://dane.verisignlabs.com/
38. Weaver, N., Kreibich, C., Nechaev, B., Xson, V.P.: Implications of netalyzr's DNS measurements. In: Proc. of Workshop on Securing and Trusting Internet Names (SATIN), April 2011
39. Wouters, P.: Using dane to associate openpgp public keys with email addresses. Work in progress, February 2014 (draft-wouters-dane-openpgp-02)

A First Look at Real Multipath TCP Traffic

Benjamin Hesmans[✉], Hoang Tran-Viet, Ramin Sadre,
and Olivier Bonaventure

ICTEAM, Universitécatholique de Louvain, Louvain-la-Neuve, Belgium
benjamin.hesmans@uclouvain.be

Abstract. Multipath TCP is a new TCP extension that attracts a growing interest from both researchers and industry. It enables hosts to send data over several interfaces or paths and has use cases on smartphones, datacenters or dual-stack hosts. We provide the first analysis of the operation of Multipath TCP on a public Internet server based on a one-week long packet trace. We analyse the main new features of Multipath TCP, namely the utilisation of subflows, the address advertisement mechanism, the data transfers and the reinjections and the connection release mechanisms. Our results confirm that Multipath TCP operates correctly over the real Internet, despite the presence of middleboxes and that it is used over very heterogeneous paths.

1 Introduction

The Transmission Control Protocol (TCP) [23] was designed when hosts were equipped with a single interface. When two hosts exchange data through a TCP connection, all packets generated by the client (resp. server) must be sent from the same IP address. This remains true even if the communicating hosts have several interfaces and thus IP addresses that could be used to improve performance or resilience. In today's networks, this limitation is becoming a major drawback. Cellular and WiFi networks are available in most cities and smartphone users would like to be able to start a TCP connection in a WiFi hotspot and continue it later via their 3G interface. Reality with TCP is different [20]. Datacenters provide multiple paths between servers, but all packets from a given connection always follow the same path [24]. Dual stack hosts would like to exploit their IPv6 and IPv4 paths simultaneously but with regular TCP they can only rely on Happy Eyeballs [29].

Multipath TCP (MPTCP) is a recent TCP extension that has been standardised by the Internet Engineering Task Force [10] to solve this problem. In a nutshell, thanks to Multipath TCP, a multihomed host can use several interfaces (and thus IP addresses) to support a single TCP connection. Multipath TCP can pool all the resources available to improve the performance and the resilience of the service provided to the applications [30]. Several use cases for Multipath TCP have already been studied by the research community including datacenters [24] and WiFi/3G offload [4,6,20]. Implementers and industry are adopting Multipath TCP quickly. As of this writing, Multipath TCP implementations exist on Linux [18], Apple iOS and MacOS [1], FreeBSD [28] and

© IFIP International Federation for Information Processing 2015
M. Steiner et al. (Eds.): TMA 2015, LNCS 9053, pp. 233–246, 2015.
DOI: 10.1007/978-3-319-17172-2_16

Solaris [7]. Apple has enabled Multipath TCP by default for its voice recognition SIRI application running on all recent iPhones and iPads. Today, there are thus hundreds of millions of devices that use Multipath TCP on the Internet.

Despite of this large scale deployment, little is known about how Multipath TCP really behaves in the global Internet. In this paper, we provide a first analysis of the Multipath TCP packets received and sent by the server that hosts the reference implementation in the Linux kernel[1]. Besides Apple's servers that support the SIRI application, this is probably the most widely used public Multipath TCP server. By observing how real users use this new protocol, we complement the existing measurement that relied on simulations, emulations or active measurements.

This paper is organised as follows. In Section 2, we describe our dataset, how the packets have been collected and the software that we used to analyse them. Section 3 describes the main features of the Multipath TCP protocol and analyses their impact based on the collected packets. Section 4 compares our work with related work. We conclude the paper in Section 5.

2   Dataset

The dataset[2] used in this paper is a one-week long packet trace collected in November 2014 at Université catholique de Louvain (UCL). It has been collected using `tcpdump` and contains the headers of all TCP packets received and sent by the server hosting the Multipath TCP Linux kernel implementation. Apart from a web server, the machine also hosts an FTP server and an `iperf` server. It has one physical network interface with two IP addresses (IPv4 and IPv6) and runs the stable version 0.89 of the Multipath TCP implementation in the Linux kernel [18].

To analyse the Multipath TCP connections in the dataset, we have extended the `mptcptrace` software [11] developed by the same authors. `mptcptrace` handles all the main features of the Multipath TCP protocol and can extract various statistics from a packet trace. Our extensions to `mptcptrace` have been included in the last release. Furthermore, we have combined it with `tcptrace` [17] and its output has been further processed by custom `python` scripts.

Table 1 summarizes the general characteristics of the dataset. In total, the server received around 136 million TCP packets carrying 134 GiBytes of data (including the TCP and IP headers) during the measurement period. As shown in table 1 (in the block "Multipath TCP"), a significant fraction of the TCP traffic was related to Multipath TCP. Unsurprisingly, IPv4 remains more popular than IPv6, but it is interesting to note that the fraction of IPv6 traffic from the hosts that are using Multipath TCP (9.8%) is larger than from the hosts using regular TCP (3.7%). On the monitored server, dual-stack hosts are already an important use case for Multipath TCP. It should be noted that the monitored

---

[1] http://www.multipath-tcp.org
[2] The anonymised packet trace is available at http://multipath-tcp.org/data/ TMA-2015.tar.gz.

Table 1. Dataset characteristics

Collection period	Nov. 17 – 24, 2014		

All TCP	Total	IPv4	IPv6
# of packets [Mpkt]	136.1	128.5	7.6
# of bytes [GiByte]	134.0	129.0	5.0

Multipath TCP	Total	IPv4	IPv6
# of packets [Mpkt]	29.4	25.0	4.4
# of bytes [GiByte]	20.5	18.5	2.0

server is mainly used by Multipath TCP users and developers who are likely to be researchers or computer scientists. These users probably have better connectivity that the average Internet user.

We have also studied the application protocols used in the Multipath TCP traffic. Around 22.7% of the packets were sent or received on port 80 (HTTP). A similar percentage of packets (21.2%) was sent to port 5001 (`iperf`) by users conducting throughput measurements. The FTP server, was responsible for the majority of packets. It hosts the Debian and Ubuntu packages for the Multipath TCP kernel and is thus often used by Multipath TCP developers.

Considering the number of connections, 89.7% of them were targeted on HTTP, 6.4% for `iperf`, 1.9% for FTP control connections and the remaining 2.0% on higher ports are likely FTP data connections.

Another important figure is the number of distinct Multipath TCP clients connected to our server. While identifying this figure exactly is not trivial, information about client IP addresses may be useful to give some feeling about the variety of clients' location. Among 790 distinct client IP addresses we observed, there are 562 IPv4 addresses coming from 464 distinct class C IPv4 network prefixes and 228 different IPv6 addresses coming from 79 distinct 48-bit IPv6 prefixes.

3   Analysis

Multipath TCP is a major extension to TCP that modifies many features of the protocol. A detailed overview of Multipath TCP is outside the scope of this paper and may be found in [10,19]. In this section, we first describe the key features of Multipath TCP. Then, each subsection focuses on a particular aspect of the protocol that is explained and analysed in more details based on the collected packet trace.

Like most TCP extensions, Multipath TCP defines a new TCP option that is used during the initial three-way handshake. This MP_CAPABLE option contains several important parameters [10,19]. A prominent characteristic of Multipath TCP is that, to be able to use several paths, Multipath TCP combines several TCP connections called subflows inside a single Multipath TCP connection. These subflows are linked together by using a token extracted from the

MP_CAPABLE option and included in the MP_JOIN option that is exchanged during the handshake of the other subflows. To support mobile hosts, Multipath TCP allows each host to advertise its current list of addresses to its peer [10]. This is done thanks to the ADD_ADDR and REMOVE_ADDR options that can be sent at any time over one of the TCP subflows. It is important to note that the subflows that compose a Multipath TCP connection is not fixed. The set of subflows changes during the lifetime of the connection since each host can add or remove a subflow at any time.

3.1 Which Hosts Use Multipath TCP?

The first question that we asked ourselves while analysing the trace was the characteristics of the clients that contacted the monitored server. Since the packet trace was collected on the server that hosts the Multipath TCP implementation in the Linux kernel, we can expect that many Linux enthusiasts use it to download new versions of the code, visit the documentation, perform tests or verify that their configuration is correct. These users might run different versions of Multipath TCP in the Linux kernel or on other operating systems[7]. Unfortunately, as of this writing, there is not enough experience with the Multipath TCP implementations to detect which operating system was used to generate specific Multipath TCP packets. This is an interesting direction for future work. Instead, we focus our analysis on the number of addresses used by the clients.

Thanks to the ADD_ADDR option, it is possible to collect interesting data about the characteristics of the clients that contact our server. Over the 5098 observed Multipath TCP connections, 3321 of them announced at least one additional address. Surprisingly, only 21% of the collected IPv4 addresses in the ADD_ADDR option were globally routable addresses. The remaining 79% of the IPv4 addresses found in the ADD_ADDR option were private addresses and in some cases link-local addresses. The large number of private address confirms that Multipath TCP's ability to pass through NATs is an important feature of the protocol [10].

The IPv6 addresses collected in the ADD_ADDR option had more diversity. We first observed 72% of globally routable IPv6 addresses. The other types of addresses that we observed are shown in Table 2. The IPv4-compatible and the 6to4 IPv6 addresses were expected, but the link local and documentation addresses should have been filtered by the client and never be announced over Multipath TCP connections. The Multipath TCP specification [10] does not currently specify the types of addresses that can be advertised over a Multipath TCP connection. It should probably be updated to specify which types of IPv4 and IPv6 addresses can be announced with the the ADD_ADDR option.

Another interesting point to note is that although the ADD_ADDR option defined in [10] can also be used to advertise transport protocol port numbers together with IP addresses, we didn't detect any utilisation of this feature in our trace.

Table 2. Special addresses advertised by clients

Address type	Count
Link-local (IPv4)	51
Link-local (IPv6)	241
Documentation only (IPv6)	21
IPv4-compatible IPv6	13
6to4	206

3.2 How Quickly Are Subflows Established?

The previous section has shown that a large number of (multihomed) hosts exchange Multipath TCP packets with our server. Our server has a single interface but two IP addresses (IPv4 and IPv6). Like the other Multipath TCP implementations [7], it never creates subflows [18] because, as confirmed by the measurements in the previous section, the client is likely to reside behind a NAT or a firewall that would block these subflow establishments.

The current implementation of Multipath TCP in the Linux kernel [18] uses two strategies to create subflows. The first strategy, supported by the default path manager on multihomed hosts, is to create a full-mesh of subflows as soon as possible. Figure 1 shows the delay between the SYN segment sent on the initial subflow and the SYN segment of the first subflow. For 88.9% of the Multipath TCP connections composed of two or more subflows, the first subflow is established within less than one second. For 46.5% of the connections, this delay is shorter than 100 msec. The longest delay between the establishment of a Multipath TCP connection and the first subflow is 360 seconds.

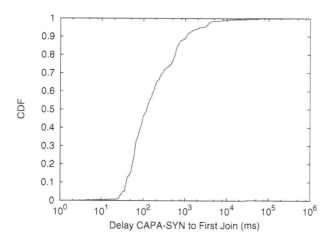

Fig. 1. Delay between the SYN of initial flow and the first MP_JOIN

For test purposes and to support local balancing over multiple equal cost paths [24], another path manager can be used on single-homed hosts. This path manager creates n subflows from the single IP address of the client to the server. An analysis of all the observed Multipath TCP connections indicates that this path manager was used by about one third of the connections that we observed.

Multipath TCP can also support backup subflows [20]. In this case, the client indicates that a subflow is a backup subflow at subflow establishment time or by sending the MP_PRIO option on an existing subflow. In the analysed trace, we did not observe any utilisation of this option.

When Multipath TCP is used over heterogeneous paths, its performance can decrease if the paths have different round-trip-times or bandwidth [22]. Figure 2 plots, for all Multipath TCP connections using two or more subflows, the CDF of the difference between the minimum and the maximum average round-trip-times over all the subflows that compose each Multipath TCP connection. These average round-trip-times were computed by using tcptrace [17]. Less than 10% of the Multipath TCP connections have subflows having the same average round-trip-times. Almost 54.3% of the Multipath TCP connections combine subflows with a spread of up to 10 msec. 13.7% of the connections have a spread larger than 50 msec. This is an important indication about the heterogeneity of the paths over which Multipath TCP is used today.

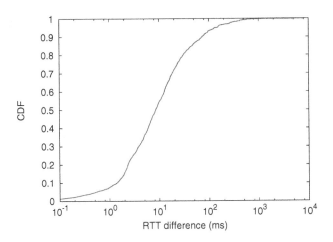

Fig. 2. Difference between the maximum RTT and minimum RTT among subflows belonging to one MPTCP connection

3.3 How Many Subflows Are Used?

In theory, a Multipath TCP connection can gather an unlimited number of subflows. In practice, implementations [7] limit the number of concurrent subflows. The Linux implementation [18] used on the monitored server can support up to

32 different subflows. We analyse here the number of subflows that are established for each Multipath TCP connection. Since our server never establishes subflows, this number is an indication of the capabilities of the clients that interact with it.

Figure 3 provides the distribution of the number of subflows per Multipath TCP connection. We show the distribution for the number of successfully established subflows, i.e., subflows that complete the handshake, as well as for all attempted ones. As can be seen, several connection attempts either fail completely or establish less subflows than intended. In total, we observe 5098 successful connections with 8701 subflows. The majority of the observed connections (57%) only establish one subflow. Around 27% of them use two subflows. Only 10 connections use more than 8 subflows, which are omitted from the figure.

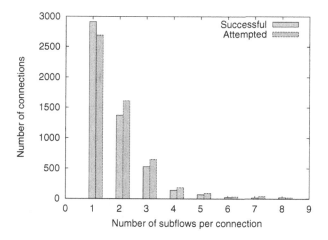

Fig. 3. Distribution of subflows per connection

The fact that many Multipath TCP connections establish more than one subflow affects the connection sizes as perceived on TCP level. In Figure 4 we show the cumulative distribution of the number of payload bytes exchanged on the Multipath TCP connections and compare it with the size distribution of the individual TCP connections. As expected, we see a larger number of small TCP subflow connections.

It should be noted that establishing multiple subflows does not necessarily mean that the payload of a Multipath TCP connection is evenly distributed over them. This will be further discussed in Section 3.6. While the MP_PRIO option has been introduced to Multipath TCP providing the capability to change the priority of a subflow, we do not observe any subflow using this option.

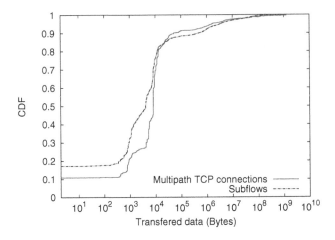

Fig. 4. Distribution of data on Multipath TCP connections and the subflows

3.4   Do Middleboxes Interfere with Multipath TCP?

The interference caused by various types of middleboxes has significantly affected the design of the Multipath TCP protocol [10,13,25]. Multipath TCP can cope with middleboxes that modify the source/destination IP addresses and ports, but also change the TCP sequence numbers or split/reassemble TCP segments [12]. If a middlebox strips TCP options, the Multipath TCP implementation in the Linux kernel performs a fallback to regular TCP [10]. The worst middlebox interference for Multipath TCP is when a middlebox such as a NAT using a Application Level Gateway changes "transparently" the payload of TCP segments, e.g. to translate the ASCII representation of an IP address. Multipath TCP can detect this type of interference by using the DSS checksum which is computed over the data and the Multipath TCP option [10,25]. Given that the TCP segments are already protected by the TCP checksum, an error in the DSS checksum is always a sign of middlebox interference.

If a host receives a TCP segment with a valid TCP checksum and an invalid DSS checksum, it sends an MP_FAIL option to inform the peer of the interference and performs a fallback to regular TCP. Among more than 5000 Multipath TCP connections that we have analysed, we observe three transmissions of the MP_FAIL option. In all three cases, MP_FAILs are sent on port 21 (FTP). This is a relatively small number knowing that the monitored server provides FTP services that are subject to middlebox interference [12] due to Application Level Gateways included in NAT devices. We did not observe the MP_FAIL option on port 80 despite the fact that transparent proxies are often reported [26]. Surprisingly, we also observe this MP_FAIL option inside IPv6 packets.

As explained earlier, the utilisation of the DSS Checksum [10] ensures that middlebox interference is detected and that the data is transported correctly. However, computing the DSS Checksum consumes CPU ressources [25] and the

DSS checksum can be disabled on a per connection basis. During the three-way handshake on the initial subflow, the client and the server can opt out the DSS Checksum. The DSS Checksum is only disabled if both propose to disable it. If either the client or the server is configured to use the DSS Checksum, then it is used in both directions. Since the monitored server was configured to always us the DSS Checksum, it was active for all Multipath TCP connections. This is the default configuration which is recommended in the Internet [10]. The DSS Checksum should only be disabled in controlled environments such as datacenters that are known to be immune of middlebox interference. We were surprised to measure that about 5% of the Multipath TCP connections established with our server requested to disable the DSS Checksum. This configuration was probably chosen for performance reasons, but it puts the data transfert at risk of undetected middlebox interference.

3.5   How Do Multipath TCP Connections Terminate?

TCP uses two different mechanisms to terminate a connection. Most connections should terminate by exchanging FIN segments in both directions [23]. Some connections terminate abruptly with the transmission of a RST segment due to problems or because the server does not want to wait in the CLOSE_WAIT state [2]. Each of the TCP subflows that compose a Multipath TCP connection can be terminated using one of these mechanisms. Above the subflows, Multipath TCP also includes similar mechanisms to terminate the Multipath TCP connection [10]. If all the data has been transferred correctly, a Multipath TCP connection should terminate with the exchange of DATA_FIN options in both directions. We observe that 89% of the 5098 monitored Multipath TCP connections are terminated by exchanging DATA_FINs. Multipath TCP also includes a fast close mechanism that allows a host to terminate a Multipath TCP connection by sending a FAST_CLOSE option inside a RST segment. This feature was included in [10] to enable a server to quickly terminate a Multipath TCP connection. It is used by roughly 10% of the observed Multipath TCP connections.

3.6   How is Data Distributed?

Since a Multipath TCP connection combines several TCP subflows, data can be transmitted over any of these subflows. The Linux implementation of Multipath TCP uses a packet scheduler [21] to select the subflow over which each data segment is transmitted. The monitored server uses the default scheduler that tries to send data on the subflow having the smallest round-trip-time among the subflows whose congestion window is open. The client could use another scheduler such as the round-robin scheduler or any custom scheduler [21].

The utilisation of the default scheduler implies that the data is not evenly distributed among the different subflows. Figure 5 shows, for connections composed of more than one subflow, how the data is distributed among the initial subflow and the other subflows of the connection. We observe that around 52% of the connections send less than half of their data over the initial subflow.

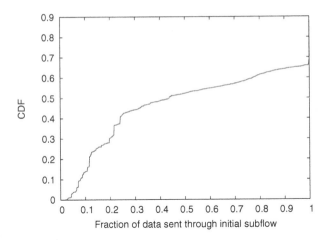

Fig. 5. Fraction of data on initial subflow over total data for connections with more than one subflow

In contrast, around 30% of the connections transfer their data nearly entirely over the initial subflow. There are different possible explanations for this behaviour. One reason could be that those connections are simply too short or too small to use the additional subflows. However, we have studied their length and size distribution and could not find any prevalence of very short or small connections among them in comparison to other connections.

Like regular TCP connections, Multipath TCP connections can be impacted by packet losses. The Multipath TCP implementation in the Linux kernel includes three main strategies to cope with losses. If an isolated packet is lost, Multipath TCP will use the fast retransmit mechanism to retransmit it over the subflow where it was initially sent. This is the normal behaviour of a TCP connection. If a retransmission timer expires, this usually indicates a more severe loss. In this case, Multipath TCP evaluates whether the data should be retransmitted over the same subflow as the original transmission or over another subflow. In the latter case (*reinjection*), data will be retransmitted over both subflows to ensure that any middlebox over one of the paths observes in-sequence data [10,12]. In some cases, such retransmissions can also occur when one of the subflows is too slow compared to the other ones [25]. If a subflow dies, e.g. due to the failure of a WiFi interface, then all unacknowledged data sent over this subflow is retransmitted over the remaining subflows. These reinjections are an indication of the inefficiency of Multipath TCP. Since reinjected data is sent over two or more subflows, a large reinjection rate will result in a badly performing Multipath TCP connection.

Figure 6 shows the fractions of reinjected data (bytes) for the Multipath TCP connections composed of at least two subflows. We provide the CDF for transmissions from the client to the server resp. from the server to the client. We observe that more than 90% of the connections do not have any reinjection.

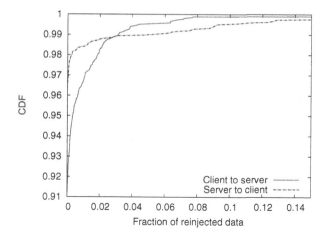

Fig. 6. Fraction of reinjected data over total data for connections

More than 98% of the connections have fewer than 2% of reinjections. This shows that reinjections are rare and that the overhead caused by them is very low in comparison to the overall TCP retransmission rate of 0.8–2.4% reported in [5]. We also observe that the fraction of reinjections is larger in the client-to-server direction than in the opposite one. The reasons for this will be the topic of future work. Finally, it should be noted that the results shown in the figure should be taken with caution for fractions above 30%. Due to the small population size and the presence of very short connections, extreme cases, such as a single-packet connection with reinjection, do have a visible impact on the tail of the empirical CDF.

4   Related Work

Various researchers have studied the performance of Multipath TCP on cellular networks and/or the global Internet. As of this writing, most of these studies have focussed on performing active measurements among a relatively small set of connected devices. We are not aware of published studies where large Multipath TCP packet traces have been analysed in details. In this section, we thus compare our findings with the main results obtained with active measurements. Although several implementations of Multipath TCP exist [7], we are not aware of published results that compare their performance. In fact, most of the published papers use the Linux implementation.

Several researchers have analysed the performance of Multipath TCP in cellular networks. Paasch et al. propose, implement and evaluate path management strategies to efficiently support 3G and WiFi interfaces with Multipath TCP [20]. The Linux implementation [18] is used by the monitored server and likely most of the clients that sent packets. Chen et al. [4] and Deng et al. [6] also perform measurements with the Multipath TCP implementation in the Linux kernel. Chen et al. focus on bulk transfers over WiFi and 3G and conclude that Multipath TCP provides performance benefits compared to regular TCP. Deng et al. analyse different scenarios. Their measurements show that the benefits of using Multipath TCP increase with the volume of data transferred. Lim et al. present other measurements with cellular and WiFi networks in [16] and focus on tuning the Multipath TCP implementation to reduce the energy consumption. Williams et al. use experiments to investigate the use of Multipath TCP (MPTCP) to augment cellular 3G connections with roadside infrastructure [27]. Ferlin et al. use the NorNet infrastructure [15] to analyse the performance of Multipath TCP in heterogeneous networks (WiFi and 2G or 3G) [9]. Their measurements show that when the difference in bandwidth between the two interfaces is large (e.g. 2G and WiFi), then the performance of Multipath TCP may suffer. They propose an algorithm that monitors the subflow performance and disables the under-performing ones.

Multipath TCP is not the only transport protocol that is capable of supporting multiple paths. The Stream Control Transmission Protocol [8] (SCTP) has been implemented in most operating systems. It was designed with multihoming in mind and support for concurrent multipath was added to SCTP [14] before the deployment of Multipath TCP. However, we have not found in the scientific literature detailed measurements of the performance of SCTP based on passive measurements. As shown in [3] only a small fraction of the published SCTP research is based on real measurements on the Internet.

5   Conclusion

In this paper, we have presented a first analysis of the behaviour of Multipath TCP based on a one-week long packet trace collected on a popular Multipath TCP server. Since the server hosts the Multipath TCP implementation in the Linux kernel, it is mainly used by developpers and researchers. Furthermore, we expect that most clients use the same Linux implementation as the one running on the server. We have analysed the real utilisation of the new features introduced in this TCP extension, namely the establishment of the subflows, the advertisement of addresses, the reinjection of data, the detection of middlebox interference and the termination of the Multipath TCP connections.

Some of our results confirm that the protocol operates correctly over the Internet. Others were less expected and provide an insight on the operation of this protocol over the Internet. Firstly, Multipath TCP hosts can use many interfaces. Some hosts announced up to 14 different IP addresses over a single Multipath TCP connection. Secondly, the subflows that compose a Multipath TCP connection are usually established very quickly. This corresponds to the default strategy of the current Linux implementation and confirms that clients mainly use this implementation. Thirdly, when two or more subflows are used, their average round-trip-times can differ by 10-100 msec for 40% of the Multipath TCP connections. This is a large delay difference that indicates that Multipath

TCP is used in heterogeneous environments. This delay difference must be taken into account by Multipath TCP implementors who are tuning their implementations. Fourthly, Multipath TCP spreads the data over the different subflows and rarely needs to reinject some data over another subflow. Finally, there are middleboxes that interfere with Multipath TCP, even in IPv6 networks.

For our future work, we will collect a longer trace to study in more details other aspects of the protocol such as identifying the congestion control scheme used on the subflows, the packet scheduler used by the client, or measuring the short term dynamics of the data transmission on the different subflows or middlebox interference.

Acknowledgments. This work was partially supported by the ITN METRICS and the FP7 TRILOGY 2 projects funded by the European Commission and by the BEST-COM IAP.

References

1. Apple. ios: Multipath tcp support in ios 7. http://support.apple.com/en-us/HT201373
2. Arlitt, M., Williamson, C.: An Analysis of TCP Reset Behaviour on the Internet. SIGCOMM Comput. Commun. Rev. **35**(1), 37–44 (2005)
3. Budzisz, L., Garcia, J., Brunstrom, A., Ferrús, R.: A Taxonomy and Survey of SCTP Research. ACM Comput. Surv. **44**(4), 18:1–18:36 (2012)
4. Chen, Y.-C., Lim, Y.-S., Gibbens, R., Nahum, E., Khalili, R., Towsley, D.: A measurement-based study of multipath TCP performance over wireless networks. In: ACM SIGCOMM IMC (2013)
5. Jerry Chu, H.K.: Tuning TCP parameters. In: Proceedings of The Seventy-Fifth Internet Engineering Task Force. IETF (2009)
6. Deng, S., Netravali, R., Sivaraman, A., Balakrishnan, H.: WiFi, LTE, or Both?: measuring multi-homed wireless internet performance. In: IMC 2014, pp. 181–194. ACM, New York, NY, USA (2014)
7. Eardley, P.: Survey of MPTCP Implementations. Internet-Draft draft-eardley-mptcp-implementations-survey-02, IETF Secretariat, July 2013
8. Stewart, R., (Ed.): Stream Control Transmission Protocol. IETF RFC **4960**, September 2007
9. Ferlin, S., Dreibholz, T., Alay, O.: Multi-Path transport over heterogeneous wireless networks: does it really pay off? In: Proceedings of the IEEE Global Communications Conference (GLOBECOM), Austin, Texas/U.S.A., December 2014
10. Ford, A., Raiciu, C., Handley, M., Bonaventure, O.: TCP Extensions for Multipath Operation with Multiple Addresses. IETF RFC **6824**, January 2013
11. Hesmans, B., Bonaventure, O.: Tracing multipath TCP connections. In: SIGCOMM 2014 (poster), pp. 361–362 (2014)
12. Hesmans, B., Duchene, F., Paasch, C., Detal, G., Bonaventure, O.: Are TCP extensions middlebox-proof? In: CoNEXT Workshop HotMiddlebox (2013)
13. Honda, M., Nishida, Y., Raiciu, C., Greenhalgh, A., Handley, M., Tokuda, H.: Is It Still Possible to Extend TCP? In: 2011 ACM SIGCOMM Conference on Internet Measurement Conference, IMC 2011, pp. 181–194 (2011)

14. Iyengar, J., Amer, P., Stewart, R.: Concurrent multipath transfer using SCTP multihoming over independent end-to-end paths. IEEE/ACM Transactions on Networking **14**(5), 951–964 (2006)
15. Kvalbein, A., Baltrūnas, D., Evensen, K., Xiang, J., Elmokashfi, A., Ferlin, S.: The NorNet Edge Platform for Mobile Broadband Measurements. Computer Networks, Special Issue on Future Internet Testbeds, 61:88–101, March 2014. ISSN 1389–1286
16. Lim, Y., Chen, Y., Nahum, E., D., Gibbens, R.: Improving energy efficiency of MPTCP for mobile devices. CoRR, abs/1406.4463, (2014)
17. Ostermann, S.: `tcptrace`. http://www.tcptrace.org
18. Paasch, C., Barre, S., et al.: Multipath TCP implementation in the Linux kernel (2014). http://www.multipath-tcp.org
19. Paasch, C., Bonaventure, O.: Multipath TCP. ACM Queue **12**(2), 40:40–40:51 (2014)
20. Paasch, C., Detal, G., Duchene, F., Raiciu, C., Bonaventure, O.: Exploring mobile/wifi handover with multipath TCP. In: ACM SIGCOMM workshop Cell Net, pp. 31–36 (2012)
21. Paasch, C., Ferlin, S., Alay, O., Bonaventure, O.: Experimental evaluation of multipath TCP schedulers. In: 2014 ACM SIGCOMM Workshop on Capacity Sharing Workshop, CSWS 2014, pp. 27–32 (2014)
22. Paasch, C., Khalili, R., Bonaventure, O.: On the benefits of applying experimental design to improve multipath TCP. In: Proceedings of CoNEXT 2013, pp. 393–398. ACM, New York, NY, USA (2013)
23. Postel, J.: Transmission Control Protocol. IETF RFC **793**, September 1981
24. Raiciu, C., Barre, S., Pluntke, C., Greenhalgh, A., Wischik, D., Handley, M.: Improving datacenter performance and robustness with multipath TCP. In: ACM SIGCOMM **2011** (2011)
25. Raiciu, C., Paasch, C., Barre, S., Ford, A., Honda, M., Duchene, F., Bonaventure, O., Handley, M.: How hard can it be?. designing and implementing a deployable multipath TCP, In: USENIX NSDI (2012)
26. Weaver, N., Kreibich, C., Dam, M., Paxson, V.: Here Be Web Proxies. In: Faloutsos, M., Kuzmanovic, A. (eds.) PAM 2014. LNCS, vol. 8362, pp. 183–192. Springer, Heidelberg (2014)
27. Williams, N., Abeysekera, P., Dyer, N., Vu, H., Armitage, G.: Multipath TCP in Vehicular to Infrastructure Communications. Technical Report Centre for Advanced Internet Architectures, Technical Report 140828A, Swinburne University of Technology (2014)
28. Williams, N., Stewart, L., Armitage, G.: FreeBSD kernel patch for Multipath TCP July 2014. http://caia.swin.edu.au/urp/newtcp/mptcp/tools.html
29. Wing, D., Yourtchenko, A.: Happy Eyeballs: Success with Dual-Stack Hosts. RFC **6555**, April 2012
30. Wischik, D., Handley, M., Braun, M.: The Resource Pooling Principle. ACM SIGCOMM Computer Communication Review **38**(5), 47–52 (2008)

Author Index